…

DENALI
SUMMER

DENALI
SUMMER

FAYDRA STRATTON

Maitland, Florida

© 2023 Faydra Stratton

All rights reserved. No part of this book may be transmitted in any form or by any means, electronic or mechanical, including photocopying, recording, or by any information storage or retrieval system, in part, in any form, without the permission of the publisher.

Orange Blossom Publishing
Maitland, Florida
www.orangeblossombooks.com
info@orangeblossombooks.com

First Edition: November 2023

Library of Congress Control Number: 2023909735

Edited by: Arielle Haughee
Formatted by: Autumn Skye
Cover design: Sanja Mosic

Print ISBN: 978-1-949935-83-7
eBook ISBN: 978-1-949935-84-4

Printed in the U.S.A.

DEDICATION

For Shata—the reason I had my own Denali Summer once upon a forever ago. Swiss Miss!

CONTENTS

Chapter One	1
Chapter Two	8
Chapter Three	17
Chapter Four	25
Chapter Five	40
Chapter Six	56
Chapter Seven	62
Chapter Eight	71
Chapter Nine	86
Chapter Ten	92
Chapter Eleven	105
Chapter Twelve	120
Chapter Thirteen	132
Chapter Fourteen	139
Chapter Fifteen	156
Chapter Sixteen	167
Chapter Seventeen	178
Chapter Eighteen	191
Chapter Nineteen	201
Chapter Twenty	217
Chapter Twenty-One	223
Chapter Twenty-Two	231
Chapter Twenty-three	242
Chapter Twenty-Four	244

CHAPTER TWENTY-FIVE 254
CHAPTER TWENTY-SIX 263
CHAPTER TWENTY-SEVEN 268
CHAPTER TWENTY-EIGHT 283
CHAPTER TWENTY-NINE. 291
CHAPTER THIRTY 298

DISCUSSION QUESTIONS 305
ACKNOWLEDGEMENTS 309
ABOUT THE AUTHOR. 313

Graduation

What they say:	vs.	What I hear:
Are you excited?		You! Should! Be! SO! Excited!!!
Have you picked your major?		Why haven't you figured out what you want to do?
What made you choose ETBU?		East Texas Baptist University? Really? But why?
You and Chris going to try the long distance thing?		High School ♡s don't last.
I married my high school sweet ♡.		You and Chris will last FOREVER
Congrats!		Congrats! Here — have a card with $ inside.

class of 2019!   *what's next?!*   *Go Tigers ☺*

CHAPTER ONE

If I burp pizza stink in Chris's face when he tries to kiss me goodnight that's what he gets. Graduation Eve was meant to be girls only—catch-up time with my sisters who are all spending the night at home before the big day. But Chris wanted to give me my graduation present and no, it couldn't wait, and fine. Except he's been at my house through two movies and four boxes of pizza, and he's still working up the nerve to give me whatever-it-is. Obviously it's a bigger deal than the Keurig I said I wanted for my dorm. Almost three years together, and he's first-date shy. It's not like him, and I'm part loving it and part wishing he'd hurry the hell up.

When we step onto the front porch, he doesn't run to his car for a big ol' box but scoots his hand into his jeans' pocket and pulls out a ring. He pinches it between his thumb and pointer finger, holding it up between our faces. How, when I'd said "coffee maker," had he heard "gold ring?"

Chris grins like a puppy about to pounce on his favorite toy. I inch back a step.

"I couldn't do this before with everybody around, but I've been itching to get this ring on your finger all night." Chris pulls my left hand toward his chest. "You know I see us together forever—"

And it hits me. This isn't just a ring. This is a promise ring.

My heart thuds heavy and loud in my head. It's in my chest but also in my ears and even my stomach somehow. Chris goes on talking, and I wonder what a heart attack feels like. Does everything slow down? Do your eyes blur? Does your chest get as tight as my chest is feeling? It's seizing up and constricting. And pain. I feel pain. My attention goes to a moth dancing around the glow of the porch light. Stupid, happy, oblivious moth.

"While you're at ETBU and I'm at A&M, I promise nothing's going to change." Those words—*nothing's going to change*—draw my eyes back to his face, and the rest of his monologue mutes behind them. "Once you transfer over to A&M, we'll get engaged for real." *Nothing's going to change.* "We can even get married while we're in school. My parents did. We can rent our own little apartment together." *Nothing's going to change.*

I'm frozen as he slips the delicate gold band, an infinity symbol looped into its design, onto my finger. His deep brown eyes tear up as he kisses me lightly on the lips.

I'm supposed to be elated, squealing in delight so loud even our old, practically-deaf neighbors could hear. I'm supposed to be surging with love, squeezing

CHAPTER ONE

Chris as hard as he's now squeezing me. When did he start squeezing me?

I'm in love with this boy. Smart, never-has-to-study Chris. Chris who loves the same country songs as I do and sings 'em loud and proud and adorably off-key. Chris, my first time. Tender and slow and nervous. He's been mine for so long, and he wants me so much, and what is wrong with me right now?

I need to sit down.

I wiggle away from him and settle myself onto the top step of the porch. Chris asks me to say something, but I'm concentrating on my breathing. It's really hard to get air. Chris has long since carried on about me joining him at A&M, and until this moment I hadn't discounted it as an option. One option. One of many other possible options.

I stare at the ring on my finger and twist it around to admire it objectively. It's pretty enough that I wonder which one of my sisters helped him pick it out.

Chris settles beside me. "You're so quiet."

"It's beautiful," I say, then exhale slowly, my feeble attempt to expel some of the tightness in my chest. Wanting to come up with more to say, I mumble, "Thank you."

That's it. That's all I got.

After almost three years together, I'd thought that being at separate colleges would be good for us. That it would help me decide if Chris was the love of my life or the love of my high school life. Now it's as though Chris has decided for the both of us.

Nothing's going to change.

"It's a lot to take in right now, probably, but I figured tomorrow would be crazier." Chris pulls me into him again and rests his chin on my head. "I love you Dawn Everly Wilkes, and I can't wait to love you forever."

It's probably my nerves and the extra pizza not letting me love this moment, but I'm not. I'm not loving this moment. I didn't see it coming, and I hate surprises. But Chris is all lit up by hope and yellow porch light, and I can't disappoint him.

"I love you too," I whisper. Someday, when we are way down the road of marriage and kids, I want that answer as part of our story.

Because it's been a pretty good story.

It started sophomore year when Chris and I were partners for a biology class project on genetics. Mrs. O'Day, our teacher, has been assigning the same project every year, and I swear from the looks of her, that's been for about one hundred years. At least.

First, we had to take an inventory of our own observable features as well as more specific things like which hand did we favor for writing? Could we roll our tongues? Did we have a widow's peak or dimples? Then we had to figure out genotypes and phenotypes for a kiddo who might have our DNA. Since we're both White, brown-eyed, and his hair is only a few shades deeper brown than my brownish but more blonde-when-my-highlights-are-fresh hair it was pretty easy. Even when we tossed dice or coins depending on the worksheet instruction no surprise recessive traits emerged. All went smoothly until we had to name her. (The "her" also determined by a coin toss.) We bickered until finally agreeing to write three names each on slips of paper, scramble them on the lab counter, and draw a first and middle name. Apparently, neither of us were taking it seriously at that point because I

CHAPTER ONE

wrote Cinderella, Jasmine, and Belle while Chris went with a water theme—Lake, River, and Ocean. At least we drew one of each.

"Ocean Belle" has been a very opinionated presence in our relationship ever since, beginning with the first time Chris asked me out. One week later, at that same lab table, he said, "Ocean Belle thinks you should go to the homecoming dance with me."

My heart calms a little at the memory. "Ocean Belle approves of this ring," I say.

"Of course she does," he laughs. "Someday she'll want you to pass it on to her."

Nothing's going to change.

Maybe that's not such a bad thing. I kiss Chris lightly on the lips, thank him again, assure him it's perfect, but then remind him that tomorrow is a big day, and he should go on home. He looks disappointed, but then he yawns which makes him laugh probably on account that it's clear his own body agrees with me.

He leans in for yet another kiss. "You are my favorite person in the whole world."

"Of course I am," I say, grinning. I blow him another kiss and slip inside my house.

My three sisters are waiting for me with the wake-the-deaf-neighbors squeals I couldn't muster. They're a chorus of "lemme see!" the second I'm through the front door.

Apparently, I was the last to know.

"It's so pretty!" the twins say together.

"Chris has good taste," agrees Darlene.

"Does he?" I ask. "Or did you do some consulting here?"

Her eyes sparkle. "He maybe texted me pictures from the store. Your man's not stupid."

Texting my oldest sister to make sure he bought the right ring. His place in my family is so entrenched, I should have seen this ring coming. Why hadn't I even considered it?

Mama and Daddy are hanging back at the end of the hall, smiles plastered to their faces.

"Let the girl breathe," Mama says, coming down the hallway, shooing away my sisters with a dish towel. "All right, let me take a look."

"Everybody knew but me?" I ask.

Daddy nods. "That boy's been raised right. Asked me first."

Of course he did.

"This doesn't affect our deal though," Mama says.

"I know." In order for my parents to pay for college, I have to do at least one year at East Texas Baptist University, Mama's alma mater, which also happens to be located thirty minutes away—and that's with hitting most of the red lights. You'd think by the sixth kid, she wouldn't care anymore, but Mama is set in her ways. I'm a good soccer player with good grades, but not at scholarship level in either category. I need Mama's deal. Plus, she'd be so let down if I didn't take it. There's no point in upsetting her for nothing.

I shut the Chris Love Fest down with I'm-tired and big-day-tomorrow excuses and hurry up the stairs to my room. Darlene will be on my trundle since Mama turned her old room into a project room. I'd like to at least be in bed by the time my sister comes up, so I can feign sleep. I'm done talking about this ring. After sliding it off my finger and onto my nightstand,

CHAPTER ONE

I collapse on the bed. My stomach weighs heavy, void of the flutters of excitement I'd expect to be feeling on the eve of my high-school graduation. But what's there to be excited about?

Nothing's going to change.

CHAPTER TWO

My entire mess of siblings, plus my oldest brother's girlfriend and her daughter, are crowded around the breakfast table when I enter the kitchen. Dale, the firstborn of the Wilkes six, lives all of ten minutes away with said girlfriend, but Dustin, kiddo number three, must have gotten in from Houston after I'd gone to bed.

I twirl to show off my graduation dress, its cheerful yellow perfect against my tan and fresh-for-graduation highlights. My brothers oblige me with whistles.

"Little Dawn—all grown," says Dale.

"Oh no," Daddy protests from his spot turning pancakes at the griddle. "Dawn'll always be the baby."

I cringe. We all have our places.

Dale fixes things. Mainly cars, but anything. Give him long enough, and he can take it apart and put it back together, usually without a video tutorial. It's

CHAPTER TWO

super convenient—he replaced the cracked screen on my phone a few weeks ago.

Darlene's the charmer, a personality trait she's long since figured out how to monetize. From neighborhood dog walker as a kid and babysitter successfully charging the highest rates as a teen, she's always hustled. Now, three years into her current venture with a direct sales company, she's got a full team under her and has already won herself jewelry and a car. Not a surprise to anyone.

Nerdy Dustin is now doing grad work at Rice in biomedical something-or-other.

And the twins. Daisy and Dolly can't get past being the double *D*s. Because they're twins with *D* names and because they have really big boobs. Never mind that Daisy graduated college a year early and is already employed full-time at the elementary school as a reading coach. Dahlia's the nurturer of the family on track to become a nurse, but she goes by Dolly, and that certainly doesn't help avoiding a boob-related nickname.

I'm the baby. Even now on my high-school graduation day. I'm not the neat freak, even though I've always kept my room the cleanest and my bed made without being told. I'm not the athlete, no matter that I started soccer at age four and made varsity by sophomore year even without ever playing travel ball because Mama said it cost too much.

For a while in third grade the twins called me Diary Dweeb. When I got my first diary for my ninth birthday, I carried it everywhere and scribbled notes and quips all day long. I've been a faithful journaler since, but not even that nickname stuck.

DENALI SUMMER

Fixer, Charmer, Nerd, Double *D*s, Baby.

Nothing's going to change.

I love pancakes, but my stomach flips a warning that food might be a bad idea. I plop into the first available seat and ask for orange juice.

"Let's not mess up that pretty dress." Mama motions for me to stand and ties an apron around me as though this baby needs a bib. When I sit down again, she sets a glass in front of me along with a small plate of eggs. "Get something in you, or you'll regret it later."

Breakfast conversation is mostly the logistics of who's going in what car to the stadium. I have to be there an hour early, and it's Darlene's job to drive me while Mama and Daddy wait at home for grandparents. That's all I know or need to know.

I manage two bites of eggs, check my makeup one more time, and we head out. I want to stop at the coffee shop where I work to pick up a paycheck and a graduation card from my boss.

About two miles into our drive, we're stopped at a red light, and Darlene looks at me so confused, I look up to make sure we didn't accidentally go the wrong way. It's the right road, and I can see The Coffee Mill sign up ahead.

"What?" Her expression is still freaking me out. It's like she's been brain-wiped by aliens and is suddenly completely bewildered. "Seriously—what, Darlene? You're freaking me out."

She narrows her eyes and looks at my left land. "Where the hell is your ring?"

"My what?" I glance down to where she's looking, and her meaning crashes into my gut. "Oh crap."

CHAPTER TWO

"Oh crap is right." She drums her fingers on the top of the steering wheel. "We have to go back."

"No." It comes out so quickly I surprise myself. "We don't have time."

"We have time. You can pick up your check and stuff later."

"But I promised I'd stop in, show Courtney my dress and all that." And I *want* to stop in.

"It's a crazy day. She'll understand if you text her and say you can't make it."

I know Darlene's right, and I know my ring-free hand will hurt Chris something fierce. "Yeah okay." But as Darlene changes lanes so she can make a U-turn, my chests seizes up like it did last night.

"No. Let's—"

"This light's about to turn. Am I going on or swinging around?"

"Go on," I mumble.

Darlene shakes her head and presses her lips tight as though she's struggling to hold her opinion inside, but when the light turns green, she continues straight.

"Chris'll understand," I say to assure myself, but Darlene hears it and shakes her head in a slow no.

As we pull into the parking lot of The Coffee Mill, Darlene can't keep it back another second. "If you don't want the ring, you have to tell him."

"I want it." Of course I want it. I've been with Chris three years. He's cute and kind, and my family loves him. *I* love him. We lost our virginity to each other. Deepening my commitment to Chris is the right thing.

"I know you, and you cannot shut up when you're excited about something. Then your guy puts a ring on it, and you're all—nothing to say. Doesn't add up."

I exhale and think on this. "It took me by surprise is all."

"Oh, knock off the clueless act." Darlene swats my shoulder. "How could you be surprised? I'm barely home anymore, but I can see Chris is serious as a heart attack when it comes to you. What else would he have given you for graduation?"

"The Keurig I wanted for my dorm?" I'd been dropping hints for a month.

This earns an eye-roll from my sister.

"Maybe I'm not ready to be promised in any official capacity, but I don't want to break up either, so I had to take it." It's the first honest thing I've said about Chris giving me that ring.

"Hell yes, you had to. You and Chris are meant for each other."

It's my turn to roll my eyes. How can anyone outside a relationship know if the two people in the relationship are meant for each other? They. Can't.

Chris decided it's time for a bigger commitment. Mama decided on ETBU. I want to make my own damn decision about something. I don't know what, but... *something*. But if I say any of that, Darlene will accuse me of pouting like a spoiled baby who can't see how good she has it. So I don't say anything else—I just leave Darlene there looking like she has more to say and go into The Coffee Mill.

The deep roast of the coffee hits my nose, and my shoulders relax at the familiar smell. My boss, Courtney,

CHAPTER TWO

isn't behind the counter but seated at a four top with another forty-ish looking woman.

They're hunched over a phone, swiping slowly, oohing and awing.

I wave, hoping the movement will attract Courtney's attention, but it doesn't. I have to stand right beside her before she looks up. "Dawn! You made it. I thought with all you had to do, you might not."

Doubt niggles in my chest. I should've gone back for the ring.

Courtney extends a hand toward the lady at the table. "This is my friend Saige. She just returned from the most amazing vacation in Alaska. Has me drooling jealous over her pictures." Then she nods up at me. "Dawn here is one of my most dependable employees, and she graduates high school today."

The friend half-smiles. "You must be sad to lose her then." And to me, "Where are you heading to college?"

"Oh, I'm not losing her," Courtney answers for me. "She'll be close by at ETBU." She hops up. "Let me grab your card and check and get you on your way."

I sink into the chair my boss has left empty and sweep away a few stray sugar granules from the table.

Saige folds her hands on the table and looks at me. Her face is tan and free of makeup, but the steely blue of her eyes are startling without any help from cosmetics. "Seems to me graduating high school should be the start of a big adventure. What made you decide to stay close to home?"

This feels a little personal coming from a stranger. The comment and question are as piercing as her eyes, but it's not like it's a secret why I'll be at ETBU, so I tell her. "I'm from a big, close family, and my mom likes to keep us close a little longer, so she has a rule that us kids all have to go to ETBU for at least our first year if we want her to pay for college."

Saige nods considering this and tucks a loose strand of grayish-blondish hair behind her ear that's escaped from her messy bun. "Where would you have wanted to go?"

Okay—so this woman doesn't do small talk. List of probing questions it is.

Somewhere I wouldn't be known as the baby of the Wilkes family, and I could just be Dawn. Somewhere with a good athletic program, so I'd be proud to be on their soccer team, but still a small enough school that I'd have a shot to walk on. But I don't need to admit that to a stranger. I've barely admitted that to myself. I say, "My boyfriend's off to A&M, so I guess there."

She cocks her head as though listening for something more and waits, but I have nothing else to add. College is a huge decision that I didn't have a say in, so I didn't give it much thought. Thank you, strange lady, for pointing this out.

When it's clear I've got nothing to add, she shrugs. "You can always adventure with your summers. There are seasonal jobs all over the world. When we were in Alaska, I'd say over half the employees were college students."

"I've never been to Alaska."

"Exactly!" She picks up her phone and brings the screen back to life, flashing a landscape of snowy mountains reflecting rosy pink in the sun's evening glow.

I'm startled by both her enthusiasm and Courtney's hand coming down on my shoulder at the same time.

CHAPTER TWO

My boss waves my check along with a shiny silver envelope before my eyes.

"Don't spend it all in one place." Her smile is wide enough that my expectations for bonus cash in the graduation card climb. "And I promise we'll have direct deposit by the end of the month so you can stop making these extra trips."

"You know I don't mind." I stand, and she holds out her other hand gripping a pastry bag that bulges with what must be a muffin. "I'm sure you didn't eat enough this morning." Then she hugs me tightly and says into my hair, "Proud of you!"

"Think about what I said!" says her friend. It's a happy sing-song chirp, but it makes me feel lame all over again. Not only have I never been to Alaska, but I've never even been on a plane.

In Darlene's car, I rip open the envelope to find a Dr. Seuss-themed card. The quote, reminding me of all the places I'll go, makes me chuckle considering the conversation I had with Saige, and the crisp hundred-dollar bill tucked inside feels like a nudge to put me on the path.

"Your boss loves you," Darlene says, looking at the money. "That's another relationship you best never screw up."

I'd been expecting twenty, hoping for fifty. Not this much. With all the money that's come in from aunts and uncles and my parents' friends—this puts me at seven hundred dollars. I haven't even gotten grandparent money cards yet. I'd planned to put all my graduation cash in my car-savings fund. That has to count in planning to go places, yet for the rest of the ride I'm not thinking about cars. I'm wondering about flight prices to Alaska.

CHAPTER THREE

Before Principal Duhy gets through the *A*s, I've learned that a flight from Dallas to Anchorage will be at least six hundred ninety dollars. That's not including all the extra costs for checked bags and whatever.

By the time we've gotten through the *H*s, I've read dozens of descriptions for Alaska jobs, all of which have deadlines for applying that I've missed. Except one. Listed three days ago. A front desk position at a hotel outside Denali National Park.

By the time Annette Zurita crosses the stage, I've read that listing so many times, I have it memorized.

All of which was a stupid use of my time because there's no way I'm leaving my job at the coffee shop and my loves-me-very-much boyfriend for the summer. But hey, at least in a graduating class of 279 seniors, it gave me something to do slightly more productive than following the class hashtag on Instagram to see what pictures people were already posting.

DENALI SUMMER

Since Chris is a Butler and I'm a Wilkes, we were miles apart during the ceremony, but afterward he finds me before joining his family. His eyes go straight to my ringless hand.

I fumble through an excuse—that I wasn't used to wearing it yet and in the hoopla of getting out the door for graduation on time, hadn't slipped it on. He says he understands but his expression, tight-lipped and concentrated, shows me he doesn't. More than once, as he pulls me through the crowd of our fellow graduates, he looks at my hand as though the ring might finally, magically appear. After we stop for a selfie with Charlet, my best friend, he mumbles, "But why'd you even take it off?"

My family and Chris's have made a plan to lunch together at the hibachi restaurant since their private room is the only spot big enough to accommodate a group as large as ours. Mama knew to book it two months out. There's no time to stop at my house to get my ring, but I can hear the wheels in Chris's brain trying to figure out how to squeeze in a stop and not be late for the reservation. Finally he accepts that it will have to wait till after. I promise I'll have it on for the class-wide Project Graduation party tonight.

"That's what matters. We'll show our friends then." I squeeze his hand and smile, regretting my decision to not go back this morning when I had the chance. I didn't mean to hurt him.

He doesn't return the smile. "I wanted to show Grams," he says.

Grams, the only member of Chris's family I've never met, lives in Florida and hasn't flown out to Texas since Chris's big brother graduated high school. That was the year before Chris and I started dating. Chris wants to introduce me to Grams as the girl he plans to marry someday. My chests constricts the way it did last night.

CHAPTER THREE

I pass the afternoon in a haze of wide-faced smiles and hugs and thank yous and entirely too much shrimp, fried rice, and yum-yum sauce. I think I'm managing the people and the attention and even an awkward introduction to Grams well enough until we're waiting on the checks and Dolly taps my shoulder.

"Come with me and bring your purse. I need your lipstick."

I nod and follow her around the table.

"Are you okay?" She asks as soon as we've ducked through the hanging black beads covering the doorway of the party room. This isn't really about my lipstick.

"Of course. Why?"

Instead of answering me she pulls me along to the bathroom. Inside, she leans against the sink and studies me. "You don't look so good."

I nudge her over and stare at my face in the mirror. My makeup is still fine. No lipstick remnants on my cheeks from grandma kisses or anything like that.

Dolly turns so we're shoulder to shoulder looking into the mirror together. "I mean you look tense. You've barely spoken two words to Chris since we got here. That boy looks like he's going to cry. What's going on?"

"What if I told you—" I trail off. What? That I wanted a coffee maker not a gold infinity promise ring? Who thinks that way?

But this is Dolly, and she can read symptoms even when you don't finish your sentences. "It's too much all at once, isn't it?"

"Yes! Why'd he go and have to add such a big thing to this weekend?"

DENALI SUMMER

"It'll be fine. All the family will be gone soon enough." Dolly's smile is all warmth and filled with the understanding Darlene couldn't muster this morning. When she pulls me into a hug, I relax against her, and my eyes sting with the threat of tears. She knows me. I'm just overwhelmed, and it will pass, and by tomorrow that ring will be my new favorite accessory.

She continues soothingly into my hair, "Just breathe, baby sis. All the craziness will die down soon. Before you know it, you'll be out on the lake with Chris, and you'll remember that boy is the best thing to ever happen to you." I pull away, and her smile grows. "You got this!"

"I got this." I echo and do my best to match her expression, but as she tugs me back to the party room, I can't stop thinking about her words. Is Chris the best thing to *ever* happen to me? At seventeen—my career undecided, my travels untraveled—and my sister thinks the best thing about my life is, and will ever be, a guy. I may not have pieced together much about my future, but Dolly's words have me unsettled.

As we step back through the black beads hanging above the entry, I glance around the room of all the well-meaning people here to support and celebrate me and Chris. I lock eyes with my boyfriend, and his face lights up at the same time a very clear and true voice in my head whispers: *the best thing to ever happen to me should be me.*

CHAPTER THREE

Or maybe I've been blowing everything out of proportion. After Project Graduation, Chris drives me home through the quiet streets of early morning. We've been together all night, but he still comes inside. Mama and Daddy won't be up for another hour or so, so we get to kissing on the living room love seat for so long that it feels so right. He's back to being the happy boyfriend because I wore the ring to the party and squealed and giggled along with our friends. Easy. Fun, even. I have no idea what I've been getting so worked up about.

After who-knows-how-long with our faces mashed, I nudge him back. "I really want to get a nap before church."

"Who needs sleep?" he says and starts kissing my neck.

"Chris!" I laugh. "You've got to go."

He groans and pulls away. "All right. But only because I'm picking you up at ten for family brunch with Grams before she flies home. She needs to see that ring."

This is the first I've heard about brunch with Grams.

"Ten! That's in like four hours." I glance at the clock on the mantel and groan. Three hours and twenty-five minutes to be exact. It's not welcome news. I was already dreading the fact that I couldn't sleep away the morning because Mama demanded we all be in church. We hardly ever go, and I begged her to just let me sleep, but they're recognizing graduating seniors during service, and she expects me to take part. It's been one event after another, but Chris has planned on brunch and Mama expects church.

It's easiest to agree.

DENALI SUMMER

After promising to put in an appearance at brunch before church at eleven, I peck Chris's cheek a final goodnight and shoo him out the door.

I tip-toe through the house and make my way along by feel, not wanting to turn on lights to wake anyone. I can't shake feeling annoyed that Chris told his family I'd be at brunch without asking me. The very first morning after I've graduated high school and my schedule has been decided by my boyfriend and my mama. I feel more annoyed at the layer of thought beneath poking through reminding me that he does this all the time, and it's never bothered me before.

Darlene's sleep breaths float up from her spot on the trundle, the only sound when I enter my room. I'm now too wired to crash. My phone's dead, so I grab my laptop. I could unwind seeing what classmates have posted since I last checked. But instead of going to Snapchat or Instagram, I search, "Denali National Park" and spend at least ten minutes looking at images. Then I find my way back to the job description of the front desk clerk.

Nothing is ever going to change unless I change it.

What if I can have the boy and the adventure? I'd only take the summer off to give myself one big change. All for me. My heart flutters with excitement. I can do this big, exciting, surprise-everyone thing.

But I only get as far as typing in my name when the ridiculousness of it all hits me, and I close the laptop.

Oh, stop being such a chickenshit. Show everyone you can make decisions for yourself. Right here. Right now.

Open laptop.

Mama will be so pissed. Do you really want to deal with that?

CHAPTER THREE

Laptop stays open.

And Chris—he'll be sad and confused, and how could you ever explain something this crazy to him?

My hand rests on the top of the computer, ready to shut it again.

If you apply, you don't have to accept.

I stare at the screen.

Oh who am I kidding? Why would I apply and not take the job?

Close laptop.

Open laptop.

Type fast.

wall stuff?　　　　　jewelry?
　　　　　　　　　　　bath mat?
　　　PACK!

Uniform:　• white button shirt 4
　• khaki pants 4 (get by with 3?)
　• black flats　• black belt

Other shoes: sneakers, shower flip
sandals x2, boots, black heels flops
　turquoise wedges?

hiking clothes:　pants 2　　purses
　long sleeve Ts 3　　　^.
　long underwear 2

Other clothes: jeans 2, black pants
　shorts 3　tops - 4 (5? more?)
Ts 5　dresses - 2　tanks - 3 4?
PJs - 3　sports bras - 3　reg bras - 3
undies - 8　swimsuit? brown belt
　What am I forgetting?　　spray

Room: Do I need hangers? Bug
sheets, blanket, throw　　Bear
　towels - 3　charger　　spray
flashlight　back up alarm clock?
　charger　speaker

1st Aid: ibuprofin, band aids, eye drops
cough drops, <u>Ask Dolly</u>.

Toiletries: shampoo/conditioner x2
lotion x3, toothbrush/paste, razors →
　　　　　　　x2

continued!

CHAPTER FOUR

My phone alarm clock goes off two-and-a-half hours later, and I check my email.

An hour after I sent in the application, an email reply from an HR person named Angie landed in my inbox. She wants me to start in the next five days. They need to replace an employee who went home after breaking her ankle slipping on some ice, and though it's not company policy, they'll pay $500 toward my flight since the short notice will likely mean higher prices for me.

I read the words over, my heart racing. Darlene shifts in the bed beside me, and I wonder if she can hear it.

Should I do this? What will my family say?

I gently shut my laptop and step over my sister, but I still bump the bed and she mumbles, "Da-awn. Go back to bed."

"Sorry," I whisper, "But I have to get ready for brunch with Chris's family, then I'll meet you all at the church." I grab everything I need, so I can get ready in the bathroom and pull the door shut as slowly and softly as I can so as not to rouse her again. I've got so much to think about, and I don't need anyone in my opinionated family weighing in.

Through my shower, my mind is a steady stream of:
You can't.
Everyone will think you've lost your mind.
Just do it!
It will hurt Chris.
If your relationship is meant to be, it can withstand this.
It's just one summer.
There goes all your graduation money and your car.
It's the experience of a lifetime.
So do it next summer with Chris.
This is your chance to show everyone you can.
This is your chance to not be the baby.
This is your chance.

The point I'm stuck on as I dry my hair and put on my makeup is—why now? Why the hurry? Alaska's not going anywhere. Okay, with climate change parts of it are, but I likely have all the summers of my college years where I could do something like this. So of course I should plan for Chris and I to do this together.

But I've been offered a job *now* and a bonus to help with the flight *now*.

Once I'm ready, I assess myself in the mirror. All dressed in a red, spaghetti-strap jumpsuit Mama bought me special for church today, all made-up so my big brown eyes look wider and deeper ("The kind of eyes I could swim in forever," Chris likes to say),

CHAPTER FOUR

and all done-up so my hair lies shiny and flat—I'm ready for Sunday brunch. Is this the look of a girl who can survive Alaskan terrain?

Probably not.

Do I still want to go?

I twist my promise ring around my finger.

Yes. Yes, I do.

The day passes in a blur, and I don't tell a soul what's on my mind. It's not until after church and lunch at the house (Mama had a casserole bubbling in the crockpot ready for us as soon as we got back) that things start to quiet and settle into the leisurely pace I love best from Sundays. One by one my siblings drift away with a final hug and congratulations and go back to their own homes and lives.

I find Daddy in the office that once upon a long time ago had been the boys' room. A border of alternating sports balls still hugs the top of the wall, but it's the only remnant of their reign here.

"What's up, buttercup," Daddy says as I inch into the room. It's his greeting for any of the Wilkes women. I plop down on the old loveseat that got retired from the living room when Mama redid it a few years back, and I pull the throw pillow into my lap, hugging it tight. Daddy's face is expectant. If I were telling him I'd be heading over to Chris's or a graduation party somewhere, I wouldn't have sat down. I'd have chirped my plans from the door.

DENALI SUMMER

"Looks like you got something on your mind," he says, watching my face for some sort of clue.

"I was thinking about doing something other than The Coffee Mill for work this summer," I begin.

"But you love it there. That doesn't make sense."

If he thinks *that* doesn't make sense wait till he hears the rest of it. I consider how to explain, but settle on spilling it all out in a rush: Chris's ring being a surprise. Saige being all sagey. Reading up on Alaska jobs through graduation. And the fact that there's one summer position available in Alaska right now, and it's been offered to me.

Daddy turns back to his computer and starts typing something in the search bar.

"What are you doing?"

"You're my baby girl, Dawn. This is the worst, good idea you've ever brought to me, but I'd be a terrible Daddy if I didn't support you because it scares me to let you go so far away. And—" he clicks a few times on his screen, "this will be easier to explain to your Mama if the flight's already booked."

Within another fifteen minutes, it's done. I leave out of Dallas on Wednesday morning.

He promises to prepare Mama while I take a nap before I'm off to my best friend Charlet's graduation party.

Charlet's party is in the fellowship hall of their Methodist church. At one end of the room, there's a

CHAPTER FOUR

buffet set up of pulled pork, baked beans, and potato salad. At the other, volunteer church ladies serve banana pudding and cake from the steel counter that separates the serving area from the industrial kitchen. There's a photo booth for people to take silly pictures and a giant matte for guests to sign that will go around a framed graduation picture of Charlet, and that's about it. This party is mostly for Charlet's parents to show off their daughter so their church friends will give her money.

Chris and I each make a plate for our dinner, snap a few pictures with Charlet, and are ready to leave within an hour.

I go back to Charlet where she's still posing for pictures and wave her toward me.

"Is it okay if Chris and I go? Or do you need me for anything?" I ask.

"I'm good. I made Parker promise to stay till the end. She nods at Parker, her boyfriend, who is now seated with Chris. They're laughing over a video on Parker's phone. "We don't even have to take care of the clean-up. It's part of the rental fee, so the kitchen committee does it all."

"God bless the kitchen committee," I laugh.

"Especially since they all added cards to my graduation present pile. When are we going shopping for our dorm? I should have plenty of cash after today."

"I'm actually going to Tyler tomorrow after work for some things. I have my dad's car all day. You can come with." I can tell her it's an Alaska shopping trip and not a dorm shopping trip then. The thing about Charlet is you have to pick your moments. In our friendship she's the Elsa, and I'm the Anna. Not just because she's the blonde, and I'm the brunette, but mostly because oh boy, she can let it go.

I hug my friend and promise to text her tomorrow when I leave The Coffee Mill.

In the car, Chris and I discuss what we want to watch when we get back to my house. I still haven't said a word about Alaska. Chris starts a horror flick, the third or fourth in a series he likes. I can't keep track of them. Dread takes hold in my stomach, hardens, and begins to ache—not because of the impending body count, but because of what I know I have to do. Usually, I'd just fall asleep, but I watch ever wide-eyed as the body count grows.

The first line of credits is barely on the screen when Chris moves in to kiss me, but I hold my hand up to stop him.

"I have something to tell you."

He eyes me, wondering what could have possibly come up since brunch this morning that is such big news I've saved it for this late in our time together.

I continue, "I figured out how I want to spend my graduation money—I'm taking a trip this summer. I bought a plane ticket."

He scoots backward. "What do you mean?"

"I'm going to Alaska."

"Alaska?" he repeats it as a question. "Like to go on a cruise?"

CHAPTER FOUR

"Not exactly. I've decided to take a seasonal job," I say. "Something different. An adventure all my own before school."

He cocks his head and grins. "Funny. Now really, what's the news?"

I'm annoyed that he doesn't believe me. I stand and walk to the window. There's an orange cat crossing the road being spotlighted by the moonlight. "It's just a summer, Chris."

His upper body falls backward on the sofa, and he releases an exasperated sigh. "Dawn, I'm tired, and this isn't funny. I'll just go home and then come get you in the morning, and we can talk about whatever is really going on."

"Can't. I work in the morning, and right after my shift I'm going to Tyler, so I can shop for hiking boots and whatever else is on my list I probably can't find here."

He pauses long enough that I can picture his confused expression even though I'm still watching the cat now slinking between my neighbors' cars. Then he asks, "You mean it?"

The details I spilled for Daddy come out again, but I leave out the part where I say the ring spooked me into being restless enough to do something like this. In this version, I blame Mama more, emphasizing needing freedom from her plans to really feel like I've graduated.

He stands and joins me at the window and wraps his arms around me before whispering at my neck, "If it's what you need to do, then I support it."

DENALI SUMMER

His arms feel so good. How can I give Chris up for an entire summer? I turn to kiss him, but he starts talking again.

"Of course if there's any way to talk you out of this, I support that more."

Ugh. Never mind.

In the kitchen the next morning before I head off to work, Mama quips, "I can't imagine what you think you'll find in Alaska, but what's done is done. Just don't get eaten by a bear."

So Daddy did his part and told her while I was at the party, and she's taking it as well as can be expected. Mama takes her coffee to the back porch, making it clear she isn't interested in any response I have for her. Mama is a damn fine pouter.

At The Coffee Mill, I break it to my boss in person. She says of course my job will still be waiting for me in the fall, but she needs to have a talk with her friend.

I announce it to my siblings in the family group text later in the morning during a lull. They weigh in (once it's established that I'm not kidding) accordingly:

Dale, Darleen, and Daisy: I'm batshit crazy.

Dustin: Totally awesome. Proud of me.

Dolly: Doesn't understand what's gotten into me, but is happy "so long as I'm following my heart."

Work stays typical for a Monday—steady, but overall, slow. By one o'clock, the end of my six-hour shift, I'm ready to clock out and concentrate on all things Alaska prep. I told Courtney I could still work

CHAPTER FOUR

my shift in the morning, but she rolls her eyes and says not to worry about it.

Charlet's only in the car a minute before she asking me what we're shopping for. I've got the whole story out by the time we're at the stop sign at the end of her street. She's so mad she insists I turn the car around and bring her home.

"I thought this was going to be dorm shopping for matchy things or new bikinis for our next lake day. What the fuck, Dawn?"

I try to say we'll Facetime dorm shopping, and it's just a summer and... But we're back in her driveway already, and Charlet doesn't waste time. She slams the car door and marches up to her garage to punch in the code. She flips me off before she ducks under the not-fully-open garage door and charges back inside.

She's always had a temper. She'll text me in an hour or so, calling herself a bitch but saying I deserve it. Then she'll call me, and we'll laugh and maybe even cry—a version of the routine we've had down since fourth grade when she moved here.

It's Dolly who comes through with the sweetest support with zero stench of a guilt-trip. When I get home with my new work shoes, khakis, and button-down shirts, plus a pair of hiking boots, Dolly's in the kitchen stirring up a batch of her homemade granola.

On the table is big, brightly patterned tote bag bursting with goodies for my trip. There's dumb magazines, a paperback, two "doodle me calm" coloring books, and a whole slew of bright pens and fancy skinny markers including glitter colors and neon.

There's also notecards, stamps, and my favorite candy. That girl loves to give.

"I'm glad you like it." She smiles and pulls wax paper out of the pantry to line a cookie sheet. "Give me an hour, and this'll be ready to go in there too."

I hug her, pinning her arms to her side, so she can't tear the paper free.

"Or longer if we're going to build in time for sister moments."

She smells like cinnamon and honey as if I didn't need another reason to count her as my favorite person at the moment.

"You're the best, Miss Dhalia. Seriously the best."

"I'm better with the use of my arms though."

After releasing her, I wander off to find Mama and ask what suitcase I can use. I'm in the attic at the end of the upstairs hallway lugging out an old brown monstrosity of a trunk-size suitcase when a text pings. She held out longer than usual, but it's Charlet.

Ok fine. Maybe I'll forgive you, but we're double dating tonight and going to the lake tomorrow, and if that means you don't have enough time to pack, I don't even care.

I text back: *What restaurant, what time? Are the guys already in?*

A stare at my phone until the next ping. *Papacita's. I'll get you at 7. Chris is getting Parker and meeting us there.*

For Mexican food she knows I like The Jalapeño Tree better so picking Papacita's is probably part of her still being salty, but I text a thumbs up and a kiss emoji and slide my phone back in my pocket.

CHAPTER FOUR

A night and a day of pretending ensues. A night out with my boyfriend, best friend, and her boyfriend with no mention of Alaska. A day with a bigger group at Parker's grandparents' lake house where we dive off the dock again and again as though it's our job. At one point, Parker's brother, younger than us by two grades, tries to ask me about Alaska, but Charlet shuts him down. Dates and lake fun, with shifts at The Coffee Mill, would have been my entire summer.

Good, but also stuck.

And I think if I'm ever going to grow, I need to get free.

Tuesday night there's another graduation party, a guy Chris knows from speech and debate, but I bow out to spend the evening with Mama and Daddy and the twins who come over for dinner too.

Chris texts me throughout the party, offering to come pick me up, but I keep insisting he stay and have fun. At midnight when another text comes through it reads:

Come down. Say goodbye.

I peek through my window to see his car in my driveway. He snuck off from the party earlier than I expected him to. I reply with a single emoji—the sleeping smiley.

Then why's your bedroom light on? Knowing you, you're still trying to figure out what to take out of that over-packed suitcase.

He knows me. That's certain.

DENALI SUMMER

In a minute I step onto the front porch. Chris's brown hair, newly buzzed before graduation to survive the summer heat, is aglow in our front porch light, and he's sweating through a peach-colored shirt.

We sit on the porch steps awhile not talking. Gnats swarm around our heads, and I scrape green paint off the concrete and pick at the chips from underneath my fingernails. Chris reaches beside him and hands me a skinny box. The kind that holds jewelry.

"What in the world, Chris? You already bought me my present." I turn the box over in my hands, reluctant to open it.

"It's for your birthday, but you'll be—" He trails off. He can't bring himself to say "gone."

I think about when we kissed in this same spot after our first real date. As in not hanging out at a school event or with twenty friends at the bowling alley kinda date. Chris had gotten his driver's license and wanted to celebrate by taking me to a fancy restaurant. Mama cried and said the last of her babies had become a grown woman.

I didn't see how putting on a dress and ordering crab cakes made me a grown woman, but that didn't stop me from falling hard that night. Chris knew how to make me forget Mama and Daddy's bedroom light still glowing right above our kissing heads when he held me there on our porch whispering sugary words and holding me through our goodnights.

That night when I looked into his face, I saw the promise of everything and that surely included love.

The night before I leave for Alaska, a few days after I'd tossed my tasseled cap into the air and mingled for the last time with a pack of kids I'd known since

CHAPTER FOUR

kindergarten, I see in his face the same promise, but I wonder what he sees in mine.

I tap my fingers on top of the box. "You're too good to me." I need to keep reminding myself this.

"You deserve that, Dawn. I want to spoil you your whole life."

Since it can't be a promise ring, I don't know why I'm so afraid, but I'm slow, picking at the tape on one end, then the other. Chris carries on about how he understands I'm changing. How he sees it's hard for me, the youngest of the six *D*s. He knows now that the ring was too big a surprise, and we should have talked about it first. He says if I change my mind and come home early because I don't like Alaska then we'll plan our own adventure. Road trip somewhere special.

"Just you and me. Think about it."

I don't answer but dislodge the top of the box and stare at a chunky silver bracelet resting on a white cotton bed. A charm bracelet—something I've talked about starting but held off because my sisters all have one. I don't like following in their footsteps. I also don't like not doing something simply because it has already been done in my family. When you're the sixth kid, it doesn't leave much undone. So, like with most things, I remained indecisive. And, like with most things, here's Chris ready to make the decision for me.

But I'd picked Alaska. All on my own.

"I don't mind you flying away. As long as you come back to me," Chris says as I rub the first of two charms, a solid silver airplane, between my fingers. "I added that one this morning before we left for the lake. Couldn't believe the jewelry store had one."

DENALI SUMMER

I inspect the second charm, a smooth, flat silver circle engraved on both sides. On one—the monogram of my initials and on the other—in tight, all-caps font, "You're my only favorite. love, C."

Oh hell. This can't still be true.

Chris's favorites list in his phone has consisted of me. Only me. It had been a gift of sorts on our one-year anniversary. "It's a metaphor," he'd said, showing me the screen, so I could stare at the absences. His parents, guys on the debate club, their faculty sponsor, his favorite local pizza spot—all deleted, all empty spaces. In that moment, I'd felt the dazzling weight of having become his whole world.

I'd always been 1/279th of a class. Or 1/26th of a homeroom. 1/16th of the girls on the soccer team. 1/14th of the grandkids on Mama's side and 1/9th of 'em on Daddy's. 1/8th of my household, and 1/6th of my siblings. Even as a metaphor, it had felt good to stand alone.

But it's time our worlds got bigger.

I reach around Chris to grab his phone off the porch.

"What are you doing?" he asks but doesn't stop me.

"We're going off to school. Different schools even. We can't be—" I scroll through his contacts till I land on his big brother and add him as a favorite, then the wings shop on the south end of town, then his boss at the movie theater.

It's as much as I can manage before Chris yanks the phone out of my hands. "We can't be what?"

I was going to say, "We can't be everything to each other," but there's a hurt in his eyes that stops me short, nudges my frustration aside. This was supposed

CHAPTER FOUR

to be a sweet goodbye. The part of me that wants him to be happy slips the bracelet on my wrist.

"It's a good memory," I say, sliding around the silver, examining it against my skin, considering its heft, whether or not I'll get used to it. "But it's okay to open ourselves up to a little more."

"You're still my favorite." His voice cracks, so I snuggle in, resting my head on his shoulder.

"You really think you'll be gone all summer?" he asks.

"That's the plan." *My* plan until I have to fall in line with Mama's required plan. My Tiger Camp Move-In date's been logged into my phone's calendar for weeks now.

"Grizzly bears and no nighttime and all that hiking. You really up for that? You get the right hiking boots and a bear whistle and everything else you need?"

I have no idea what a bear whistle is, but I nod. The scent of the neighbor's magnolia swells around us as we sit in silence, me tracing the letters of Chris's inscription with my finger, still not knowing what to think about it. The soft humidity of an early Texas summer and the steady thrum of the cicadas increases. This is home. And a whole summer away is a long time. A lot of missed days on the lake, a lot of missed date nights and movie nights and summer barbecues. Of course I'm not ready for grizzlies and constant day light and all that hiking and whatever else Alaska has that Texas doesn't.

I'm going anyway.

CHAPTER FIVE

Daddy stands gripping his third cup of coffee, hugging me at the Dallas airport's curb-side drop off. He wanted to park and watch me go through security, but I wouldn't allow it. Now he's fighting his tears.

"Isn't this what you'd do for Dale or Darlene?" I ask.

"I don't think either of those two have been on an airplane."

"Then what about for Dustin when he used to go to Florida?" The third D-kid traveled three of his high school summers in a row to Kennedy Space Center for camp. "I'll be fine, Daddy," I reassure him and hug him tight.

It's a good front, but the minute I turn away from him, tears sting my eyes. All I have to do is turn back around, and he'd understand then quietly and thankfully return my luggage to the trunk. But I've said goodbye. I won't go back.

I check my suitcase and follow the signs to security where I take off my shoes like the lady in front of me

CHAPTER FIVE

and try not to think about how naked the weird body scanner machine is making me look to the TSA guy monitoring the screen.

I find my gate in plenty of time, but I'm too scared to go off exploring in case I miss the boarding announcement. I bought a water, but I'm afraid if I drink it, I'll have to pee, which puts me in a bathroom also out of boarding announcement range.

During take-off I chew gum to keep my ears clear like Mama told me to, and it works okay. I sit by the window watching big ass Texas grow smaller and smaller until it disappears beneath a cloudy sky.

During that first flight, I don't open my Dolly sack one time. Instead I pick at my thin sweater so much I put a dime-size hole in the sleeve. The lady beside me pulls out a neck pillow and goes right to sleep which suits me fine. I don't feel like talking.

Weeks ago, I chose a schedule for this first week of the summer that had me working every morning and sunning with Charlet every afternoon. After a whole summer of more or less the same, I knew I'd be happy to continue on to ETBU. I've even wondered if I'll like it enough to stay on there to get my degree like the twins and not drop out like Darlene. (Dale never went to college. Dustin got offered so much money by other schools, he didn't need Mama's plan.)

Chris had to go and rattle me. I eye his ring on my finger and twist around the bracelet on the wrist of my opposite hand. I've been claimed by jewelry. Twice over.

I pull out my wallet, unzip the coin pocket, and drop in the ring. Then I take off the bracelet and zip it into the inside pocket of my Dolly sack.

DENALI SUMMER

Not this summer. This summer is for me.

Once I'm seated at the gate in the Seattle airport, I relax a little. Halfway there. I pull out a pack of skinny markers and the first coloring book my fingers touch. Flipping through, I settle on a wood scene—a swirl of pinecones, tree limbs, and small animals. The seats fill in around me as I make progress on the page. First comes a family of four—mom, dad, and two boys, eight-ish and ten-ish. I overhear the youngest boy pounding his mom with question after question about Alaska. Must be vacationers.

A young couple takes up four seats as well, sandwiching themselves between two giant hiking backpacks. They can't stop kissing, so I guess they're off on some adventurous honeymoon.

And then there's the cute guy all by himself at the end of my row. He wears a massive set of headphones and sits oblivious to all of us while he reads a paperback.

I make a concerted effort not to look his way again. I have a boyfriend. This trip is for me to be with me. To be out of my home that sometimes housed as many as eight people, three finches, two cats, and a dog. Away from my best friend, Charlet, who arranged with the ETBU housing department for us to be roommates without bothering to ask me first.

Away from Chris.

He's already texted me twice today. The first pinged with a flashing gif that read, "I woke up wanting to

CHAPTER FIVE

kiss you," making my stomach jump and my thoughts re-doubt Alaska all over again. I heart it but don't reply. His second text asked me to call him once I land because he wants to make sure I get in okay. I like this second text but don't have anything else to say. A few days into this trip I'll surely miss him, and I'll be the one sending him love-sick gifs, but I'm not there yet.

Do a little hiking. Make a little money. Room by myself and experience quiet. Accomplish this thousands of miles away from all things high school, Chris, and Mama. Then with a clear head, I'll know what *I* want.

End-of-the-row cute boy slides the headphones to his neck and runs his fingers through his shaggy reddish-brown hair, but I have no business noticing that. I renew my concentration on a fat squirrel's fluffy tail.

The seatbelt light above me blinks on and a flight attendant announces we're preparing for descent. I snatch my open-but-ignored journal off the tray table and toss it in my Dolly sack.

The angles and edges of the mountains take on definition as we draw closer. There's more brown peeking through the white than I expected. We come in over water, and I search the surface, expecting what? I'm not sure. Little floating ice islands occupied by polar bears? An enormous whale cresting and splashing my welcome? There's nothing but the perfectly spaced pattern of wind grooves layering deep blue over deeper, darker blue. I have not landed in theme-park Alaska, but the real thing, and the only impression she makes as the plane touches down is that she is a vast, far-reaching place. So like Texas but also not all.

A smooth landing does nothing for the jostles and bounces increasing in my stomach.

Ditto for the voice over my shoulder as I inch into the aisle and pop open the overhead bin to fetch my backpack and jacket.

"Need a hand?" asks Headphone Boy, injecting a slight second syllable on the word "hand." During treks to the bathroom, I'd noticed him a few rows behind me. The elderly couple and some other solo male passengers in the rows between us are either still gathering their things or have already ducked ahead.

"Thanks, but it's pretty light." And by light I mean lighter than a car or a small elephant but still probably heavier than a sack of bowling balls. No matter. I don't want to accept help from a cute boy, certainly not one with a soft, familiar drawl, perfect for lulling me off my guard.

My backpack contains everything I'll need for my one night in Anchorage before continuing on to Denali in the morning. And a second set of clothes I shouldn't need. And another book. And a throw blanket in case what the hostel provides is gross. Point is—I don't want to do battle with the zipper on my over-stuffed suitcase until it comes time for its summer-long unpacking, so I over-stuffed my backpack too.

I shimmy into it, drape the Dolly sack over my shoulder, tuck my jacket on top, and waddle forward a few inches before the next inevitable stand-still.

"You here for the summer?" he asks.

CHAPTER FIVE

I nod, eyes concentrating on the coat of the man standing in front of me.

"It's my second summer. I'm up from Texas."

He didn't draw out the word "Texas" with the love and reverence I'm used to hearing from fellow natives. I turn around.

He smiles when I look at him, a wide smile that pushes into his eyes, crinkling his whole face in the cheeriest way. His hair stands up, mussed, no doubt, by the headphones no longer on his ears, but hanging from his neck.

"That where you're from?" There should be no doubt, with my accent, where I'm from.

"Originally, no, but we've been there—" he stops, seemingly to do calculations in his head— "in August, it'll be four years."

Not a Texan. Not even a little bit. When he talks, I concentrate on his eyes, a golden-hazel brighter, almost orange, in the center. And his messy hair, lit so brightly by the fluorescent lights above us combined with the daylight streaming in from raised blinds in the land of the midnight sun, is flecked with a coppery red. In burnt-yellow corduroy pants and a red and orange plaid shirt, everything about him is warm, like a cozy fire standing behind me.

"I'm born and raised East Texan," I say.

"I've never been east of Dallas. In Texas, I mean. I moved from the East Coast."

I'm about to ask if that's where he's originally from, but the line of passengers shuffles forward. I turn to settle into the lumbering pace, letting his sentence be the last in our conversation. He takes the hint and doesn't say anything else when the line slows again near the exit. He's across from me at the luggage claim, but my suitcase is one of the first on the carousel. I lose him as I head outside.

After being inside airports and planes all day, I welcome the blast of cool, fresh air and wait awhile before pulling on my jacket. It must have been eighty degrees this morning when I left Dallas, but a quick check of the weather app on my phone tells me it's forty-eight in Anchorage. At seven in the evening, the sun still overpowers the cloudless sky. The wall of mountains stand even more jagged and intimidating than they looked from the air. Flat East Texas seems like another planet.

I squint in the direction of traffic, hoping to spot a cab but don't see one. Two pulled away from the curb as I arrived, so now I have to wait for the next batch or just give up and order an Uber.

The connected-at-the-mouth couple from the Seattle airport settles in behind me, wearing their giant packs.

"Where you heading?" asks the girl. "Maybe we can share a ride."

I tell her the name of the hostel I booked, and she shakes her head. "That's the one closest to the airport. We're headed downtown." She smiles in a way that makes me think she knows something I don't, and I second-guess my hasty choice made after a brief online search. But there was a moose pictured in front of the building in their most prominent website photo, and I'd kinda hoped he came with the place. Happy moose plus the fact that zero pics of former occupants sporting bed bug rashes had shown up in review posts.

CHAPTER FIVE

This could not be said of the hostel closest to the train station, my other main consideration.

"Susanna! Johnny! Where we going?" Headphone Boy, now sporting his own giant pack, joins our party. My suitcase looks even more out of place.

"Mr. Master Quesadilla Maker! Thought that was you at the airport." Johnny gives him the back-pat boy version of a hug, but before he can even pull away his hand from the first pat, Susanna rushes in with a full stand-up tackle.

"Gonna miss your food, man."

"Yeah? You won't be at the park?"

"Nah. Got gigs in Nome. Port town work this year."

I think I'm making sense of this exchange as a taxi comes around the corner. I step closer to the curb to make clear I'm claiming it.

The driver pops the trunk and steps around to help me load my luggage. As I'm telling him what hostel, Headphone Boy bumps up beside me.

"Sounds good. Me too." He dumps his pack onto my suitcase and slides it to the side, wedging it into the small remaining trunk space.

Turning toward me, he holds out his hand. "I'm Flint. Don't mind splitting cab fare, do you?"

I shake his hand. It's strong and warm. "Do you go by Flint or Mr. Master Quesadilla Maker?" *Or Headphone Boy*, I add in my mind.

He laughs. "Try my quesadillas before you make that call."

During the short ride, we realize we'll both be working at the Denali Tundra Lodge. Flint's returning to his job in the employee cafeteria and congratulates me for scoring a cushiony front desk job as they tend to be more coveted—doled out first to retired old folks still game for a summer adventure.

"I'm replacing someone who broke her ankle."

He nods. "That would explain the late start. Front desk clerks usually come in the first wave. There's more training."

"What do you mean waves?" I'm a little unsettled thinking I'm behind in what I'm supposed to know, but there's nothing I can do about that now.

"Start dates. They bring in a wave of employees at a time."

It must have worked out that I'm in with Flint's wave. At least there will be other newbies with me.

The car crunches up a gravel driveway and the hostel stands a pleasant violet that matches the bluebonnets dotting the front lawn. No sign of a welcome moose though. A pair of guys with shaggy beards and striped knit caps are lounging on the lawn and call out friendly hellos. I pull cash for my half of the cab ride and gather all my things.

Flint looks over my luggage. "No camping gear? Or is it tucked away in that...I'd call it a suitcase, but it looks more like a pod. How much in over-weight charges did you have to pay?"

It had cost a lot, but Flint doesn't need to know that. The employee website didn't list camping gear on the packing list. It was emphatic about having enough dress-code work clothes and mentioned bringing bedding and towels but nothing about camping gear.

"No comment," I say, frowning. I'm trucking around more volume and weight than anyone else I've met, and it might be all the wrong stuff.

CHAPTER FIVE

Flint accepts this answer without further prodding. "It's all good. You can borrow, or there's a small gear shop near the hotel that rents. Eventually you'll figure out what you want to buy." He nudges me with his elbow. "Let's check in. I want to dump my stuff and make some dinner."

The idea that he's "making" supper catches me, but I follow him up the gravel path.

It's good to kick off my boots. Too bulky to pack, I had no choice but to wear them on my flights, but I was a fool not to have broken them in better. Wearing them once for a two-block dog walk so Rusty, our old mutt, could do his business in the empty lot around the corner wasn't enough to prevent today's giant heel blisters. My flip-flops are heaven.

I stare down at my pedicured toes, gold and navy, because Charlet wanted us to wear ETBU colors on our toes to graduation. It couldn't have helped the blister issue to have had my dead foot skin sloughed off before today's main boot debut. At least I packed Band-Aids.

I park my suitcase at the end of the bed, leave my backpack on top of it, but put my wallet and Mama's good camera in my Dolly sack to take with me. "Be trusting, not stupid" is a long-standing Wilkes motto.

Flint is searching cabinets in the first kitchen I come to.

"What's the plan?" I ask, pulling up a stool to the counter.

DENALI SUMMER

"That depends. What do you have?"

I stare at him blankly.

"For dinner? Did you pack any food for dinner?" he clarifies.

Was I supposed to? "Can't we order pizza?"

"Expensive airport lunch and cab fare—that maxed today's budget." He shakes a box of macaroni. "This is cheap."

Knowing he might not make it to a store tonight, he came prepared. I feel like even more of a rookie. A rookie who soon learns she does not need Band-Aids for her heel blisters, but moleskin. Of course Flint has this magical camping product and promises to get some for me after we eat. He shares food. He shares moleskin. Me—I'm the rookie baby who's now ignored six texts from her boyfriend when clearly she should be tucking her tail in and heading on home to him.

Flint finds the right-sized pot, fills it with water, and turns on the heat before moving back toward the fridge to pull out a bottle of ranch dressing and a Ziplock bag with carrot and celery sticks. These aren't the nubby, ready-to-eat things either. These are carrots that were peeled, trimmed, and sliced long-ways down the middle. This is celery that came in a connected leafy bunch that someone rinsed and cut.

"Did your mama get up at the crack of dawn to prepare you snacks?" I ask as Flint goes back to check the water and then dumps in the pasta. If she did, I'm a little jealous. My own mama, still pouting over me springing this trip on her, didn't do anything to help. The only calories I can contribute to Flint's spread are two candy bars, a big unopened bag of Skittles, half of Dolly's home-made granola, and a quarter of

CHAPTER FIVE

a container of spicy lime peanuts—what's left of my Dolly sack food contents.

Flints shakes his head. "I pack my own snacks." He finds plates and sets one before me. "Ranch?"

I nod, and he pours a small salad dressing puddle for me before sliding the bag of prepared veggies my way then goes back to stir the pasta shells. After a few more minutes, he's dishing them onto my plate.

"Veggies and carbs and a little dairy. Hopefully you've already gotten enough servings of protein in today. As your summer chef, the balance of your diet is important to me."

I roll my eyes, but then remember my manners. "Thank you. I appreciate a summer chef with a wide repertoire. I had a burger for lunch."

He laughs again and somehow the sound of it warms the whole room.

We're quiet while we eat, but twice I hear my phone buzz and rattle in my bag. I ignore it and think over the questions I don't ask: whether or not Flint is in school or floats around seasonal jobs. Where in Texas he lives. Where he moved from. What Denali will be like. If it matters that I've only ever tent-camped once and that was at a KOA with newly renovated bathrooms. If there will be other single girl travelers like me. If…

"Your phone keeps buzzing." Flint nods at my bag when it goes off a third time.

"I've already checked in with my mama and daddy, so whoever it is," I let a shrug finish my sentence. Just like I've kept in my questions about him, I don't want to go into very much about me. Might give the wrong impression.

"You're not a talker then, huh?"

DENALI SUMMER

"Tired," I lie.

I couldn't be less tired. I'm wide awake, thinking about my morning train ride. I've never been on a train. Not even a city subway. And my brain is stressing over my alarm not going off causing me to miss my train. Then there's my new boss and who I'll be working with and what Denali will be like and if I'll end up being lonely in my requested single and... all of it. My nerves are pinging every corner of my mind. I am most definitely not tired.

"Go and rest." He stands and reaches over for my empty plate, stacking it on his own. Even "The Baby" helps in the kitchen at my house. Setting the table or cooking or cleaning. Something. But Flint has done everything. In Alaska I'm an even bigger baby than before.

"I'll be in this common room or the other, reading or seeing if any other Denali workers check in. Come find me if you can't sleep," Flint says.

"Thank you so much for supper. I'll have to pay you back somehow."

"You don't have to, but if you can cook, I don't mind taking a night off," he says.

"I know a few recipes well enough." Mama would not abide a daughter who couldn't cook by the time she graduated high school.

"Then I'll sneak you in the kitchen sometime and see what you can do."

Everything about Flint has been friendly and casual, either because I've kept it that way or because that's how he is, but this sounds like we're planning a date. I can feel my cheeks pinking in a blush. But that's silly. This wasn't a date. Boys and girls have

CHAPTER FIVE

to eat, and sometimes they eat together. That will happen this summer, and it's not cheating.

"Sure." It's a squeak of an answer, and I think on if I should say anything else, but then I'm reminded of one of Daddy's favorite expressions: "Never miss a good chance to shut up," so all I do is smile and skirt out the door.

I'm just not sure what to do with boy attention. Between everyone at home knowing I'm with Chris or the twins taking all the attention in the first place—it's not something I've had to consider in a long time.

A text chat with Charlet and one finished woodland color sheet later, a girl in my dorm hands me two, soft, nude-colored squares.

"Moleskin. From that cute guy in the orange and red flannel."

"Thanks." I turn the sheets over in my hand, not sure exactly what to do.

"You cut it to whatever size you need. The back peels off. Do you have scissors?"

"Yeah, in my bag. I'll get up in a minute." I have nail scissors, but they're tucked deep into my suitcase. I drop the moleskin squares on my bed and turn to a new coloring page. A minute later a small pair of scissors fall into my book.

"Mine were easy to get to," she says.

Obviously. Because everyone is a better packer than me. But I take the scissors and cut out two heel-sized strips from one of the squares before tossing the excess in my Dolly sack and the scissors back to their owner.

When she leaves again I wonder if she's going off to hang out with Flint. She's on the tall side, wispy thin with long, straight hair—the look guys at my high school usually went for. Only when those girls ran out did shorter, fuller-thighed girls like me get flirted with. Before Chris, I'd had a two-month relationship in eighth grade and had been asked to one dance in ninth that didn't turn into anything.

If she does go out to be with Flint, I'm sure he'll be as nice to her as he was to me. He's probably like that with everybody. I picture them side by side on that old plaid couch in the common room where we had supper, choosing a movie and sharing popcorn. Meanwhile, I'm lying in the girls' dorm bored and restless. I might have been capable of coming all the way to Alaska, but now I can't seem to leave my room.

After playing a few games on my phone, I read over Chris's texts again and realize I never called him.

I shoot him a text, knowing it's too late in Texas for him to see, but at least he'll know I didn't forget him.

Sometime between the scrolling and the berating myself again over packing mistakes and being too chicken to return to the common room, I fall asleep.

On the Train

Mountains shed snow
like giant chocolate
sponge cakes shaking
off confectioners sugar

Hmmm. I've brought
Mama's analogies to
Alaska ..

Time to see with MY
eyes!
(Easier said than done?)

Ground cracks, bursts
gives way to shrubbery,
moss (no simile - it is what it is)
So much NEW

Arriving in Alaska's springtime

Her beginning ...

(Mine too)

CHAPTER SIX

The morning quiet of the hostel common room stirs my homesickness. I'd hoped to see Flint, crack jokes about having another leg of our route together, but I'm alone doodling in my journal, downing Dolly's granola and some water from the sink, wishing the Uber I scheduled would hurry up.

My trip journal is lame. Spending money on a new one for this trip when I had a blank journal seemed more lame. It's made from recycled paper and came free by way of Daddy by way of Mr. Shobert, head of our city's sanitation department and fellow member of Daddy's Kiwanis club. Mr. Shobert had passed them out at an April meeting along with refrigerator magnet reminders on what could and could not be recycled in our county. Apparently, our corner of Texas still isn't ready for recycling glass.

National-park-summer-worker me opted to appreciate this free gift and its low environmental impact rather than expand her carbon footprint by

CHAPTER SIX

driving my car to the mall and buying some glossy covered, chemically treated option with an inspirational quote hanging above an adorable wide-eyed fox or owl. Unfortunately, being responsible isn't as cute.

At this time at home, Mama is in the kitchen starting coffee then she's off for the middle school where she's principal. They still go the rest of this week and next before their summer starts. Daddy is coming in from walking Rusty, about to tap on my door to make sure I'm up for work before heading off to the tire store his daddy's family is now three generations deep into owning. The phone alarm trilling this morning was a poor substitute for Daddy's door tap and Rusty's low bark.

But by time I go from car to train, the new view pushes thoughts of home to the corners of my mind. I can't take my eyes away from the mountains stretching across the horizon. The thick browns of the lower ridge lines are coming back to life but still seem groggy from the snow's release—like the sun-leathered face of a wise old matron returning to her duties after a long-needed nap.

When we slow for the first stop at Wasilla, there's a rustle in the bushes below my window. A fox darts from a low bush, pounces on a mouse, and sits upright to gulp down his meal. I watch in awed disgust as mouse tail twitches against fox face before disappearing.

As we near Talkeetna, we're told to prepare our cameras for our best chance to catch a view of Denali, the mountain. The voice on the PA announces that she's such a big mountain she has her own weather system and usually stays under cover.

DENALI SUMMER

"She's beautiful, but camera shy—a lot like my wife," our guide says. I immediately think of a time Chris was trying to take my picture at Parker's grandparents' lake house. Maybe it was over spring break.

"All this time together, and I hardly have any good pictures of you," he'd whined when, at the sight of his phone held in picture taking mode, I'd pulled a towel over my head.

"Maybe I don't take good pictures."

In spite of the thick cotton, he'd heard me. "You take beautiful pictures." He tugged the towel down from my eyes and stared into them. "You'll take those duck-face selfies with Charlet. Why won't you let me take pictures of you?"

Because silly selfies are quickly lost in feeds and likely don't get looked at after the day they're posted. But Chris will keep them on his phone. Hell, he'd frame 'em for his room. I'm not good with that. Growing up, when we had to take pictures of all six *D*s posed around Mama and Daddy against some studio backdrop, I always looked the worst. Even as a baby and a chunky toddler when my cuteness should have been stealing the show from a brace-faced Dale and an unfortunately permed Darlene, I managed to be wiggling awkwardly, working myself up so I'd turned red and my hair sprang every which way from static. We took a new family picture every three years or so and what-crazy-face-is-Dawn-going-to-be-making-this-year became the running joke of the family complete with awful, acted-out examples from my brothers. This carried on between picture session and proof delivery. Sadly, my photo results never disappointed,

CHAPTER SIX

and the next few days I suffered through their impersonations of my picture face.

That day at the lake, after much begging from Chris who said his mom was working on a scrapbook of high school to give him at graduation and had demanded more photos of us, I'd agreed to a couple photo and a group photo. He stole another one when I'd been swimming and turned to wave. In it, sun flare sparking off the lake streaks past my face so that one side of it is lost in light. It's eerie but also beautiful—the first time I'd attached that word to a photo of me.

Later that day, a friend snapped a shot of Chris and me jumping off the dock, hand in hand, our tan bodies in brightly colored swimsuits spread against the backdrop of green pines and white clouds. The deep inky blue of the water calm but somehow expectant of the explosion of spray about to be brought on by our impact. That picture looked like a real estate ad beckoning others to join the fun of lake life. Even I could admit that.

I asked Chris for copies of the prints and hung them in my room—in a collage frame I'd found at the craft store the perfect size for the patch of wall I'd chosen. I didn't bring it to Denali, but it'll get put up in my dorm. Thinking about that day makes me miss Chris. At Talkeetna I have cell coverage, so I call him.

"Hey! I knew it! You miss me already!" His voice bounces with enthusiasm.

"I'm not sure how long I'll have coverage. I'm on the train, but we're stopped at a town."

"Is it gorgeous?"

"Amazing."

DENALI SUMMER

"Take lots of pictures and post them when you can. I want to see everything you're up to."

He's being sweetly excited for me now, not like the upset Chris I left on my front porch step. He misses me, and sitting all alone on this train that feels good. I rethink my reason for calling.

"I got all your texts from yesterday," I start.

"Good. I didn't know if they were getting through, not sure how much of Alaska has made it on the grid."

I'm not about to admit that I was never off the grid yesterday. "I don't know what it will be like at Denali, so don't..." I want to ask him to stop texting me for awhile because I came here for me. To be with me. And the constant pinging of all things home and boyfriend isn't helping me be here. But all I say is, "Don't get mad if I go awhile without texting or something. Just assume it's weird cell coverage."

"You know what could be cool? Writing letters. Whenever you think of me and don't have any bars, write me a letter. I'll keep 'em coming for you too."

Oh Chris. Turning my attempt to blow him off into a romantic gesture.

"Sure. That'll be sweet," I say. "Good idea."

The line is silent for a few seconds. I can hear the TV in the background and wonder what he's watching, remembering times we'd pick the same show to watch separately together from each of our homes, texting reactions throughout the episode. I absolutely do not miss home enough to wish that's what I was doing today.

"Chris?"

"Still here, just thinking. Missing you."

"I miss you too."

CHAPTER SIX

"I'm used to telling you about my day, Dawn. I like texting you as things happen. I like the idea of letters, but it makes me a little sad too." Somewhere around him there's a succession of gun fire and an explosion—not something I'd have wanted to watch. "Hold on," he says, "let me pause this movie."

I can't have another conversation about Chris being sad about my decision. A woman seated near me lifts the lid off her steaming coffee to pour in a sugar packet and the scent signals my stomach that it's ready to take a trek to the dining cart.

"Hey, the train's starting up again, so I have to go."

"You be safe. No going out to the bus and munching on the wrong mushrooms."

The bus/mushroom reference is an Alexander Supertramp thing from *Into the Wild*. Chris has read the book and made me watch the movie with him a long time ago. I hadn't even thought about that being near where I'm going.

"You know full well I don't like any kind of mushrooms."

Our connection grows fuzzy. I think he's saying goodbye.

"Can't hear you anymore. I'll..." I don't want to say write, because I'm not sure when I will. And I don't want to say *I look forward to your letter* because I'm not sure I am. I hold the phone against my face not knowing what to say until the call goes dead.

CHAPTER SEVEN

Denali remains cloud-cloaked the whole train ride even though the sky beyond her peak is blue and clear. I guess she'll show herself when she's ready. I've got all summer to wait.

At the Denali train station, the shuttle for my hotel stands waiting. As soon as it deposits me and a handful of other passengers, all older couples I take for tourists, we're greeted by a line of twenty-something bellboys in the required hotel khakis, black work boots, and hunter-green polo shirts embroidered with the hotel logo. Blond, tall, broad-shouldered, with matching grins. It's as though they're fraternity brothers from a house that requires the same look from all its members and had to learn this particular smile instead of a secret handshake.

I'm trying not to stare, so it takes me a minute to realize that the last two in this group of four are actually twins. I immediately want these guys to meet

CHAPTER SEVEN

my sisters and have a double wedding. The pictures would go viral before you could say viral. Oh. My. God.

"Ma'am. Where to?" Says one twin, his grin growing wider around a southern accent thick as tar.

"We-ll," I draw out the word on purpose. "I'm not sure. Is there a place for employees to check in?"

"About time we got another girl joining the team." He stops to shake my hand before taking my bag. "I'm Jake." He points to his name tag. "And that's my brother Josh. Those other two," he indicates to the first set of bellboys who are already disappearing inside the lobby, "are Sugar and Dylan. We're all here from Alabama so they call us the Bama boys. Roll Tide."

"Sugar?" I'm more interested in this than the football comment. Whether Roll Tide is meant to be a cheer or a taunt makes no difference to me. In our family we root for Dallas and the Lobos, our local high school team where all us *D*s, and even Daddy, attended. Whatever happens in between high school and the pros only matters in terms of who takes our Lobos boys or where our Cowboys draft them from.

"He don't like his given name. Where you from?"

I suppose I'll learn how a boy gets a nickname like Sugar another time. "East Texas."

"Just you or you got a friend or boyfriend coming too?"

"Just me."

"Brave. I like that." He winks, and I know I am in so much trouble.

Jake won't let me carry anything, not even my Dolly sack, and doesn't comment on the size or weight of my suitcase, so he is my new favorite person.

"Not going to tease me about this suitcase?"

DENALI SUMMER

Jake shrugs. "Girls like their stuff. I have a little sister. This is probably what she'd bring."

That's me all right. Doing little sister things. "But I should have brought it all in a pack." I press the point because if I'm going to be seen like a little sister nuisance I want to know. What will people really think about my lack of hiking gear?

"You can borrow. I hardly use mine. Bama boys prefer day hikes and fly fishing. Great fishing right here off the Triple Lakes hike and not far into the park at Horseshoe Lake." He points around in the air which I take to be his way of directing me toward the general location of these fishing holes.

As we continue, Jake jabbers on about Angie, the director over all the employees. I'm guessing this is the same lady who emailed me. He says she's a stickler for fully clean uniforms and over-the-top politeness no matter how belligerent a guest might be.

"Josh got a fleck of mustard on his pants at lunch one day, and she made him go change. We have to wipe the mud off the tops of our boots throughout the day too." He looks down. "I'm overdue."

We head around the side of the hotel, pass a volleyball court with a sagging net, and continue further down the path until we come to a building that looks like a double wide trailer. A sign on the door reads "Staff only."

Jake stomps up the ramp, my suitcase thudding loudly behind him as it hits each groove between the boards. He knocks on the door and waits and knocks again before glancing at his watch. "She might be at supper."

CHAPTER SEVEN

He pulls my suitcase against the wall. "Your stuff'll be fine here. You hungry?"

"I could eat," I say. An understatement. The turkey panini and fruit salad I ate on the train are a long distant memory.

"All righty—let's go to The Zoo."

"The Zoo" is about half the size of the Fellowship Hall at the Baptist church we rarely attend. At least the seating area is. The open, cafeteria style-kitchen looks equally big. A pair of men who look Hawaiian? Asian? and then it occurs to me maybe they're Inuit? Anyway, they stand behind the shield of glass, dishing out food to a whole line of men. Only men. A glance around the tables reveals that I have brought the female count up to five in a group of about thirty. It's like a very weird and picky rapture scenario took place before I got here.

"It's not quite a zoo yet. But this weekend it'll be crazier. By then, all the summer employees should have checked in," Jake says. "There's Angie." He points to the third woman in my room-scan count. "I've got to get back to the lobby." Another wink and I'm on my own.

I go for the food first. Moving through the line, I opt for grilled fish and salad instead of nuggets and fries.

"Healthy girl. Good choice."

This man, I check his name tag, RJ, doesn't look old enough to be my dad, but he's at least been-at-it-awhile teacher age. Maybe I should be okay with his complimenting me like I'm a five-year-old, but I'm tired of being made to feel young or inept or both. I want winky Jake back calling me brave.

Flint's copper-colored head is nowhere to be seen as I continue sliding my tray along, select the largest bowl of chocolate pudding from the row of desserts, and smile at RJ as I do.

I walk toward Angie who notices me before I can introduce myself.

"My new front desk clerk!" she says. She has a short, dark crop of tight curls, gray at her temples. Her face is weathered but friendly, and I appreciate when she motions for me to sit at her table.

"Glad you found The Zoo. After you eat, I'll get you your schedule, name badge, and room key. Was the ride up okay?"

I nod, my mouth already full with a bite of salad. The zesty dressing burns at my throat. Reaching for my drink, I realize I forgot to get one.

"What'll you have?" A man across from me says rattling the ice around in his empty plastic cup. "I'm going for a refill."

"Water's fine. Thank you." I swear, somebody stamped helpless on my forehead.

"Bus? Or did you splurge for the train?" Angie asks me.

"Train," I say.

The man beside her lets out a low whistle. "Fancy."

Do other people take the bus? That must be what Flint did. Was I wrong in that decision too? Then again, this heavily bearded man with black-lined fingernails and a dark splotch on the side of his shirt the size of my fist might think a lot of normal things are fancy.

CHAPTER SEVEN

Our table mates introduce themselves and include their job with their name. The bearded man is a bus mechanic which explains why he's not at the standard of clean Jake said Angie expects. The man who sets my cup of water before me is a bartender. Maybe that's why he was so quick to notice my lack of a drink. The rest are bus drivers. They all look about the same age as Angie or older. She points to the table beside us filled with much younger guys. "And those are all bus washers."

"We have that many busses?" The table erupts, finding my question very funny. I guess we do.

After catching her breath, Angie explains, "Narrated tourist tours and hiker shuttles run through the park all day, every day. You'll have to get that down in order to direct guests which to choose. The buses also pick up any hikers coming in from the backcountry who need a lift." Angie points to another young table, this one with a girl. "All of that crew? Raft guides. River tours launch right here, so you've got to memorize that schedule too." The girl at the rafting table, who's Black, was already looking badass with hair cut down to the slightest bit of fuzz, and now that I know she's a raft guide, she has all my respect points.

I guess there's no table of front desk clerks. My job offer email warned of crazy hours, so I suspect there's no all-together, end-of-the-day quitting time for us.

A group of ten, evenly split guys and girls, walks in and the volume of the room doubles with their animated chatter. "Housekeepers," Angie says. "They hold the keys to the storage closet with clean linens, soaps, shampoos, and lotions. So if you need any of that, make a friend quick."

"No, ma'am, I've got sheets and towels and all my toiletries." I may not own camping gear, but I have enough of my favorite shampoo and lotion to last me through the summer. And then some.

"Ma'am," she repeats. "That makes me feel old. It's Angie. Or HR Angie. There's a Snack Shack Angie too. Lots of staff, lots of names, so keep your name tag on. It really helps." She nods at my tray. "You going to finish, or can we go?" Glancing me over she adds, "You don't look like the type to eat much."

I'm not sure how to take that, and my mind is spinning with all the details she's thrown my way. I have a job. In a new place. I have to learn a gazillion names and figure out how to be a front desk clerk. I take one more bite of pudding before dumping the rest of my food and follow HR Angie out the door.

HR Angie hands over a huge packet of information and a key, then shows me to my room. A room which contains two beds. A room that's connected, by way of a grungy bathroom, to another room with two beds. All these beds are still empty, but I suspect my nights of having a quiet single will be few.

"I thought I'd be getting a single."

"Singles go to staff with seniority." HR Angie sounds like she's reciting a line from the employee handbook I should have already known. She taps my information packet. "Happy reading. If you have any questions you can text me; my cell number is in the packet. There's usually coverage. If not, come by the trailer."

CHAPTER SEVEN

My first shift starts tomorrow at five a.m. If I read every word in the packet of information Angie said I'm supposed to memorize so I can help the hotel guests, I will not have time to sleep between now and then.

I make my bed, unpack my clothes into two of the four dresser drawers and take care to only fill half the closet. The remaining clothes will have to live in my suitcase which, no matter how hard I push, won't fit under the bed. I try lifting the bed up and kicking the suitcase under with my foot, but this move sends me crashing on my butt and dropping the bed with a loud bang as the thick wooden legs pound the linoleum floor. From the floor, I consider asking Mama to send up a rug. She could have a cheap one shipped from Ikea. How long might that take?

There's nothing left to do but leave my stupid suitcase standing upright at the foot of my bed. This kinda, sorta blocks the door to the bathroom, but until I hear a roommate complain, that's its spot.

I gather the remaining clutter from my bed—phone, earbuds, mini wireless speaker, a rogue pen—and dump it all in a basket I brought for these things. My room key came clipped to a hotel lanyard, my first souvenir, and I toss it in the basket too, then set the basket on the nightstand between the beds.

I also have a framed picture of me and my sisters, the best one of us taken at our last family photo shoot. I'm squinty, and my bangs are messy, but overall, it's about as good as it gets from me. Staring down at my sisters makes me teary and lonely. I have not run into Flint or Jake again. There are no new texts from Chris.

That's what I wanted.

Except maybe not as strongly right at this moment.

DENALI SUMMER

If Darlene were here, she'd be pulling me out the door to meet my surrounding dorm-mates, comparing the rooms to take inventory of who brought what. Darlene is all about appraising potential resources. Dolly would be asking if I'd eaten enough, and Daisy would have brought more to make the room homier and colorful. She'd be setting everything about and covering the plain walls with pictures.

But it's only me.

I place the frame beside the basket and grab my lodge information packet. I have bus tour, river rafting adventure, and guided hike schedules to memorize. These aren't the only entertainment options. There's a husky kennel with dog demonstrations, horseback riding across the tundra, and helicopter rides over the park or to a glacier. I've also got to learn tomorrow's restaurant specials and sort through pages of hotel policies. It takes every ounce of control not to call home and cry to Mama. But there's not time for that.

Somehow the most clueless girl in Denali has been appointed keeper of all the knowledge. I've got a lot of catching up to do.

CHAPTER EIGHT

At five a.m., the front desk night worker isn't interested in telling me anything, doesn't even introduce himself. He just shuffles off droopy eyed, his fatigued stagger so much like a drunk's I wonder if he'll make it to his room. The lights on the phones are all off, and I hope they stay that way until someone shows up with instructions.

At about 5:15, a woman who looks like my granny on Mama's side—short and rounding with a sleek bob of silver hair that touches right at her chin—comes rushing at me.

"I am so, so sorry," she says. "I hope you haven't had any calls or anyone come up."

"No, ma'am. It's been quiet." I show her my packet. "I've been reviewing this."

"Perfect. Did you get anything to eat? The Zoo doesn't open till six, and technically you're not supposed to take your break till at least seven. I keep a basket of breakfast snacks on that shelf," she points past my feet, "for the morning shift. Granola bars, yogurt covered raisins, stuff like that."

She really does remind me of Granny who still carries lollipops and baby wipes in her purse, never mind that all her grandbabies are grown.

"And I'm Wanda. Can't believe I skipped introductions. I manage the front desk staff. I swear I'm never late, but a moose mama and her most adorable calf were plodding through staff housing right as I walked out my door, so I had to run back for my camera. They hung out at the volleyball court posing, and I lost track of time."

I have yet to see anything bigger than a fox. The train conductor had promised at least three of Alaska's big five: bears, wolves, moose, caribou, and dall sheep, but all we passed were caribou. I was in the bathroom at the time, so I even missed those.

"Are they still there?" I ask, hoping she'll let me run out and check. I'd love to get a picture on my phone to text Mama and Daddy.

"No, I left when they did. They're deep in the woods by now." She pats my arm. "You'll see plenty of moose this summer."

I want to believe it, but until I spot more animals, they feel as elusive as Mount Denali. I introduce myself too, and Wanda starts off by telling me how happy she is to have the front desk spot filled.

"When Mary cracked her ankle, I didn't know what we'd do!" Then it's a string of the usual polite questions: Where am I from? How was my trip up? When she asks why I chose Denali for my summer break, I hesitate, not sure which answer to give.

CHAPTER EIGHT

I'm here because Chris gave me a promise ring, and I was zero parts elated total parts scared. I'm here to show Mama I can still do my own thing before falling in line with her plan. I'm here to show my family I can be something besides the baby, and there's more to me than Chris.

All of that. All of that is why I'm here, but for Wanda, this coworker I don't yet know, I settle on: "Someone at my work talked up Alaska so well, I came as a chance to get away before college."

Wanda considers this. "I thought college was a chance to get away."

Not when college is thirty minutes from home, and I don't have a meal plan because Mama expects Charlet and I will still take advantage of free home-cooked meals at her house or mine. If we want to eat closer to campus, we can always go to the twins' apartment. Dolly still has a year of college left.

So, no. I will not be getting away. Not even a little a bit—just taking different classes in a different set of buildings.

Before I figure out how to explain this, we're interrupted by a hotel guest approaching the desk. He's looking for the morning paper and a hiking guide. Wanda explains that the papers usually arrive closer to six, and the first guided hike begins at eight.

He humphs. "How about breakfast? Can I at least get breakfast?"

"Snack Shack opens at six. The restaurant opens at eleven for lunch service," she says. It's a chipper but no-nonsense tone I'll have to start using too.

"Thirty minutes until I can eat?" His frown deepens. "You do know that the sun rises at four a.m. around here."

"Yes, sir," Wanda says through a small, professional smile. "That's why all the rooms come with thick, sun-blocking curtains. If there's any sort of gap letting the light in so you can't sleep, I can send maintenance out to replace or adjust them."

He stares at her not sure how to respond to her offer and finally mumbles, "My curtains are fine," before walking away.

Wanda turns to me. "We get a handful of early birds throughout the week complaining about late start times. You can remind them that Oxbow Trail is nearby and well marked. If that's not good enough, the first bell boy starts at six, and he can escort people there if needed."

The Bama boy who goes by Sugar strides in as if on cue. He's early for the first bell boy shift.

"Morning, ladies. Ms. Wanda and—," his eyes flicker to me then up, down, and all over me, "I did not get the pleasure of meeting you yesterday."

Sugar's dark blond hair tufts at the front, a cowlick he's opted to ignore rather than tame. His eyes are chocolate, and they're steadily trained on me.

"I'm Dawn from East Texas. The new front desk clerk at your service."

"Dawn from East Texas that is a relief. I never did get good service from a West Texas girl."

At this hint of a tease my eyes squint to the glare I usually reserve for my brothers. "I imagine not. Everybody knows those West Texas girls are useless," I say.

CHAPTER EIGHT

But Sugar is already tired of the joke. "You met my boys last night, didn't you?"

"I met Jake. He carried my luggage and helped me find HR Angie."

"Jake's a gentleman, that's for sure. May be why we're such good friends." He looks me over again. "What are you doing after your shift, Dawn from East Texas?"

"Not sure. Maybe that nearby hike? Oxbow?"

He shakes his head, vetoing my choice. "It's covered in tourists, and it's not much more than a mile. Oxbow is for if you want to go on a walk after dinner. I'll take you someplace better."

I hesitate. This feels datey. I came here to get space from a guy not replace him. But considering the guy-girl ratio of this place, if I'm going to have friends this summer, this is how it's going to be.

"What's your plan?" I ask.

"My shift ends an hour after yours, so you take a slow lunch and get changed, and by then I'll be off and ready to get you on a trail."

A tattoo sneaks past the end of a short shirt sleeve stretched tight by his ample bicep. Do I really want to commit to spending my afternoon with this guy? In the woods. Alone. I can hear Darlene in my head: *Stop being so damn cautious*. And the twins chorusing together: *It's just a hike! He's hot! Why not?* My own voice has nothing to add.

"Hiking would be great. Thanks."

It's slow for the next hour until those going on the first park bus tour begin filling the lobby asking where to wait, scheduling activities for tomorrow, or, if they're checking out in the morning, arranging baggage pick ups and shuttle rides. I'm swamped and overwhelmed and making up half my answers when suddenly the bus driver, a man I recognize from supper, comes inside and lets them know the bus is open, they can pick their seats.

"Departure in ten minutes," he hollers before leaving. And snap, everyone's gone. Even those still in line don't bother to use their last ten minutes.

"Happens that way every time," Wanda says, watching them file outside. "It'll be dead for forty or so minutes until the eight a.m. tour folks show up. You'll want to take your break before they come or once they clear out. I'll go whichever you don't pick. Doesn't matter to me."

I choose the later break time. No Flint in the breakfast line as a I choose pancakes and a fruit cup. A scan of The Zoo shows an empty seat with the raft guides. A tall, pale skinny guy stands up and pulls the chair for me when he sees me approaching. My body relaxes at this swift gesture of welcome.

The conversation is a rapid ping pong of their have-you-ever... bush-whacked, been in the back country, tent-camped outside a camp ground, seen a grizzly, gone rafting... and my no, no, no, no, and no.

The whole group of them are aghast and excited by my answers, claiming the right to be the ones to take me out first, show me what to do. I explain my gear problem, but they dismiss it, offering to lend me anything I need. Their quick generosity so astounds me, I don't feel like the baby or the rookie or the helpless one. I just feel friendship.

They want to know when my first weekend is and argue about what section of the park I should start

CHAPTER EIGHT

with. Names of sites whirl around me: Savage River, Primrose Ridge, Teklanika. By the time I have to go, they're still undecided but make me promise to sign up for an afternoon of white-water rafting this week.

"How much is it?" I ask, standing up with my tray. I still have graduation present money, but I ought to pace myself. At least until I get my first paycheck.

"Free. Everything's free for staff if there's spots open. And they make spots come open for front desk workers so you know what you're talking about when you promote it to guests," says Jonelle, the girl I'd mentally deemed a badass yesterday.

All the activities I read over last night reenter my brain in a rush. "That's fantastic," I say.

"It so is," she agrees.

After my shift, I run to my room to change out of my uniform and into hiking clothes. With fresh moleskin added to my heels, I ease my feet into my boots and grab my backpack which I stuff with a light jacket, bug spray, a water bottle, Mama's nice camera, and a paperback.

I'm the last in the lunch line before they shut it down. Still no Flint, and I'm starting to wonder if I'd misunderstood where he said he'd be working. The room is mostly empty—no jovial raft guides, only a couple from the housekeeping group and two bus washers. I pick an empty table in the corner.

Sugar finds me reading.

DENALI SUMMER

"Head buried in a book. Must be one of them smart East Texas girls." He sits down and nudges his shoulder against mine. "You ready?"

He's already changed too. "Sure, where we going?"

"Healy Overlook. I hope you have strong legs or you might be sore in the morning."

Oh great.

He explains that we have to take the shuttle into the park because our trail begins at the visitor center. During the ride, he goes into more detail about our hike. "It's about five miles, a slow grade through the taiga for the first bit and then a steady incline."

"Doesn't sound too bad."

"It's not. Until the last mile. Even with switchbacks, it has a pretty quick elevation gain. But it's worth it," Sugar says.

His hand finds its way to my knee and stays there as he talks, so I'm listening but also trying to ignore the electrified sensation pulsing out from beneath his palm. I don't want his hand there, but I don't know how I'm supposed to move it. I feel like I'm the star of *The Bachelorette*, and my first one-on-one date has turned out to be with the frisky guy of the house. Or was supper with Flint my first one-on-one? Not the point, I scold myself. Besides, if I were the bachelorette the audience would know I've left a guy back home, and they'd hate me.

Friends. I'm making friends, and I need to concentrate on the words of this new friend. Switchbacks I think I get, but taiga? I ask Sugar what it means.

"Land of little sticks on account of a lot of the trees being skinny and pitiful. It's the arctic forest part of the land before the tundra."

CHAPTER EIGHT

That word I know.

"And why do they call you Sugar?"

He laughs. "Don't waste time do you?"

"Guess not." And here I'd been thinking the same about him.

"My last name is Sweet, and my first name is... not what I want to be called." He squeezes my leg, and the jolt rides all the way up my thigh. I shift, angling my leg so maybe his hand will slide off, but nope, not happening.

"Would you tell me if I guessed?" I ask.

"It's not Rumpelstiltskin. I'll tell you that."

When we get off the bus, Sugar points to the Visitor Center. "Final chance to pee indoors for the next three hours. Longer if you hike slow."

This reminder alone should earn him a rose.

At the trailhead, Sugar has me go first to set the pace. I pull out my camera to be ready should we spot any wildlife and begin walking, attempting a rate that won't bore Sugar but won't kill me. Soccer season ended in February, and I'm not in my best shape.

The trees may be puny but they provide enough cover that there's not much of a view. It's mostly compact gravel but stretches of trail are threaded through by roots, and I have to concentrate on my footing and not conversation. But these are Alaska roots! If only my family could see me now.

The footfalls of our heavy hiking boots on the path take on a steady rhythm. Our noise is punctuated by the trill of a robin or chirp of a sparrow. There's a bridge crossing and aways after that we get our first break in the trees and glimpse of a valley view. A small yellow flower dots the sweeping greens of the nearest slope. The bright blue of the late afternoon sky is only lightly dotted by thin lines of wispy clouds. Sugar suggests we stop and hydrate. I chug half my water bottle and suck in a long breath of Alaskan air, crisp and deliciously dry. I do not miss Texas humidity one bit.

"It's been," he takes out his phone and checks the time, "thirty-five minutes, so the climbing and switchbacks are about to start, but then we'll be past the trees and into all the views. There's a few steep parts and a few big boulders to scramble past, so we'll take an easy pace. No need to wear you out on your first Denali hike."

Oh yes, I would very much like an easy pace if I'm to be rock scrambling. These are not moves a girl learns in the flatlands of piny East Texas.

Above us on the trail, I hear a chorus of giggles and the thumping of multiple boots. A minute later, three girls, high school-age but still, I think, younger than me, troop by saying "Hey-ey" in unison as they pass. One flashes a line of metal braces. Clad in brightly patterned leggings and pastel knit caps with large, fuzzy poms budding out from each side like animal ears, they're quite a sight.

My sisters and I do that too. We have many sets of matching silly things that we've bought special for some party or outing or trip. The outfits on these girls make me smile. Sugar's glance seems to be showing appreciation as well—for their asses. If Chris were here, he'd never ogle like that.

"You go ahead. I want to watch your footing at the steep parts," I say, self conscious of where his gaze has been so far during the hike. My own pants are stretch material, wide at the bottom so they can come down

CHAPTER EIGHT

over my boots, fitted over my knees, more snug as they continue up.

"If that's what you want." He tucks his water bottle in the mesh pocket at the side of his backpack. As he heaves the pack over his arm, it slides the sleeve of his t-shirt, and I get a glimpse of his tattoo—a charging, tusked elephant with demonic red eyes. A crimson-colored *A* loops wide beside the animal.

"Jake said ya'll were fans, but that's quite a tattoo."

"You like it?" He holds the sleeve and grins like a little boy who's pleased he's been caught in the act—of what I'm not sure.

"I'm not a Bama fan."

"But you like tattoos on guys, don't you?"

I'm not sure. Chris doesn't have any. Daddy and Dustin don't either. And Dale, poor Dale once had a girl's name scripted on his chest, his big gesture of commitment because he knocked her up after senior prom. He revealed the tattoo when he proposed, but while he'd been getting tatted, she'd been having an abortion. Obviously, she turned him down. But he's got Jesslyn and her daughter in his life now, and he had the tattoo of prom girl covered with a tattoo of his first car, a red Camaro. So it all worked out.

I'm not supposed to know about that first tattoo, but even little sisters nine-and-a-half years younger can clue in when a tattoo shows up then gets changed right quick. Plus, Darlene can't keep a family secret to save her life. So yeah, by the summer before fourth grade, I already knew about sex and abortions. Thank you, oldest brother and sister.

"Don't suppose it matters much either way. As long as a guy doesn't have some other girl's name or something raunchy I never want to look at, tattoos are fine."

"It's cute how your accent gets thicker when you're thinking through something."

I blush.

"Southern accents—now that's what I like on a girl," he adds.

I swat at his arm. "I have a boyfriend, you know." Good. Now I've said it.

Sugar looks all around. "Don't see him."

I roll my eyes. "We're here to hike. Let's get going."

"What's the hurry? Sun won't set till about midnight."

"You do know I started work at five this morning and will again tomorrow." And the next three days after that.

"Quit your worrying. I'll get you home in plenty of time for your beauty rest." Sugar sets off, and it's harder, but we take more water stops. When the growing stitch in my side pierces too sharp, I use picture-taking more shots of the valley and ridgeline view as an excuse for extra breaks.

After an hour, we come to a section where the gravel path narrows tighter than I'd like at the edge of the cliff. It's a stretch that lasts about twenty feet. Beyond that it seems to widen again before the final ascent.

"Are you kidding me?" I say, eyeing the path. I'll have to walk it foot over foot, tight-rope style to fit.

"It's not as narrow as it looks, and you can lean onto the mountain side if you need to."

Oh. I'm going to need to.

A few steps onto the narrow part of the path, Sugar slips, releasing a cloud of dust into the air as a burst of

CHAPTER EIGHT

scree slides down the side of the mountain. He leans to his other side and grips at a root.

He turns and says, grinning, "Still here."

We continue on to the small, scratched-up sign that announces the end of the maintained trail, and a little beyond to a rock cluster at the edge of the ridgeline. I toss down my pack, and a groundhog climbs onto a nearby rock. He lets out a quick succession of high-pitched chirps, like whistle-blasts from a coach demanding our attention.

"Look at that marmot's belly. Stupid tourists been giving him granola bars," Sugar says.

I turn out my empty pockets as though it might mean something to this fuzzy, over-sized squirrel, under-sized beaver.

"Sorry, buddy. Nothing to share even if I wanted to," I say, bringing my camera up to take his picture. He lets out two more blasts and scurries away.

Sugar chooses a rock and sits down then takes off his shirt, using it to rub the sweat off his face. It's about sixty degrees—generally the weather southern boys pull out their hoodies, not take off their shirts. So I'd guess he's done this to show off his back and further test his theory that I like my guys tattooed. An ornate cross stands colorful against a backdrop of black Polynesian symbols. A fierce-looking rat sweeps across the shoulder opposite his Bama mascot. Plump, realistic women's lips part for the beginning of a kiss. There's even a Quidditch snitch from *Harry Potter* shaded masterfully as though it's zooming through the other pictures, impossible to catch. It's a whole collage of stories.

Twisting to rub an empty section on his lower back, Sugar says, "I want to put something from this trip here. I'll know what it should be by the end of the summer."

"Like a grizzly?"

"If I have an encounter and live to tell the story, sure. But I was thinking more like a scenic picture of my favorite fishing spot. I don't have any landscapes."

"I'll definitely be rooting for landscape lake over a grizzly-slashing paw."

Sugar puts his shirt back on, and I settle next to him on the rock. We sit, sides pressed together, eyes on the view. It turns out, not everything is bigger in Texas. The sky, still bright as candy, outlines the cut of each mountain. The closer peaks are greens and browns, but deeper in the distance snow caps remain prevalent, and farther still there's an entire mountain of white.

"Is that Denali?" I ask, pointing out the all-white peak.

"Sure is. Not the best glimpse of her from this spot but still impressive on such a clear day."

We're quiet a good long while before Sugar asks, "What's a girl with a boyfriend doing leaving him behind for a whole summer?"

"Taking a little time for me."

"And he was okay with that?"

Ha! Not at all. "I didn't give him the choice."

He studies me, but it's not the flirty-with-a-touch-of-lusty I've gotten from him before. It's a respectful, who-are-you type of gaze. "Dawn from East Texas, who does what she wants without being held back by a guy. Strong willed aren't you?"

CHAPTER EIGHT

"I don't know about that." I've always felt more like the pushover tag-along, but yes my decision to come to Alaska was quickly and strongly willed.

"You are. I can tell. And that boy of yours better appreciate it."

Jake called me brave. Sugar says I'm strong willed. But what seems more important than these new labels is that on my first full day at Denali, I have climbed a mountain.

This will be my summer for everything.

CHAPTER NINE

Or confusion. This will be my summer for confusion.

When Sugar and I get back to the hotel from our Healy hike, we go straight to supper, and there, at the first table with a very cute Hispanic girl I haven't met, sits Flint. He's not wearing his headphones, and this time he's in plain blue jeans, but his button-down shirt is red and so are his Converse. Red continues to be his thing, and I continue to approve.

"Gabby," says Sugar. "Who's your friend?"

Flint stands up and extends his hand, while Gabby, from her seat, says, "Flint, this is Sugar. Sugar, this is Flint." Her voice is flat like a little child being forced to apologize.

"And Dawn, I already know." Flint lets go of Sugar and reaches out to hug me.

"I'm kinda sweaty," I say, backing away. His squinty, to-his-eyes smile dims, and I feel bad.

"It's still good to see you," he says and sits back down.

CHAPTER NINE

"You too. I have not forgotten I owe you a supper." As soon as I say it I feel catty—like I brought this up now only so Gabby could hear. Standing beside Sugar, I have no business staking a claim on Flint. Okay, even not standing beside Sugar, I have no business staking a claim on Flint. Because Chris. Duh.

Sugar and I continue on to the food line, and gutsy me chooses lasagna—never mind that the bus washers in front of us joke the meat sauce consists of road-kill caribou. When we return with our trays, Gabby has left, but Flint's still at their table. I'm pleased to see he's waited for me. Then I scold myself for assuming his waiting has anything to do with me. Then I scold myself again for being pleased in the first place. There's a lot of inner mental chatter going on during the six-foot walk from the drink station to Flint.

I immediately ask how he got a day behind me in his travels.

"I'd always planned on being in Anchorage an extra day."

"You never said that."

"You never asked."

Good point.

"Bama boys did that too," Sugar says, interrupting. "Day in Anchorage, but then we did three nights in Chugach at a campground, and two more nights at Riley Creek in the park. And then," he emphasizes the then, "we reported for bell hop duty."

This explains how Sugar already knows so much about the hiking when it's his first year at Denali. I'd assumed it was because the Bama boys had first wave employee start dates. Wanda told me at work today I was between the third and fourth wave, which starts showing up tomorrow. I expect this wave will bring me a roommate and two suite-mates.

"Four of them came up from Alabama together," I clarify for Flint. "Two are twins, so don't think you're getting double vision."

"Thanks for the tip." Flint grins.

Sugar nudges me. "The creek past Riley Creek campground is another spot I want to show you soon."

I attempt a smile through my lasagna-stuffed mouth. Sugar has pulled the same catty move I did in front of Gabby. Flint looks from me to Sugar and back to me. I keep smiling, and it makes it hard to swallow.

"They put me on breakfast for tomorrow, and I've still got to unpack, so...I'll leave you two to your dinner," Flint says, standing.

"I have morning shifts this whole week," I say, willing him to also hear: our schedules match! It can be you and me hanging out tomorrow!

"See you sometime in the morning then," says Flint.

"You met him coming up?" Sugar asks as soon as Flint disappears.

"Yeah, same flights. He's from Texas too. How do you know Gabby?"

"First wave employee. She works in the gift shop."

When Sugar walks me back to my room, he asks if he can come in, but I insist that I'm too exhausted for company. As soon as I close the door on him I remember I left my backpack on the floor by my chair at supper. Standing with my hand on the inside knob, I wait long enough for Sugar to be gone, open it a sliver and peek around to confirm it's safe, then run back to The Zoo.

CHAPTER NINE

I practically crash into the River Rat Pack, my new name for the rafting guides. Jonelle and Elijah are walking hand in hand, confirming my suspicion that they are a couple. The whole group of them have wet heads as though they've come from a swim.

"Aren't you supposed to stay in the raft?" I ask.

Another of the guys, I'm still having trouble with their names and he's not wearing a name tag, laughs. "The occasional polar plunge never hurt anyone."

Jonelle sidles up to me and says, "We were in our dry suits. It's not that bad."

"I'll take your word for it," I say.

"No!" she says as though remembering something. "You'll do it! Tomorrow! I checked the schedule before we walked out. I've got two spots open on my two p.m. You have to come."

Her voice drops again, "Maybe with Zeke. He thinks you're cute."

"Which one's Zeke?" I whisper.

She points to the younger, skinnier version of the two river rats I've decided are brothers. The one who pulled out the chair for me yesterday.

"Sure. Sounds fun." *What the heck*, I think. *I'm here to make all the friends.* If they think I'm cute, so be it. But I'm not saying yes for Zeke, I'm saying yes for my next adventure.

"Awesome! Guys, Dawn's coming on my two p.m., and there's room for one more."

Bigger brother nudges little brother and says, "Zeke'll go," and they all laugh.

DENALI SUMMER

Back in my room, I feel a pang of guilt. Flint, Sugar, Zeke... The names are on repeat in my mind as I shower and get ready for bed. Am I right in thinking that all rafting dates and hiking dates and meal-prep dates and camping dates are presumed casual?

This isn't something I'd be worrying about after a shift at The Coffee Mill.

My sister Daisy is working an all-girls camp this summer. Once she finishes her summer school reading coach duties, she has six weeks off, and she'll be working those as a counselor at an overnight camp. When she applied, she'd asked me to come too, but I'd never seriously considered it. I'd been to that camp as a kid. At some point or another each of my sisters has worked there. Why hadn't I thought to apply there when Chris gave me that ring?

My Denali identifiers come back to me—because I'm braver than that. Because little 'ol me, brimming with bravery and strong will (Mama would call that piss and vinegar.), needed an Alaska adventure.

Maybe. Or maybe my number one identifier is Expert Problem Avoider.

Whatever. I've made my bed, and now it's time to lie it in. After the world's longest day, it's about time. I twist Chris's ring off my finger and plop it into my nightstand basket and sink into my pillow.

Day	What & With whom	Sightings Animals (not UFOs)
Thursday 5/23	Train · just me	Fox (and briefly) a mouse
Friday	Mt Healy Overlook w/ Bama Boy Sugar Sweet	McFatty the Marmot
Saturday — was graduation only a week ago?!	Nenana River rafting — Jonelle, Zeke, random tourists	Dall sheep
Sunday	Solo hike! Horseshoe Lake Trail (and then Flint)	no beavers just an attack moose!

↗ is okay, attack had strong but he of zero concept personal space!

CHAPTER TEN

Wanda beats me to the desk in the morning. I walked crazy slow, willing a moose to cross my path. No such luck.

At breakfast, Flint's smile, as he dishes up my waffle and side of sausage, is the same for me as it is for everyone else. My face returns this same expression of friendship; my brain accepts that this is good. I've only downed two bites of sausage when Sugar and Jake (I'm able to confirm which twin because he's wearing his name tag.) plop into the chairs on each side of me.

"Dawn from East Texas! Feeling good or feeling sore?" Sugar asks.

I woke up so stiff it was as though someone had syringe-injected concrete into my leg muscles. "Alabama Sugar whose real name is... Carlton?"

"Ha—not even close. One guess a day. Tomorrow, I'll let you ask a question first."

CHAPTER TEN

"I'm feeling good," I say. This is a little true considering I'm not moving at the moment, and the two ibuprofen I took first thing this morning haven't worn off yet.

Jake takes a banana off my tray and peels it. "You want this?"

"Yes," I snatch it back. "They have plenty of food up there, you know."

These boys are as bad as my brothers.

Sugar bumps his leg against mine. "You up for another hike then?"

"I'm rafting," I say, grateful for the excuse. I'm not ready to make Sugar my exclusive hiking partner. "Jonelle invited me on her two p.m. Zeke's going too."

"The high school kid?" Jake's back with his own banana, and his words are muffled through a big bite.

"He just graduated. Same age as me."

"You're fresh out of high school?" Sugar looks at me as though he's reconsidering how old I look.

"Sugar's a cradle robber," Jake laughs.

"How old are ya'll?" I know they're college guys, so eighteen to twenty-two, right? Which doesn't seem like such a big deal. The twins dated some seniors when they were freshmen. Not that I'm talking about dating anyone.

"Josh and I are twenty. Dylan's twenty-one. Sugar here, he'll be a senior, but he's taken his time along the way."

"Been red-shirting grades since kindergarten." Sugar grins as though this is a point of pride.

Now it's my turn to reconsider his age. "How many grades?"

DENALI SUMMER

"Well, kindergarten, then I got on a roll for a while but sorta stalled out between middle school and high school. Did an online thing for an extra year before ninth. Took a year off before college and another year before I started my major to intern just to be sure I was making the right choice."

Which means he's four years behind making him twenty-five or twenty-six. Dale's only one year older than that. Dale, who's likely to become a step-dad to a five-year-old before the year ends. Dale, who's been working full-time with Daddy since he passed on Mama's ETBU offer. Dale, who expanded the tire store to include an auto body shop which he's been overseeing completely since the day he turned twenty. Sugar suddenly seems both younger and older at the same time.

"Didn't realize you were such an old man," I say. "I should be asking if you're the sore one today."

"A little more experienced, but not old yet," Sugar says to me but his eyes drift from mine to the door where Gabby has entered and taken a food tray.

"Speaking of experience." Jake holds up his hand, and Sugar meets it with a fist bump. I'm pretty sure the conversation took a hard right toward locker-room grossness.

I don't see how she could have heard them, but Gabby notices our table and scowls.

"Break time's over," I announce and push my chair back.

"Enjoy your raft ride," Jake says.

"Don't fall in the water," Sugar adds.

I point to Jake, "I will," then point to Sugar with the other hand, "I won't."

CHAPTER TEN

A few more guest calls to the desk, and I think I'll have the phones down. Yesterday I kept hanging up on people instead of placing them on hold, but so far today I've managed holds and transfers. Now if I could consistently transfer the calls to the right person, that would help. Room 127 didn't want to hear about the package that had arrived for Room 172. Go figure.

Between walk-ups and calls, I pump Wanda, who's on her fifth Denali summer, for park hiking and camping tips. I don't tell her I'm trying to gage what I can manage doing by myself in case she proves the over-protective grandma sort. I take notes in my journal, words crammed in and around mountain doodles. Accomplishing even half this Wanda-list would add up to quite the summer. But seeing as I've already hiked Healy, and I'm on my way to raft the Nenana, I'd say I'm keeping pace. If only my family could see me now.

As long as I don't fall out of the raft and drown.

My siblings have a let's-make-fun-of-Dawn group texting exchange they keep adding me to where they've all placed bets. It started off with whether or not I will die (Dale), come home early (Darlene and Daisy), or stay the whole summer (Dustin). So far Dolly has stayed out of it beyond liking and disliking their texts. Then they started discussing, assuming I die or come home early, what will have caused it. Dale's put his money on an animal attack. Darlene says I'll fall on a hike and break something. Daisy says I'll miss Chris too much—and on this Dolly agreed so they're willing to split their winnings. Meanwhile, Dustin, my new favorite, last wrote:

She's tougher than you think, ya'll. Stop being assholes.

Jonelle is every bit the professional as she gives her safety speech and instructions. First, she reminds the clump of tourists huddled in the gray gravel at the river's edge that those with heart conditions, epilepsy, or women who may be pregnant may not ride. About twenty feet away, her boyfriend Elijah is leading a similar talk for the tourists signed up for the oar boat he'll be paddling that will launch at the same time as us.

"If you didn't catch these restrictions when you registered, that's okay. We'll give you a full refund, and if you choose to wait on the rest of your party, there's complimentary hot chocolate in the office. Anybody need to bow out?" Jonelle scans our group and gives us a second before calling Zeke to her side.

"I'm such a fantastic guide that even my fellow guides want to ride with me when it's their afternoon off." She pats Zeke on the back. "Zeke here may look twelve," Zeke blushes but she ignores this and keeps talking, "but he's every bit as accomplished and capable as I am on this river. He'll be helping me right now as we distribute paddles and helmets and get you fitted with the right drysuit and life jacket."

Zeke approaches me with a helmet. "I think this'll fit," he says, handing me my piece of

CHAPTER TEN

protective bright-yellow plastic. I rub my fingers over the scratches and grooves that have roughed the exterior, and he seems to read my thoughts. "Those are mostly from being dropped or tossed into the storage shed too hard. Not from river rocks. Well, maybe this one." He fingers a little chip at the right temple area and our hands touch. "This one could've been a river rock."

He has bit-down nails and stubby fingertips but long, gangly fingers on long, gangly hands that spring from sleek, narrow wrists. The surge of puberty has stretched him into a tall, wiry thing, but left him baby faced and concave in places most guys our age have filled out. There's a hint of brown fuzz above his lip that solidifies his stuck-post-middle-school-growth-spurt look.

He gently pushes a few strands of hair away from my face and places the helmet over my head. "It's a good fit though." The eyes staring into mine are the sharp blue of early nightfall. Sugar is definitely the sexier of my adventure-date partners, but these eyes alone keep Zeke a contender in the looks department for a girl who might be interested. A girl who's not me, obviously. The shy smile that emerges between his sentences doesn't hurt either.

By the time Zeke has found me a satisfactory drysuit, life jacket, paddle, and booties for my feet, Jonelle has outfitted all but one of the other six passengers. As Zeke brings the remaining man his gear, Jonelle catches my arm and whispers to me, "Go easy on him, heartbreaker."

DENALI SUMMER

I attempt a look of exasperation and innocence. Whatever this becomes on my helmet-squished head results in a deep laugh from Jonelle.

I follow her to a stretch of compacted dark sand. For about twenty feet the shore is clear of the boulders and most of the smaller rocks that line the rest of the shore. The raft is one shade darker than the slate gray of the roiling water.

Once our group has the raft at the water, Jonelle points Zeke and me to the front two spots before commanding everyone else to fill in. After a final shove, she jumps into the middle back spot and releases an exhilarating whoop.

"Let's do this!" she yells, sinking her paddle into the water. Our raft team answers with a collective cheer and paddles through a calm stretch of river toward the choppier waters ahead. We don't actually have to paddle. The Nenana's steady flow hauls us along at a brisk enough pace, but it's nice to work off our initial excitement.

Zeke pulls his paddle into his lap. "Are you cold?" he asks me.

"Not so far." Jonelle had warned me last night to wear long johns underneath my clothes. I also opted for wool socks. A glacial river underneath an inflated boat makes for a chilly ride, especially in the shadows of its rock-carved path.

"Wait till our first rapid, and this water hits you." He shudders his head and shoulders. "It'll wake you up, that's for sure."

"Are we near?" As I ask the question, Jonelle calls from behind us, "All right, Razor Back is up ahead,

CHAPTER TEN

and the river's high, so we get to start off with a level four. All forward!"

Everyone sinks their paddles in the water with renewed vigor. Within seconds, we're being bounced—

"Like cowboys on a bronco!" hoots the man behind Zeke.

Yes, exactly.

The river dips, the raft dips with it, and we take in a wave that leaves me paralyzed for a second. So cold. My face. My neck. So, so cold. No words. Just cold.

We take another big bounce and dip before Jonelle yells, "All back!" She proceeds to steer us to the side for a few hard strokes and then reissues the all-forward command. Through my river-splashed face, I can see Elijah's bright-yellow raft up ahead. If the banana boat with only one oar-paddler can make it, so can we. I concentrate on my paddling. Dip and pull and keep moving to stay warm. Dip and pull again. My arms feel stronger than ever before, and I'm loving every second.

"And stop!" The raft straightens, and we're back to a smoother section of river. The sunlight sparkles along the rippling water bright enough that I wish I had sunglasses. "Great paddling, team! Everyone lift your paddles up and give each other a paddle high five!" Jonelle stretches her own paddle toward the Alaskan sky and eight paddles raise to the air in response, tapping their celebration, creating a giant round of paddle applause.

"That was awesome!" I yell to Zeke.

"One rapid down, eight to go. You cold yet?" he asks.

"I'm cold, and I'm fired up all at the same time," I laugh.

DENALI SUMMER

The next three named rapids are rated as threes. One is aptly called Cable Car because the jostling current swirls begin shortly beyond a cable previously used for cable cars. Zeke extends his paddle towards it.

"There used to be an old cable car up there, but they removed it," he says.

He brings his paddle back toward the water in sync with Jonelle's next, "All forward!"

As soon as we're through this stretch, Zeke points toward the mountainside.

"Check out the Dall sheep."

Four white sheep graze between the rocks. They're low enough that I can make out that one is larger, and none have the larger curved horns of a ram. Probably a mama with her lambs. Never mind that I don't have a camera with me, it's my first "big five" sighting.

I wave in their direction. "Hey there, Dall sheep," which can't, of course, be heard by the actual Dall sheep.

"Ever seen them before?" Zeke asks.

I shake my head. "Haven't been seeing a lot of animals. Just a marmot on Healy and now these guys."

"Seriously? There's that moose and her calf always walking through housing. I usually see them on the volleyball court at night when I'm coming back from the rec room."

Yes, rub it in. The moose appear for everyone but me. "Haven't seen 'em." I shrug, though this gesture is probably not detectable with all my gear. And, considering Dale's bet, that I'll die by animal attack, maybe I no longer want to.

"Don't worry about it. You'll end up having some crazy animal stories by the end of the summer. Last year, my brother and this other guy were in the

CHAPTER TEN

backcountry crossing a little river braid when three caribou came crashing toward them. Micah about shit his pants. Never did figure out what spooked them."

"Watch for caribou on river crossings. Got it." I turn to get a final look at the sheep which are now ascending higher up the ridge line. From a distance they're like large dandelion tufts blowing up the rock face. I'm greedy and impatient for more sightings, but at the same time enthralled and absorbed by my surroundings even without them. I am in a freaking raft on the Nenana River drifting between mountains, the silt in the glacial water gritty against my skin, the temperature exhilarating. At home, after a shift, I'd be with Chris watching a movie or with Charlet or one of the twins painting our nails or watching stupid videos. In Alaska, I'm being commanded to get my paddle back in the water because we're approaching another rapid.

At The Knife, our last class four, I experience one bounce high enough that I think I might come down outside of the boat rather than in, but I lean the right way and manage to land in my spot. In fact, we don't lose any passengers overboard, except at one area of particular calm where Jonelle said we can jump in if we want to. Our crew only has one taker, a twenty-something man who I think wants to show off for his young bride and performs a surprisingly agile back flip off the side of the raft. He swims for a bit, taunting his wife to join him, but when it's clear she won't budge, Zeke helps hoist the man back into the raft, yanking at his life vest to get him up and over the side.

DENALI SUMMER

We pass the still-scattered train wreckage at the Train Wreck class-four rapid and obey Jonelle's final, "All forward!" We hit a big wave and enjoy some fun rollers that take us down closer to a bridge, but Jonelle aims us toward a stretch of dark silt beach without many rocks. We paddle until we've slid to the point that half the raft is wedged onto the land.

At the take-out, Elijah's oar-rafted passengers have already stripped off their dry suits and booties. When he sees us angling toward the beach, he shuffles to the water's edge to offer his hand to each passenger as we exit. Once we reach him, Zeke jumps out to help with pulling while Jonelle continues to steer and push us forward by digging her paddle into the shallows.

Jonelle collects tips and hugs and, from me, a promise for whatever candy or snack food she might want sent in Mama's first care package. When I see that she has her phone along, I make Zeke take a picture of us together. Then he hands the phone off to a tourist, and we get one of all three of us. After the pictures, it's back to business—Elijah and Jonelle directing the gear placement before we load the vans for the return trip to the lodge.

On land, Zeke recedes into shyness, and it's a quiet ride. The only time we talk is to make plans for me to sit with River Rats during supper in an hour.

While on the river I've gotten two new texts and an email. The first text from Chris:

Sent you a letter today! Love you.

Went rafting today—I'll write you about it soon. Love you too! I send back.

The second text is from Mama, and it's... problematic.

CHAPTER TEN

Dale and Jesslyn talking about a wedding at the end of the summer. Might have to bring you on home a little early. Stay tuned for when they set a date.

No one else has said anything about a wedding. Is this a joke because she saw what my brothers and sisters have been texting? I decide to ignore it.

The email is also annoying. Someone by the name of Mrs. Hume is introducing herself as my ETBU freshman guidance counselor and asking me to schedule a phone call to discuss my fall schedule.

It's still the beginning of summer. I do not want to talk about fall schedules. Especially when I have no idea what I'm majoring in. I should just keep my phone turned off until August.

Back at the hotel, all I want to do is take my sweet time during a very hot shower, but I see someone at the door as I near my room. It's a headphone-wearing Flint, wedging a sliver of paper above the doorknob.

He turns and sees me approaching but has to squint and shield his eyes from the sun before he seems to decide it's me. He slips off the headphones. "I was leaving you an invitation."

"Oh yeah, big party tonight?"

"If you consider a foursome playing Spades in the staff rec room a big party, then yes. Absolutely."

"Who's playing?"

"Me, Gabby, hopefully you, and Bus Washer Ben."

"I don't know Bus Washer Ben. Is he a worthy opponent?"

"I hope so."

"Sounds good. What time?"

Flint nods toward my door, so I step past him to remove the paper he's left there and scan his neatly scratched words. "I can do eight o'clock," I say.

"It's a date then."

"Wait. Am I being set up with Bus Washer Ben?"

"No," he says, "not at all." It's my turn to squint against the sun framing his face, and I can't tell if he's smiling. "See you at eight."

"Should I bring anything?"

Flint pulls his headphones away from his ears and says, "We have cards, but you can add snacks if you have any," then he snaps them down and walks away, dissolving into the sunlight with every step.

Hiking, rafting, and friends. Forget going home early. I may never leave at all.

CHAPTER ELEVEN

With ten minutes to spare before closing time, I make it to the gift shop. A gal's first big five sighting deserves a souvenir, so I want a stuffed Dall sheep.

Gabby stands on a step stool reorganizing a high shelf of stuffed animals. There are birds mixed with the bears, which can't be good. The Dall sheep are at the bottom, a risky move putting their white fur so close to the well-trodden floor, but they're not my shelves to keep organized.

I squat and sift through the selection then hold up a lamb and an ewe, "Which one should I get?"

Gabby looks down, noticing me for the first time, "Little kids like the lambs. I like the mamas better. Who's it for?"

"Me. Wanted to commemorate my first big five sighting today." I set the lamb back on the shelf and bring the ewe with me to the snack section near the register. Gabby follows me and moves behind the counter.

"What do you like?" I ask. "I'm picking up stuff for our card game later."

"Flint told you? Wasn't sure who'd he get for a partner. Thought you were hanging out with Sugar."

"I'm hanging out with lots of people." I hold up a pack of trail mix, but Gabby shakes her head.

"Don't waste your money on that. Flint can make up a big bag of gorp from the kitchen supplies."

"Gorp?" Is gorp a word for trail mix that I don't know about?

"Good 'ol raisins and peanuts. Gorp. Flint adds chocolate chips too."

This conjures an image of Gabby packed tightly in the kitchen supply room with Flint giggling over food prep. And that doesn't bother me one bit because being bothered wouldn't make any sense at all when I have a boyfriend.

She sweeps her thick, wavy brown curls away from her face and yanks a hair elastic from her wrist to slink it into a messy bun then reaches for a bag of spicy chips I've never tried. "These are my favorite."

I set them on the counter next to my Dall sheep. "Okay and a bag of these," I toss a bag of salt and vinegar, my chip of choice, on the counter, "And..." I take one of each candy bar and add them to my pile. "These."

"That all?" Gabby asks. Two short words but I can feel the mocking in her question. It's not as though we have to eat it all. And in this area I won't apologize for being my mama's daughter—any kind of gathering should always have more than enough food.

"Do we need drinks?" I ask.

"There's a Coke machine in the rec room."

CHAPTER ELEVEN

"Then this seems good." I pull a fifty from my wallet and wait for her to ring up my loot.

"Fifties in your wallet? You sure you're not a tourist?"

First of all, who cares what I have in my wallet? If she thinks I'm spending too much, I can put her stupid spicy chips back. Second of all, I am a tourist. I'm a working tourist. What's wrong with tourists? Third of all, I get a ten percent employee discount on everything, which makes my twenty-five-dollar stuffed animal just over twenty dollars and my dollar candy bars are under a dollar and all of that seems very reasonable to me.

But I will not say any of this. I've agreed to Spades with her tonight, so I will play nice. Southern girls can play nice all day without anyone ever calling into question our sincerity. It is our spiritual gift.

"It's graduation money. I have a lot of relatives."

I've never been a pageant girl, but I've been in many a local parade propped on the back of Daddy's bright red 1969 Pontiac Firebird convertible. This car usually lives on display at the tire store, a mascot I suppose, but it comes out for parade occasions, and I have perfected a remarkably wide, visible even from the back of the crowd, parade smile. This is the smile I bestow upon Gabby when I hand her my cash. Then I deliberately sink my voice deeper into its southern accent of obliviousness when I thank for her my change.

The River Rats cheer when I enter The Zoo. Jonelle's strong voice rising above the rest hollers, "Dawn the Nenana River Queen!"

I slide through the food line, quickly grabbing a salad to counter balance my junk fest later. The only empty chair at the River Rat table is next to Zeke. As

I slip into it, I catch the eye of Bama Jake who's eating with his brother and some bus washers. He winks. Of course.

"You seemed like you were having fun, right?" Zeke asks.

"Oh she had fun," Jonelle jumps in. "How can you not have fun on the Nenana with me as your capable guide?"

I swim so much I thought I had good upper body strength, but Jonelle's arms are ripped. She was definitely a capable guide.

I pull my Dall sheep out of the bag to show Zeke, and he laughs. "What will you name her?"

I only have to think a second. "Nenana."

"That's perfect."

Elijah launches into a story of a time when Jonelle wasn't quite as capable that includes a raft-flip and impersonations of a very excited tourist. We're all teary eyed laughing he tells it so well. Even Jonelle can chuckle at the expense of her former rookie self. Zeke's brother Micah follows up with the tale of his first time being the lead guide and getting so stuck in an eddy he had to wait on the next raft down the river to come to their aid. Passenger flying overboard stories follow from everyone. Before I know it, the cheap plastic clock on the wall says five past eight, and I've got to run. Maybe it's the athlete in me who had to run a lap of the track for every late minute past the set start time for practice, but I hate being late. I sprint the whole way across the grounds between the two buildings.

When I rush into the rec room, Flint, Gabby, and a curly haired, shaggy goatee wearing guy I presume is

CHAPTER ELEVEN

Bus Washer Ben are already seated around a table. It's in a cluster of three heavy wood tables, each for four people. At one end of the room sits a behemoth of an old TV in front of a floral couch and a plaid recliner with mismatched throw pillows. At the other end is a dart board, foosball table, and two doors—one marked storage and one marked "The Shitter" in a painted-on cursive that is equal parts elegant and ironic.

"Sorry I'm late. Lost track of time at supper."

"No worries," says Flint, "The cool kids are supposed to be conventionally late."

I glance at the clock in this room which is the exact same make as the one in The Zoo. "In that case I'm still about ten minutes early so you're welcome."

There's a thick wooden counter that runs along the wall nearest the table they've chosen where I set out the chips and candy bars. "My snack contribution."

Bus Washer Ben immediately stands up. The sweet smell of pot wafts from his clothes as he leans across me to select his favorite from my supplied candy selection.

"I like this girl. She gets invited every time," he says.

I refuse to make eye contact with Gabby, and yet the smirk I was trying so hard to cast toward the floor, comes with my face when I glance up and catch her looking at me.

After grabbing a candy bar for myself I take my seat across from Flint.

"I assume you know how to play?" This is directed at me, but Gabby doesn't wait for my answer. Instead, she begins to deal, flinging the cards with enough force that we have to block them from sliding off the table.

DENALI SUMMER

Poker is the preferred Wilkes card game, but no matter what I'm playing, I cannot be intimated at cards. Period. Between Mama, my brothers, and Darlene, I've been taught how to play out any hand because bluffing your damn way to glory is more impressive than a lucky deal any day. As for the twins, they only ever play the first few rounds before complaining the rest of us are too competitive and not any fun. Daddy's like the twins, wishing the rest of us wouldn't take the game so seriously, but he generally sticks it out till he's forced to fold or flies in under the radar of the rest of our shenanigans to slowly steal all our chips away.

I'm a poker girl, but yes, Gabby, I can play Spades, thanks for asking.

As the last card slides across the table, she says, "Predict your tricks. Let's go."

Flint exhales. "Okay, okay. You do know we didn't put any money on this?"

The first deal sends me a ridiculously good hand of both red aces, the diamond king, and a lot of high spades. I claim seven tricks for my team, a genuine expectation, no mind games needed. Flint looks impressed but says he'll take two more, so our team has bid to win nine of the thirteen rounds. This feels very doable, but I'll have to be careful not to catch more rounds than I predicted with all my trump-card spades.

When we do win our nine tricks this earns a tight-lipped congratulations from Gabby, but when we win out our predicted eight the next three rounds she looks like she could piss fire. If I knew her better, I'd be laughing and teasing her. This face on Darlene, and I'd be in tears. This face on Dale or Dusty, and

CHAPTER ELEVEN

I'd be squealing and trying not to pee my pants. This face on Gabby I have to ignore. Blame the cards. Be a gracious winner. Which is not one ounce of fun. Flint looks bewildered by Gabby's attitude. Bus Washer Ben seems oblivious and ready for another candy bar.

Flint and I are potentially one hand away from breaking the 500 points we need to take the whole game when three out of the four Bama boys, the twins and Sugar, roll in, carrying a six-pack and discussing movie choices.

"Who wants to watch a movie?" Sugar hollers to the room.

My table mates don't answer. I study their faces, but it's as though they're all deaf or the Bama boys are ghosts they can't see, or I don't even know. A twin, it's so hard to tell which one when they're together and name tag free, deposits the beer on the coffee table in front of the couch while the other bee-lines it for The Shitter. Sugar approaches our table and announces the movie, perhaps to entice us.

I recognize the title. It's about some couples' game night getting derailed. Chris convinced me to see it in the theater even though I'd suggested we watch Black Panther for the second time.

"Go away, Sugar," says Gabby. Once again our dealer, she begins flinging out the cards with the same vigor she's applied since the beginning of the game.

"We still have at least one hand to go," I say, as if this helps explain why Gabby wants him to leave our table as quickly as he's come.

"Great. You're almost done. Finish up, then come over." Sugar sinks a hand onto my shoulder and squeezes. He doesn't wait for another response before ambling over to the couch and popping open a beer.

Gabby mumbles something that I'm fairly sure is a nasty insult in Spanish, and while part of me wants to get this stupid game over with, another part of me wants to delay getting sucked into the expectation of joining the Bama boys once we're done. I deliberately overshoot my bid by at least three tricks. As my first "misstep" since I've sat down becomes apparent, Gabby's demeanor slowly softens with each trick she claims that I don't.

"Not ready to be done then?" she asks, writing mine and Flint's first negative of the game on the small pad of hotel stationary where she's been keeping score.

"Maybe I got cocky."

This earns an eyebrow raise of disbelief.

Flint deals the next hand, and I stare at cards so good we can make back the points I lost us in the last round and still win the game. I'm deciding how I'm going to play it when Zeke and his brother come in and station themselves in front of the dart board.

And I'm done. I don't want to have to decide who to talk to and worry about if I'm being flirty. It's time to get back to my room, maybe doodle out a page about potential college majors, see if anything speaks to me, and then be responsible and email back that guidance counselor. Or maybe just crash. It's been a long day, and I don't have to keep going because other people want me to.

I make a good bid, resulting in a win that lands us at 510. As soon as this score is tallied, I thank them for the game, grab my stuffed animal, and excuse myself

CHAPTER ELEVEN

from the room, leaving all the uneaten candy bars and mostly-full bags of chip in my wake.

About ten minutes later, when all I've done is started a new page in my journal where I've written and crossed off nursing, written and crossed off teaching, written and crossed off tire sales, written and crossed off mechanic, and written biomedical engineer but not yet crossed it off, there's a soft tap at my door. I pull at the curtain to see Flint standing there, shoulders hunched, hands shoved in his pockets, staring down at his red Converse.

I open the door about three inches. "Hey."

"Hey," he echoes, eyes searching mine as if he doesn't know what to do now, forgot whose door he knocked on, or what he's doing here.

"Hey," I say again.

He's still studying me, like I'm a critter he doesn't want to spook. He rubs the coppery stubble growing from his not-recently-shaved face before asking finally, "May I come in?"

I left the rec room in a hurry to be done with boys for the day. I didn't want Zeke to invite me to play darts. I didn't want to squish on the couch with the Bama boys and deal with Sugar's floating hands. I didn't want Flint to see me making a choice to spend the rest of my evening with either Zeke or Sugar. And I certainly don't want to have to explain any of the above to Chris.

Alone, I can keep journaling or color a page or read a few chapters in the quiet of my still roommate-free room. Alone, I can be in my thoughts. Alone, I can be alone.

DENALI SUMMER

But I am a sucker for properly asked questions and tallish boys in red Converse with a day or two's growth of coppery facial stubble. I didn't know this about myself, but Alaska is about discoveries, right?

"Sure." I pull the door all the way back so Flint can move past me. He plops onto the naked mattress across from mine.

"Here." I toss my throw blanket at him. "You can put that under you."

He stands to fold the blanket neatly in half and stretches it over the bed, smoothing out the wrinkles before settling back down. He leans against the cream-colored painted cinder block of the bare walls on his side of the room and stares at me. I'm conscious that the completed coloring pages I've taped in a line to decorate the wall by my bed may look childish. I'm also conscious of the fact that I've already changed, and my pajama shorts are silky and tiny, and the blanket I would have drawn up to cover myself is beneath Flint's butt. I grab my pillow and pull it into my lap and grab Nenana the Doll sheep to set her on top of the pillow.

"Sorry that card game ended up being so lame. Ben's usually funny, but when he smokes he goes boring-level mellow. And Gabby…" Flint doesn't appear to know what he should say about Gabby, instead he scoots forward and reaches for the picture of me and my sisters from the nightstand between the beds.

I finish his sentence instead. "Gabby's not joining my fan club any time soon."

Flint ignores this. "You have three sisters?" he asks.

"And two brothers."

CHAPTER ELEVEN

"Wow. Big family." He sets the picture back on the table. "I have a little brother. That's it."

"How old is he?"

"He'll be a senior next year. Which seems crazy."

I can remember Darlene, Dale, and the twins coming over for the first day of my senior year. I expect Dustin would've come too, but he was already back at grad school. The twins fussed over my hair as Mama insisted on taking pictures. For as long as I can remember, Mama's had a row of eight-by-ten pictures on the wall leading to hers and Daddy's bedroom of each of us on our first day of kindergarten. Underneath it she'd hung a second row of eight-by-ten pictures of us kids on our first day of our senior year. As she snapped the pictures, both Mama and Dolly got teary when Darlene said, "Now you can finish your picture row, Mama."

Meanwhile Dale and Chris leaned against Chris's car, laughing and enjoying the spectacle of the Wilkes ladies enforcing yet another ritual on the youngest.

"If he'll be a senior, he doesn't sound like such a little brother," I say.

"He is to me. I can't seem to break my habit of wanting to protect him. Our dad works a lot, so right now I'm living at home and commuting. I'm hoping he'll come to UNT with me, so we can get an apartment together near campus."

Clearly, I'm not the only babied baby. "What about your mom?"

"My mom—," he pulls a foot to the frame of the bed and takes a sudden interest in adjusting the laces of his shoe, "—left Virginia Beach to live in Roanoke with her new soon-to-be-husband before the divorce to my dad was even finalized. Didn't see her much after that, haven't seen her once since we moved out to Texas."

"Oh." An absent mother is such a foreign concept to me I have no idea how to respond. Charlet's mama teaches math at our high school and was so involved in high school gossip, she knew it before we did. Chris's mama never did go back to work after having babies, but she ran any and every fundraiser for the speech and debate team and volunteered to chaperone anything that ever needed a chaperone. And my mama, my mama in spite of being a busy middle school principal and community advisor to the Junior League, East Texas Literacy Council, and probably ten other organizations I don't know about, still didn't have her focus divided enough. She could keep tabs on the behaviors of every Wilkes child as well as any boyfriend, girlfriend, or best friend of a Wilkes child. And those boyfriends, girlfriends, and best friends knew it. Three years of Mama-void would be dull indeed.

One summer is nice though.

"Sorry," Flint says. "Didn't come here to get into all that."

Then why did you come? "That's okay."

He runs a hand through his hair. "Are you—," he pulls up the other shoe, "are you interested in Sugar? I think that's what has Gabby acting weird."

"I don't know Sugar all that well."

"You went hiking yesterday."

"I imagine I'll be hiking with a lot of people through the summer." I'm mindful that I should work in the whole I-have-a-boyfriend fact too, but I want to see where this is going first.

CHAPTER ELEVEN

"Well, Sugar has his sights on you. I thought Gabby was mad about something that happened with Sugar, but now it seems she's mad he's moved on." He shrugs. "I don't really understand it."

"Mighty nice of you to come by and explain something you don't understand."

He cocks his head, and I toss Nenana at him. I'd have pegged him in his chest but he reacts quickly enough to catch it.

"Yes, I'm making fun of you," I say.

He pitches my sheep back. "Says the girl who brought a suitcase the size of a moving pod."

"I guess we've come to the point of the evening where we play catch with a stuffed animal while lobbing insults at the same time?"

He laughs. "The inevitable ending for a night that began with a belligerent game of Spades."

"Next time I'll have to insist on poker."

"I believe you have one hell of a poker face." He keeps Nenena in his lap and lightly brushes her fur back and forth.

"Have to with a family as big as mine."

Flint stays another ten minutes or so before tossing back my sheep and announcing he'll leave me alone. "We both have early shifts in the morning."

I stand up when he does, so I can lock the door behind him. He turns back to me, and our faces are so close my cheeks flush and gut stirs. "Good night," he says, low and soft.

"Good night," I echo, studying the sparks of gold in his hazel eyes.

DENALI SUMMER

He pauses, his hand on the doorknob, and looks as though he has something else he wants to say, but he simply nods at me and walks into the still-bright night.

Hello my name is not actually Sugar

slim shady

Do I care?

Brad Brian Pinky Brain Darian
Ross Joey Chandler Hopper
Dustin Lucas William Benjamin
Colton MACK! (try that next?)
Lancaster Wellington George
Tobias Kaden (Caiden Kayden?)
Blue Silver Gray (Grey?) Ash
Slate Clay Shepherd Cooper
Gage Axle Jayden Jason
Jaxon Leo Noah Cain Able
Owen ~~Martin~~ Roberto Carlos
Eddie Ajani Mason Xavier
Nicholas Sebastian Flounder Eric
~~Ricardo~~ Bear Cub Lion Ed
Simba ~~Mowgli~~ Horace (try that)
Cody Yancey Piero
Drew
Kenji Benji Davis Joel Ryan
Walt Jesse Saul Gus
Jeff Austin Scott Matthew
Tuna Barry Barney
Gabby Olaf Kristoff
says Rodney Carlton Banks
Helmut Kevin
Flynn Jay Klaus Eugene

CHAPTER TWELVE

Sugar's real name is not Mowgli. He sits with me at breakfast, and I'm relieved to see that Gabby is not in The Zoo to witness. He also tells me he'll be fishing on the Triple Lakes trail with Dylan, the non-twin Bama boy, after his shift. I don't appear to be invited.

"Have fun fishing, Martin!" I say as he leaves.

"One guess a day," he laughs over his shoulder.

I'm happy not to be included on this fishing excursion. Three days at the lodge, and I'm offtrack on Mission Me. Not Chris's me. Not Mama's me. My own me. I'm hoping I can get her sorted out well enough that she'll come back to Texas with me. At the *end* of the summer. No more texts about a wedding, and no follow-up from Mama, so I'm still letting that go.

At college, I'd like this version of Dawn to help me do things like pick my own major instead of falling in line with whatever Charlet decides for herself. (I can hear her now: "If we have the same major, we'll

CHAPTER TWELVE

always have a study partner!") Or what Mama pushes for. ("There's a teacher shortage, honey. Just think about it.")

Sugar can't help with that. Neither can Flint or Zeke.

Wanda assures me during our shift that there's a large beaver dam at Horseshoe Lake, so if I camp out long enough I'm guaranteed to see one.

That's what I set off to do. With Mama's good camera in my backpack accompanied by a book—I have every intention of committing to my beaver stake-out for as long as it takes.

Once the park shuttle passes through the touristy section everyone around here calls Glitter Gulch, it's only another mile before I'm at the trail head. I'd been warned that this was a popular trail, that I'd be hiking alongside plenty of tourists, but a misty gray sky appears to have kept away my potential trail-sharers. I'm so very by myself that as I begin the ascent to the overlook I wonder if I made it clear enough to Wanda that this was my plan. If anything happens I'd prefer someone knew where to find me. I'd been vague about my afternoon with everyone else, so it'll be left to Wanda to send help. Or, and this seems like the better goal, I could not need help in the first place.

At the overlook, I've been promised an amazing view of the Nenana, this lake and that river are cousins related by water-linking marshes. I'm hopeful, given enough time, the cloud problem can be fixed by a steady increase of sun to force the shedding of gray and releasing of blue. So I pace myself slow and will the sun to emerge as I climb.

It's too short a walk. The overlook sign peeks out from ahead on the trail with no changes to atmospheric light or color. In fact, the mist feels as though it's strengthening into a rain. Without the sun breaking through the clouds, it's a cool landscape of gray gravel beside dark waters outlined by darker tree silhouettes. I take out my jacket and forgo taking a picture.

From this point the trail descends sharply. The muscles I woke coming down from my Healy hike are awake again now and sending pain signals of resentment at this all-too-soon reuse. Another ten minutes go by before an elderly couple pass me on their return trek.

"We saw three beavers at the dam. You're in for a treat," the wife says.

I spy the beaver's lodge before I'm at the trail's end, but no beavers. I continue on to the dam hoping the three beavers spotted by the couple before me are still at work, but I can't find them. The blanket of heavy mist thickens the quiet as I continue to stare, willing a beaver to emerge from lodge side or dam side. When nothing stirs after a considerable amount of time, I scout around the lake's edge for a tree-protected area that still offers me a view of beaver construction while I wait. Spotting a small trail offshoot, I follow it farther around the lake to a cluster of tall spruce not far off the bank, positioned in a semi-circle as though beckoning me to take shelter in their midst.

I use my jacket to cover the ground because I'd rather have a dry butt than shoulders. My camera's at-the-ready in my hands, my gaze stuck to the calm lake surface, expectant of an animal-caused disturbance to its flat sheen. Enough minutes pass that I feel as though I might fall into a trance, so I set the camera down and pull my backpack over it for protection. I

CHAPTER TWELVE

sink my eyes down into my book, figuring that beaver activity, should it ever come, will be loud enough to catch my attention.

Three chapters later, I'm disturbed by the chatter of a family of hikers, the tense reprimands of a mother calling her two young sons away from the lake's edge, the low bark of the dad finalizing the expectation they obey. The mom is able to position the boys for a photo in front of the beaver's lodge before they retreat back up the trail.

The weather relents, and the traveling clouds take the mist with their retreat. I scoot away from tree cover closer to the water's edge and strip another layer, plopping my long-sleeve tee near the shoreline. I'm left in only a tank top so the newly present sun can warm my shoulders directly. My boots and socks are next to go, tossed behind me to land where they may. I stretch my toes toward the water and yank my pants up to expose my legs past my knees before re-opening my book.

When I hear the first splash, I lift my head, expecting to see a new set of rambunctious hikers tossing sticks or stones to break the water's stubborn calm. Instead I see a bull moose. A bull moose whose antler rack appears to be, from point to point, significantly longer than my own body. The sight of him both thrills and alarms me from the tops of my pinking shoulders to the bottoms of my lake-kissed toes. But there's a good stretch of water between us, a comfortably wide expanse separating my vital organs from those potentially piercing antlers. This situation is fully okay, fully Alaska magic. The reasonable thing to do is take a lot of pictures.

DENALI SUMMER

He's far enough away that I have to zoom, but not so far away that a full zoom leaves me with anything but a close-up of his face. Its bored gaze steadies in my direction. He doesn't move again until he dips his wide brown muzzle toward the water and raises it, water dripping like a shimmery beard. And I happily snap away, catching all of it until the image in my view finder blurs unable to re-establish its focus point. I drop the camera from my face to see what's happened and discover the moose on the move. In my direction. With astoundingly long strides that cover almost half our distance in only four steps.

Time to scramble. I secure the camera strap over my head then toss my shirt, water bottle, book, and jacket in my backpack. By the time it's zipped, the moose has splashed ahead another impressive step. The water covers him to his chest, but he doesn't appear to care. His sights are fully on me, or my stretch of shore, or a berry bush beyond me. Whatever it is, I'm in his way, and I have to move. Fast.

I snatch one sock from the dirt and stuff it into the nearest boot then scan the ground for their matches. The second sock lays atop a low bush, but I still can't find the other stupid boot. I yank my backpack to my shoulders and clutch my single boot to my chest where it bumps my camera. The moose strides closer so that now he's three steps out and zero zoom level away from a closeup.

"Hey, moose!" I call in alarm. "Give me a second, and I'll be out of your way." Then under my breath, "Holy hell, where is that friggin' boot?"

Wilkes kids are conditioned to know that if you drop an F-bomb you best be hurt to the point of an

CHAPTER TWELVE

emergency room visit. Apparently, this is so ingrained in my psyche that it is unalterable even under possible moose attack.

Another splashy step and my heart stops, but a glance behind me shows he's turned, so in terms of the distance between us, it's a lateral move. Unfortunately, it's also a step that puts the moose closer to blocking my escape route.

I finally catch sight of my lost boot behind a tree in a way that doesn't appear logical, but there's no time to consider physics or the geometry of bounce trajectory or whatever math high school supposedly equipped me with to solve the mystery. The moose's next step is at a diagonal putting him a little closer to me and a little more in the way of my path. I'm now cornered between a lake, a moose, and the steep, seemingly unclimbable hillside behind me. Not a single trail offshoot marks this way, but I don't have a choice. Climbing is my only option. I tie my boots to my backpack, ignoring the discomfort as they thump against the side of my thigh.

Tackling the steep terrain at a very inelegant crawl, I pull myself forward with branches when available, by clawing into the earth when they're not. But I keep at it, not looking back at the moose, not thinking about what might happen should I lose my footing. When I reach a level patch of earth wide enough to sit safely, I take a moment to catch my breath and pull on my socks and shoes. I'd like to snap a final shot of this would-be attack-moose, one with my phone so I can text it to Dale along with: *I did not get killed by this moose today. Also, screw you.*

DENALI SUMMER

But the moose is now hidden in tree cover so, next time.

Sweat rolls steadily down my neck and between my boobs, but I can spot the marked trail above me. I can do this.

Another three yards and I'm able to pitch my backpack up to the trail before clambering the final bit. Elbow to the trail, I'm about to hoist my body when I spot a hand stretched in my direction.

"Need some help?" It's Flint's voice.

I shake my head and feel the anger rise within me. To be spotted like this, looking foolish and inept on one of the easiest trails in all of Denali—why is he even here?

He steps to the edge and peers past me. "That's quite a climb. Don't think it's the way you're supposed to go though." He waves to the trail around us. "Thought the rangers had this part marked well enough."

"Oh, shut it." I inch a comfortable distance from the edge and cross my legs to sit and rummage through my backpack until I find my water bottle.

After a good, long, heart-rate-settling, anger-cleansing chug I'm ready to speak again. "Did you come here to find me?"

He settles down beside me. "I did. Wanda seemed to think I should. She came through the line at dinner and asked if I'd seen you this afternoon, said she couldn't believe you weren't back four hours after you'd set off on a one-and-a-half-hour hike."

"And here you are."

"Here I am. What happened down there?"

I rummage again, until my hand connects with my camera and pull up the moose pictures. The creature's

CHAPTER TWELVE

face, now small and docile in the confines of my display screen, appears so unthreatening I feel silly all over again.

Flint reaches for the camera. "That's some moose. In all my hikes, I've never come across a rack that wide."

That makes it a little better. "Yeah, and he and his rack decided to pay me a visit at my reading spot, blocking my path back to the trail. I had nowhere to go but up this way."

"Steep. No wonder you're so sweaty."

I dab at my face with my shirt before becoming self conscious I've probably pushed sweat-hardened bangs every which way, framing myself in spikes and tangles. When Flint looks off down the path, I attempt a quick finger comb to settle it flat again.

"Did you see any beavers before the moose came after you? Last time I hiked down here they were all posing outside their lodge like models for postcard day."

"No beavers." Because, as I have come to accept, the animals of Denali don't like to do for me what they do for everyone else. The beavers I'm supposed to see stay hidden while the moose I'm not expecting decides he wants my patch of lake shoreline even if he has to trample me to get it. "Just the bull moose with no respect for a lady's personal space bubble."

This doesn't fetch a smile. Flint's golden-hazel eyes are concentrated and searching, as though he wants to find the accosting moose. He shakes his head slightly. "I'd stick to hiking partners till you've got a little more experience in the park. Alaska's not exactly Texas."

"Ya think?" I know my tone is rude, but his comment feels rude too. Not having experience doesn't mean I have to be talked to like a kindergartner who doesn't understand the distance of Alaska from Texas.

"I meant that..."

"I chose what is usually a well-traveled trail within two miles of a ranger station. I came equipped with water, good boots, and the right clothes. I told another person where I was going. What the hell else am I supposed to do?"

"Have a hiking partner. Like I said." He says it quietly though, less confident in pushing his point.

"Do you hike alone?"

"Yeah, but it's my second summer, and—"

"Did you hike alone last year?" He kicks into the dirt, and I keep going before he gets a chance to make more excuses. "I'll bet your very first Denali hike was a solo." Again, no comment from Flint. "It was, wasn't it?"

"Yeah, but—"

"And you've hiked solo off-trail in the backcountry."

"Yes."

"But I'm a girl."

"That's not what I said."

"It's absolutely what you meant. Guess what? Sometimes I'm going to hike and camp with other people, and sometimes I'm going to do it alone. And, while it's nice Wanda was worried about me, today would've worked out fine even if you'd never come."

I hold my hand to take back my camera, zip it into my pack, then take off on the trail.

From behind me Flint hollers, "Sorry I came to help you. I'll know better next time." It doesn't sound like he's walking after me, and I refuse to turn and check.

CHAPTER TWELVE

Flint's words sound too much like Mama's words at dinner the night before my flight: be careful, have a partner because you don't know what you're doing, don't take risks... I thought I'd left all that in Texas.

My footfalls hit the compact trail in heavy thumps as I speed-walk my way to the shuttle pick-up site. When the shuttle pulls over for me, Flint has barely come into view, and runs the last ten yards or so.

"Thanks for waiting," he pants to the bus driver before sinking in the first empty aisle seat. He pulls his headphones out from his back pack, sending his hair wild and adorable, but does not turn, does not look at me. Instead he stares, rigid and straight, so that I don't even have the satisfaction of his profile in the steady light of the evening streaming through the windows.

Fine. He can insult me and be mad at me. Fine.

I want to shower and crawl into my bed. I'll sleep off my frustrations and settle things with Flint in the morning. What matters is that I've made it back ungored, so Dale can't win the stupid family bet.

But as I approach my room I'm stopped, wrapped from behind by two thick arms and rocked back and forth in this backward hug. Upon release, I'm spun around to face Sugar.

"Where've you been all afternoon?" he says.

"Hello..." I'd meant to have something ridiculous to call him, but I forgot to plan this ahead. "Brian."

"Not Mowgli or Martin or Brian. You're not very good at this game, Dawn from East Texas, but I have an offer. I'll give you the first initial if you go camping with me." His hands are still on my shoulders, and he's grinning like a little boy who's caught a lizard. I have a weird and funny image of Sugar attempting to attach a lizard to his earlobe, something my brothers always did with their lizard catches, and suddenly it's impossible not to match his goofy grin.

"Good. You're in a good mood, so you'll say yes," he says.

Not exactly and not necessarily. "When would we go?"

"When's your first set of days off?"

"Sunday and Monday. Why, when are you off?"

"I'll switch with one of the boys, don't worry about that. We can leave Saturday after your shift. Do a two-night trip."

He's not warm-smiley like Flint but mischievous-smiley. It's tempting. Flint thinks I should have an escort when I go off in Denali. Okay then. He can watch me make plans with plenty of willing escorts.

I'm still not quite ready to answer Sugar because I don't think I should be alone with him for two nights in the backcountry. "Can we get other people to go?"

He pauses but decides not to probe the reasoning. "Sure. Two more guys came in today so it will be easy to get another Bama boy, and that Bama boy can find him a tent mate."

I interpret this to mean that Sugar expects he and I will be sharing a tent and not me and the girl. There's no doubt the other Bama boy will bring a girl.

This is a detail that can be worked out later.

I'd hoped to get off the trails and into the backcountry with my weekend, but, being gearless, didn't know how to go about asking. Now I'm being offered a trip.

"Then let's go camping."

CHAPTER TWELVE

"Awesome. I'll visit the ranger station in the morning, see what sections of the park are available, and get our reservation permit."

I knew nothing about our need for permits. This reminder at how little I know sends a tiny sliver of forgiveness through the anger I'm still harboring for Flint.

Sugar hugs me from the front this time and jogs off in the direction of the rec room. Finally, I can shower and relax in bed for the rest of the evening.

Or maybe not.

As I near my room, I hear music blaring, seemingly from inside even though I'm sure I didn't leave any music on. I reach for my key lanyard and twist open the door.

"Hello?" I say. There's no response. The door snags, and I have to push harder. When it's open enough for me to fit through, I'm accosted by an explosion of clothes and the smell of lavender and orange popsicles.

Final wave has arrived.

CHAPTER THIRTEEN

I'm short, but my roommate is shorter. Like might not even be five-feet-tall short. She's wearing a white dress cheerfully pocked by bright red cherries, and her look is topped by a shock of highlighter blue hair that, in spite of its pixie-ish cut, maintains impressive volume. Her back is to me and this hair is bouncing as her head bobs in rhythm with the music still blaring. It's coming from my wireless speaker, so like my sisters and Charlet, I've got me another share-without-asking type in my life. Even Mama borrows my shoes. My stuff is your stuff no matter where I go.

"Hi! I'm Dawn." It comes out more of a yell than I'd meant for it to.

The girl twirls around, the thin sweater in her hands falling out of its fold during the turn. "Oh hey!"

Pineapples splash across the light-yellow fabric. How many fruit-clothing items does a person need?

"I'm Vanessa. Excuse the mess. It takes me awhile to nest and sort and situate. I'll have every bitty thing

CHAPTER THIRTEEN

off your bed in a bit. Oh, but that—" she points to a large-sized, flat-rate shipping box in the middle of my bed, "that came for you."

I move a stack of brightly colored clothing, all happily patterned and more suited for visits to read to kindergartners than anything Alaska related, and grab my box. It's sooner than I expected any packages to arrive, but it's Mama's handwriting with a postmark indicating she shipped it off Tuesday, the day before I even left.

Ha! Someone wasn't quite as pissy as she'd let on.

At the top of the box lies a batch of vacuum-sealed cookies with a sticky note that reads, "Graduation batch two—I knew your brothers would eat up the first set." Underneath I find a sealed plate of Texas Gold, the yummiest, sugariest bites of heaven a girl could ever hope to taste. They're made with yellow cake mix and cream cheese and who knows what else because I prefer them to remain a mysterious miracle of Mama's kitchen. On this batch, the sticky note reads, "I did a lot of baking while you were upstairs packing."

Under a layer of bubble wrap there's a mishmash of stuff: a box of granola bars, two water-flavoring squirts, postage stamps with sticky note that reads, "No excuses" (She must not have known Dolly gave me some too. My family sure is expecting a lot of hand-written letters.), an ETBU long sleeve t-shirt, an ETBU plush tiger, a book titled *How to Survive Freshman Year*, and a card with twenty bucks inside also signed by Daddy. Which reminds me that I still haven't emailed that guidance counselor.

Oh Mama—amazing and annoying all rolled together.

Vanessa stands over me and points at the plate of Texas Gold. "Please tell me those are Ooey Gooey bars, and you're about to open them up and share."

"In my family, we call it Texas Gold, but you can taste-test the difference," I say, peeling away the seal and setting the uncovered plate on the nightstand between our beds.

"Girls!" Vanessa calls in the direction of the bathroom. "It's snack time!"

There's a quick clatter of doors before two girls race into our room. They're remarkably identical in that they're both about the same height (a little taller than me, considerably taller than Vanessa), both have long, straight brown hair parted at one side, both wear skinny jeans and tight-fitting tees with nary a muffin top to disrupt the line of one stretch material to the next, and both have on glasses with thick plastic frames. The differences are that one girl has pale white skin and blue glasses, while the other sports bright-orange glasses and darker skin. Not exactly Black though, maybe she's part Black but also Asian? Anyway—she's not a skin-tone you see much in East Texas.

The darker girl steps forward. "I'm Shelby," she says, "and I come running for free food. Obviously."

The other girl giggles. "Me too. I'm Kendra."

I take the plate of Texas Gold and hold it out to them before introducing myself. They're moaning their approval of Mama's baking skills when I ask, "Did ya'll know each other before coming up here?"

"Oh, yes," says Vanessa. "We met freshmen year. We'll be seniors in the fall."

"Go Owls!" squeals Shelby, and the three of them do a spirit finger thing in the air.

CHAPTER THIRTEEN

They're the same age as the twins, but announcing their mascot and shaking appendages doesn't clear up the school for me. "What college?"

"Florida Atlantic," says Shelby.

"Where's that?"

"Boca. Not far from the beach, and you can even get to South Beach in Miami in less than an hour."

I'm not sure what beaches she's talking about, but I nod like I do. I'd guess a lot of things are across or around or over by popular beaches in Florida.

"What brings ya'll to Alaska?" I ask.

Instead of answering, Shelby asks, "You have the cutest accent. Where are you from?"

"East Texas." I'm conscious not to drawl out Texas.

"I just love how you talk!" Kendra adds.

I look at them, wondering if they're being condescending. I sure hope my new roommates aren't the type to equate southern, slower speech with a slow mind. Taking your time around words, adding a few syllables here, a softening swallow of vowels there—it's an easy slide into conversational melody. Southern talk can be like Sunday supper, hammock lounging, and sun-made tea—all good things that don't need rushing.

These girls know as much about East Texas as I do about South Florida—nothing. But they seem eager to learn and begin by pounding me with quick, melody-free questions: Where's my town in relation to Austin or Dallas? (No where near Austin, two hours due east from Dallas.) Do we get as crazy for high school football as *Friday Night Lights* makes it seem? (Actually, yeah we do.) Do people listen to anything other than country music? (Yes.) Do people wear cowboy boots everyday? (No.) Does everybody boycott abortion clinics in their spare time? (Seriously? This is a Texas stereotype?) Do I want a wall built to keep out Mexicans? (Eye. Roll.)

Dear Lord, these girls are trying my patience.

Except it's only Shelby who's asking the questions. Vanessa makes her bed, and Kendra moves over to help her stretch out the lime-green sheets splattered with ice cream cones. So it's not just fruit, and it's not just clothes—any food print on any type of fabric for Vanessa will do.

When she pulls out a pink fleece blanket sporting a purple unicorn it's as though a time warp lands me at my first sleepover in fourth grade. Charlet had a unicorn party for her birthday. We made fleece tie blankets and used puff paint to color in the unicorn head Charlet's mama had already pre-drawn on one side with fabric marker.

It was the same set of girls for every sleepover all the way from fourth grade through high school. And now here I am, with a new set of girls. It's weird.

The unicorn gets no comment from Shelby or Kendra who've, no doubt, seen it before. Since I'd realized I didn't have a single, I'd been hopefully imagining who my roommate could be, but in no instances did I come up with someone like Vanessa. I didn't occur to me either that my roommate and suite-mates would all know each other, leaving me as the odd woman out.

"You never did say what brought you all to Alaska. You like to camp?" I ask.

Vanessa snorts and goes back to folding sweaters while Shelby reaches for another Texas Gold bar and settles on my bed. I cringe. But she eats delicately, one

CHAPTER THIRTEEN

hand placed below her food to catch crumbs. I can unfurl. I hate crumbs on my bed.

"I do," Shelby says. "These girls are being good sports tagging along. This is my last chance at an extended girlfriend getaway as a single lady. I made an Alaska adventure a requirement for my bestie bridesmaids."

"Bridesmaids?"

Shelby pops the final bite into her mouth and juts out her left hand where an impressive square cut diamond encased by many more baby diamonds takes up a considerable amount of her skinny ring finger. "He took me to Cabo for spring break and proposed!"

"Is the wedding soon?"

Shelby nods. "We're having a beach wedding this December and then a Christmas ski vacation in Canada for our honeymoon."

Cabo and Canada—this girl gets around on a bigger budget than I've ever hoped for.

"You're so blessed." Kendra sits beside Shelby on the bed and pats her leg. "We're blessed too, getting to have this time with you before Baxter steals you away to the beach."

"My fiancé's family has a vacation condo on the water," Shelby explains. "That's where we'll be living our last semester of school."

This is the part of the conversation where I'm supposed to show off my promise ring and explain my own I'll-be-married-in-college-too plans, but my naked finger reminds me, it's still in my junk basket and has been for days. I never can seem to remember to put it on.

We'll bond over that another time then.

DENALI SUMMER

"Sorry, ladies, but I've been up since before five, and my shift starts at five again tomorrow, so I'm going to hit the shower. Then it's my bed time." This is my not-so-subtle way of saying: ya'll be gone by the time I get back.

Kendra and Shelby don't stir from my bed.

It's like they didn't even hear me. Instead, they dive into more questions, wanting to know where I'm working, what I've already seen, who I've met, what the hot twin bellboys are like, and on and on and on. Somehow during all this chatter I find my way onto the bed as well, curl up with Nenana, and drift off.

I wake up disoriented as to why I'm on top of the covers in my clothes. Movement in the bed across from me coupled with a loud exhale brings the previous evening back. A you've-overslept panic grips my chest, and I spring up to grab my phone to check the time.

It's only two o'clock in the morning.

A quick sweep of the room with my phone flashlight reveals surprisingly cleared surfaces, all clothes disappeared. The beam also shows a white towel with a giant yellow happy face emoji now hanging on the wall over Vanessa's head like a poster.

I reset the alarm on my phone to give me time to shower before my shift then strip off all my dirty clothes and slip under my sheets for another two hours of sleep.

CHAPTER FOURTEEN

The hotel wakes slowly. First with requests for newspaper delivery and late check-outs, then a trickle of rooms want more towels before we get inquiries about openings for the morning park bus tours. Later in the morning it's people wanting room key replacements, restaurant or bus or activity reservation confirmations, upgrade finagling, and early check-in demands.

I didn't expect to find a kindred spirit in Wanda who's maybe fifty years my senior, but she's fierce about Gin Rummy, our favorite time-passer in the first hour of the morning. That's about as much as I need to call her my friend and not just my co-worker.

We're deep into our morning when I use a lull in guest requests to tell Wanda my moose story. She's so tickled, I'm worried she'll pee. But when I tell her about Flint's botched rescue, she gives me a Grandma Look.

DENALI SUMMER

A Grandma Look is different from a Mama Look in that Mama Looks are stern without an inch of sympathy. A Mama Look says: child, you done something wrong so listen up. And then comes the tirade. A Grandma Look infers disapproval, but still gives you room to explain. It says: you've perked my ears because I'm not so sure you did the right thing, but let's keep talking this through.

I choose my next words carefully. As in, I decide to eliminate all the words explaining how I stomped off, leaving Flint behind me on the trail and how I didn't speak to him the rest of the evening.

"Of course, it was good of him to come, and I appreciated that, but he sounded so condescending telling me I have to always have a hiking buddy anytime I go out."

"You should have seen the way he tore off from his dinner shift when I told him you weren't back yet. He clocked out three hours early and lost pay on your account. That boy has a heart of gold."

"Right, but..."

"But he was concerned and acted in your best interest at a cost to himself. Does he really have to say all the right things as well, or can you cut him some slack?"

"I suppose." The eyebrow height of The Grandma Look raises, so I add, "I'll talk to him. Next time I see him. I'll hold up the food line if I have to."

We're interrupted when Sugar approaches the desk escorting two couples my parents' age who need to check-in. Wanda enters their information then hands off the keys to Sugar so he can deposit luggage in their rooms while they finish check-in. Once she's

CHAPTER FOURTEEN

processed their payment and collected signed receipts, she lets me promote the rafting excursion. There are exactly four spots open for today's six p.m. tour. I must have a little of Darlene's salesmanship in me because they sign up.

As the couples walk in the direction Sugar carried their things, Wanda says to me, "I don't know what to think about that Sugar. Seems like there's a story to him that might not be all good."

"Why do you say that?"

"Something Red said."

Red, who's in charge of hotel maintenance, is Wanda's husband. I didn't put this together until this very morning when I saw Wanda leaving the silver airbus parked alongside staff housing I knew belonged to Red. I might have considered it her walk of shame, but she wears a delicate wedding band. I can't imagine Wanda with a husband in the lower forty-eight and a summer honey on the side.

They're an unexpected pair. Red's gruff and hairy—arms and legs so covered in their wiry tangle you can only assume there are limbs under all that. When he's not handy-manning here in Alaska, he must be handy-manning somewhere else at home. I can't imagine him doing anything else. Wanda, on the other hand, used to be an elementary school secretary, retiring only last year. She's neat and put together like a suburban grandma/school secretary often is with her well-trimmed hair and a pleasantly rounded middle. She's also prone to wearing exceptional jewelry on regular days. Today a strand of thick pearls peek from the collar of her uniform Tundra Lodge button-up shirt.

DENALI SUMMER

Wanda doesn't say more because a pair of young boys I recognize as belonging to a family who checked in a few days ago are approaching the desk. They want to know if there's a hike they can do in the hour before they're supposed to meet their parents in the hotel restaurant for lunch.

"The only thing close enough to fit your timeframe is Oxbow Trail," I say.

The younger boy rolls his eyes. "We've done that a thousand times already."

"We've done it twice," corrects the older boy, before punching his brother in the arm. "Stop being so whiny."

They continue to argue in a way that doesn't make me miss my brothers.

"Or, you can go to the take-one, leave-one book shelf," I point to the books along one wall of the lobby, "and read till they get here."

The older brother shrugs and wanders over to the books, but the littler one pulls out a phone and slinks away to the nearest couch.

"That's why their parents have gone and left them behind. That younger boy reminds me of my grandson. I don't volunteer to babysit much."

"How many grandkids do you and Red have?" I decide to confirm my theory. I mean, I'm mostly sure but not exactly sure.

"I have four, and Red has one. Red's my second husband. I met him here at the park."

Summer romance knows no age limits. "I want to hear that story."

"How about you come to the husky kennels with me today after our shift? We can brush some dogs and swap some stories."

CHAPTER FOURTEEN

As I'm agreeing, I look up to see Vanessa, clad in a long green skirt, silky white blouse, and her pineapple sweater, bouncing through the lobby with Shelby and Kendra flanking her sides, interlocking arms at the elbow. Vanessa, so much shorter than the other two girls, has to raise her arms. It's as though she's a small child they're about to swing. I bet they could too if they had any strength in their bean-pole arms.

"Here come the room invaders," I mumble as they near our desk.

"Roomie!" Vanessa greets me cheerfully, but the trio does not stop. They pass us and turn toward the snack shack.

"I'd guess the one in the middle's our new baker," Wanda says, watching the swishes and thrusts of their silly group walk.

Job assignments were covered in last night's never-ending conversation but not until the haze of sleep had begun to overcome my brain. The information tickles there, almost ready to resurface. Food. All of them would be working with food. Shelby and Kendra as servers in the restaurant, Vanessa in the snack shack. That was it.

"I thought all they had were cookies, and the dough came frozen."

"She requested a spot in the restaurant or snack shack—where ever she could bake. Sent pictures and recipes. Marvin bought a new display case for cupcakes, cookies, tarts, brownies, and who knows what else. He's caught her vision, that's for sure. Red's supposed to be installing the new case today. If that girl can create half as much as she claims, I'm gaining ten pounds this summer."

DENALI SUMMER

Marvin, the general manager, almost never comes out of his office, the trailer he shares with HR Angie, but the department managers often have to go in there for meetings. Wanda's mentioned him enough to give me a sense of the man. I add, "pushover for baked goods," to my running tally of mental notes I'm keeping on the biggest boss.

Wanda usually stays into the afternoon shift to go over the log book comments with the next two to take over the desk. If the check-ins bottle neck, she ends up staying longer. Today, when I wave off to go change out of my work clothes, she promises she'll be right behind me so as not to delay our husky grooming plans.

I'm through lunch and Wanda still hasn't made it to The Zoo. It occurs to me she has a kitchen in the airbus and doesn't have to come eat all her meals in the employee cafeteria; we hadn't explicitly chosen this as our rendezvous point. But I continue to dawdle. The tables have all cleared, and RJ is wiping down the counters. Flint's disappeared into the supply closet, and I'm staking out his exit. I did not, as I'd promised Wanda, hold up the lunch line which consisted of me and two housekeepers behind me when I'd come through. Now that it's me, RJ, Flint, and a pair of bus drivers in the far corner of the room, I'm feeling gutsier. A minute passes, two, five. What could he still be doing in there?

RJ switches off the kitchen light, and a surge of worry hits my stomach. Did I miss Flint leaving? Is there a back exit? I approach the line again, and RJ makes a sweeping gesture toward all the empty bins around him.

"All cleaned up. We're closed," he says.

CHAPTER FOURTEEN

Yes, I can see that. "I'm looking for Flint."

"He's stocking." RJ reaches behind him to grab his keys.

"Can I go back there?" I'm surprised by my own words, but once they're out, I'm glad.

"Shouldn't." But he pushes his way through the door and makes a show of the fact that this access into the kitchen is not locked before he leaves The Zoo.

I push the door open to the kitchen and continue on through the supply closet door.

"I'll be done in a second. I only have to—" Flint turns. "You're not RJ."

"Disappointed?" I mean it as a joke, but once I've said it, I realize he could be.

He doesn't answer. Instead, he pushes back a giant can of baked beans before grasping a second from the floor and setting it on the shelf. Then another. Then another.

"I'm sorry."

There's a slight delay to his rhythm, a pause of his arms in the air, and I know I have his attention.

"I shouldn't have gotten mad on the trail yesterday. I appreciate that you came looking for me. Wanda told me you clocked out to do it, which makes it even sweeter. I felt silly after that climb, and I've taken to getting downright pissy when other people tell me what I can't do. It started the closer I got to graduation, and it's only gotten worse. Coming out here is kind of a big fat, oh yes I can.

"I'm the baby of my family, and I've had the same boyfriend since early in tenth grade, and everyone expects they know me and can persuade me to do what they want. So I came to Alaska alone where I can hike or do any damn thing I want to without a sibling or a parent or a boyfriend or anybody telling me that I shouldn't, or there's a way to do it better, or my plan isn't as important as this other idea they've come up with. I—"

I've run out of steam, and I'm not sure what I else I need to say. Already, I can hear the echo of these words filling in the spaces between us. Their pout, their fuss. A tangent like this at home would be met with, "Is she done yet?" by any one of my siblings, and promptly ignored, as though I'd said nothing at all. But here the words feel like they're inflating, louder and fuller and whinier; Flint stares at me, his eyes a mixture of surprise, but also, possibly, delight?

"You've never said so much all at once." He grabs the last can from the floor and adds it to the shelf then smooths his hands on his black and white checkered chef pants. "And all of that is helpful to know."

Helpfulness wasn't really my goal here, so I'm not sure what to say. Luckily, Flint keeps talking.

"I'm sorry too. On the trail yesterday I was concerned, maybe a little scared for you, but from now on..." He stops, considers. "From now on, you have my word that I will always lean toward confidence in your abilities."

Flint is someone who hears what I have to say, doesn't make fun of me or talk over me, but apologizes and says he'll trust me moving forward. How has this never worked at home? Will there ever be a time when I can say what I'm feeling at home and get this kind of response? I'm flooded with gratefulness toward Flint and toward my past self for taking this

CHAPTER FOURTEEN

Alaska risk. Even if, when I leave here, I go home and stay in East Texas for the rest of my life, I'll know how I'm supposed to be treated, how things can be.

"Thank you." I want to say more, but I'm afraid I'll cry.

Without the rows of cans at his feet he feels closer; I shift forward and lean onto the wall shelves.

"As for this boyfriend. Is he still your boyfriend?" Flint asks.

I can't help but blush at this change in subject. "Um. Well, yes, technically." Technically? Where did that come from?

"Sounds complicated."

"I'm sorting through my feelings on that." This makes it sound like I'm considering breaking up with Chris, which isn't exactly what I meant. "Whatever happens—I think it's good for us to have this summer apart."

"You got far enough away that's for sure."

"Part of the point."

I'm so conscious of our bodies in this tight space. Is leaning nearer to Flint an old habit of flirting? He'd only have to come a few inches to rest his chin on my head, brush a kiss anywhere on my face.

These are not helpful thoughts.

But I'm warm and aware and alive and interested in ways I haven't been in such a long time. I want to know if Flint's resisting the small distance between our faces or if he's immune. I want to know why this is where my thoughts have turned when I came in here to apologize.

Flint steps away and scans the room. "Looks like I'm done in here. What are you up to this afternoon?"

DENALI SUMMER

For a second, I consider rain-checking Wanda and telling Flint I'm free, but I've never been the kind to cancel plans on one person because another person came along. Mama taught me better than that. "I'm supposed to go with Wanda to the kennels. I thought she'd be in here for lunch, but now I guess I need to go find her."

"Sounds fun. I'll probably be with her lesser half. Red asked me if I wanted a few more hours today helping him on that snack shack case. I should check how it's coming." He motions toward the door which I'm mostly blocking. "After you," he says, one hand on the metal cord that hangs from an uncovered bulb, waiting for me to open the door.

The Zoo has emptied, the overhead lights all shut off, only a few puddles of sunlight pool around the windows with open curtains. It's still a dingy employee cafeteria—walls lined with dark wood paneling, mismatched posters in cheap frames, and faded floral curtains. The smell of foods past mingles with the scent of cleaning supplies present. But in the empty, quiet, almost-dark the mood has changed; it's as though we're trespassing in an abandoned space. I like being here alone with Flint.

For no reason other than it feels right, my voice drops. "When can I cook you that supper?"

Flint's voice answers at normal volume. "How about you figure out what you need, write me a list, and then we'll pick a date. If we have everything, we could do it tomorrow. After the dinner shift."

I promise to get him a list by the end of the day.

CHAPTER FOURTEEN

Wanda and I take the old, mud-splashed blue Camry that lives parked behind the HR/big boss's trailer. Until now, I didn't know it ran. Wanda says it's shared by the managers, used mostly by Red if he needs to drive to the Home Depot in Fairbanks.

"Usually I take the shuttle, but we lost time re-finding each other. This'll be faster."

"I should've thought to come to the airbus sooner."

"No, no. We never said. I'm glad you talked things over with Flint. That makes it worth running a little behind. Not so sure the dogs will feel that way, but they'll get over it."

"You go a lot?"

The car rattles instead of responding directly to Wanda's twist of the key. She holds her hand steady and gives it a little gas. "Come on, fussy car. It's your buddy, Wanda. Wake up for me."

Her little pep talk works—the rattle quickens until the engine groans to life.

"This thing runs on prayers more than anything," Wanda says, eyes in the rearview. "I go Monday, Wednesday, Friday, and sometimes Sunday. Those huskies know me well."

The car's a stuffy mix of cigarette smoke and spicy aftershave, the latter likely caused in part from a faded cinnamon air freshener fallen to the ground by my feet. I crack the window. "Do you have a favorite dog?"

DENALI SUMMER

"Oh, yes. Wait till you meet Opal. He takes a while to warm to new people, but he and I have become best pals."

"How many dogs are there?" I ask.

"At the moment thirty-five, which is high. They usually stay closer to thirty, but four are about to retire by the end of this year, and the litter coming only has two pups." Wanda taps the horn and waves to someone outside. It's HR Angie, and I wave too. Three minutes later, we're pulling into the visitor center. "From here, we hoof it. There's no parking at the kennels."

We haven't been walking long when Wanda asks me, "Do you fancy Flint, or is there another boy you'd have preferred come after you yesterday?"

"I'm trying not to fancy anyone."

"Why's that? Don't believe in summer romance?" Wanda's arms are bent and swinging in power-walk mode, but we're going an average pace. She's only a smidgen taller than me.

"I have a boyfriend back at home. We've been together a long time, but—"

"But?"

"I honestly didn't realize there'd be so many guys here."

Wanda stops. Just stops. Then looks at my face, I guess to see if I'm being serious, and then she howls, high-pitched and long. The giant laugh folds her in two.

I wait beside her on the path. "Why's that so funny?"

"A pretty thing like you who clearly has some boyfriend issues to sort through and comes to Denali. Oh, Dawn. That is too much."

I stare at her, waiting for more.

CHAPTER FOURTEEN

"Women like camping too, but it's still an activity heavily preferred by men. Ditto for the raft guiding and everything else there is to do around here. And look at the jobs—bus driving, bus washing, bellman, maintenance, those raft guides—all heavily preferred by male applicants. None of that occurred to you when you applied?"

Another Alaska fact known by everyone but me.

"I didn't think much on who else would be here. I was only thinking about getting myself here."

Her face stills. "I can relate to that. If I go back four years to when I first came, I didn't have a good sense for what I'd be getting into either. I'd been widowed two years. A friend suggested I look into seasonal hotel employment, and I did. Considered Alaska straight away. My late husband and I were supposed to do an Alaskan cruise for our thirty-fifth anniversary, but he died a year short of that plan.

"I came for escape. I came to honor Richard, my first husband. I did not come to meet Red." Wanda smiles to herself. There's a happy memory tucked into that smile, but she's keeping it back. "I still met Red."

"When did you know he was the one?"

"It crept up on me through the summer. By the end of it, I didn't want to leave him. So he said I didn't have to, said we could get married."

"You got married after one summer!"

"No, I had to warm to the idea first. I hadn't even told my kids or grandkids about him. Their dad and I had married while still in college. He'd been my whole life for a very long time. I had no idea how my kids would react to a new someone. And my daughter, well, she had her own plans for my life. She'd been expecting me to move close to her as soon as I'd retired. She'd met with realtors, trying to find a house she could go ahead and buy then rent till the time came for me to move in."

"What'd you do when you were apart from Red?"

"I had work to keep me busy. Red and I wrote letters and video-chatted. At Christmas we holed up in a Virginia cabin for five days, our gift to each other. I still hadn't told my kids what I was up to. I lied and said I'd been at a women's retreat."

"You naughty girl!" I elbow Wanda lightly. Ha! To think of parents lying to their kids when it's supposed to be the other way around.

"The next summer," Wanda continues, "I made my plans to return to Alaska, but my daughter pitched a fit. She'd bought a two-bedroom bungalow a ten-minute drive from her house, and she'd expected we'd spend the summer fixing it up. She wanted me to pick out kitchen cabinets and granite colors. That is exactly what I was running away from. I did not want to be puttering around my bungalow, growing tomatoes, baking cookies, and waiting for family to drop in. I wanted to get back to the man I loved, the man who understood my life was not winding down but gearing up for new adventures."

Adventure. That's the word my boss's friend used that had gotten my own mind spinning. How could I be seventeen and already feel stuck? So I'd come to Alaska and proven to myself I could have an adventure, but is that it? Or will I go home as stuck as I ever was—adventure itch scratched, back to Mama and Chris making all the decisions?

CHAPTER FOURTEEN

Wanda finishes her story, "At the end of that summer, with lupine braided into my hair, we got married on the Savage River Bridge, vows led by a park ranger. A sunrise wedding before the tourist hikers showed up. Marvin and HR Angie stood with us as our witnesses."

"Did your daughter freak out?"

"Oh yes. We talked about having a local reception, but she wouldn't have anything to do with that. Refused to come. Wouldn't visit. Didn't even want to see Red at Christmas."

"Did she ever come around?"

"Yeah. She got tenants in the bungalow, and the rent's higher than the mortgage, so she's happy about that. Red offered to customize an organizational system for her closet to free up room for more shoes—the beginning of winning her over. My third summer up here my son came with his family and sold her on why I'd fallen in love with this place. End of this school year, she worked with my principal to throw me a hell of a retirement party where she all but gave me her blessing to spend my time how I pleased. I don't need her permission for diddly squat," Wanda shrugs, "but it was still nice to hear."

I don't need permission for diddly squat—maybe I can adopt that as a motto.

"Will she visit Denali too?"

"That's the plan. They'll be coming end of July. Same time as—" Wanda shakes her head. "Never mind. Not a booking you'd care about."

Excited barking grows louder, and the trees give way to a wide gravel clearing. Wooden bleachers line the back of the cleared area.

DENALI SUMMER

"This is where they do demonstrations for the tourists." Wanda sweeps her hand toward the rows of seats.

"Three times a day." My activity information is well memorized by now.

"Seats will start filling for the four p.m. as soon as the next shuttle pulls up."

Our feet crunch along, and we pass a storage building and a ranger trailer station before the long row of kennels, high-fenced structures connected by dark wooden posts between each new kennel. Inside they all contain matching log-cabin-style dog houses with flat roofs. A tall brown door with a lighter brown name plaque screwed toward the top lets us know who we're passing. At the first kennel, a dog named Banjo, sleeps atop his dog house, uninterested in the growing volume of commotion as more dogs catch sight of us.

The dogs scuttle to the fencing beside their doors, and stand upright, whining their request for release and play time. Wanda greets them, holding her hands up to their paws.

"Give me a second," she says to a large black dog. "You know I have to gather my things first."

Wanda marches past all the dogs to another storage shed, but I'm looking down at the end of the kennels where Gabby nudges a dog back and closes his door.

Wanda retrieves two leashes and two large dog brushes, handing me one of each.

"Gabby comes out here too?" I ask.

Wanda nods. "Every other day. She and Toklat, he's the biggest beast out here, love each other to bits."

CHAPTER FOURTEEN

I pull at a tuft of white hair clumped in my brush and release it to float through the air. Gabby's a softie for big 'ol fuzz balls. Not what I would have guessed.

Wanda fetches Opal and directs me to take out Timber, a smily dog with a white underbelly and face. Timber nudges into me with the full strength of the sled dog I know he is, and I stumble back.

"Easy now," I say. I'm used to dogs, but our Rusty is a mid-sized mutt, and Chris's family has a little poof of a Pomeranian. Timber, on his hind legs, could put his big paws on my shoulders and dance me around.

I click the leash onto his collar and lead him outside. He rubs along my legs, so I bend to hug his neck from the side, earning myself a happy lick on the face before he bumps me over onto my butt and attempts to crawl into my lap.

"Timber's a cuddler. Did I forget to mention that?" Wanda calls from beside Opal, who stands still during his brushing, patient and calm.

Timber isn't as accommodating as Opal, but I manage a good enough rub down, a cloud of red and white fur floats behind him as a I work. Wanda and I brush three dogs each before the tourists begin ambling around us, passing time until the next demonstration. Many of them offer to help, and I listen to Wanda explain repeatedly about approved volunteers handling the dogs. I guess Wanda's approval is all I needed, and I'm grateful to have it.

CHAPTER FIFTEEN

Chicken and broccoli casserole with twice-baked potatoes. I present my list to Flint, hoping I'd calculated correctly that the kitchen has what I need.

"Can you do a cracker crust instead of a cornflake crust for this casserole? We only have sugared cornflakes, not the plain."

The Wilkes family is a house divided as to which casserole crust style is better, so I'm practiced at both. Which is to say, I can spread crunched crackers as well as I can spread crunched cornflakes and sprinkle either with butter with equal ability. "Sure," I agree.

"Then I've got what you need."

So now I have a supper date with Flint, but before I can feel happy or guilty or anything, Sugar strides over and grabs the chair across from us.

"What do I do if I need meals to go for a backcountry trip? Is there a form or do I tell you?"

CHAPTER FIFTEEN

Food. For camping. Because Sugar and I are going camping. And we'll probably need food. It's a good thing he's planning this trip.

"What do you need, and when do you need it?" asks Flint.

"Dinner for tomorrow, three meals for Sunday, breakfast for Monday. For two people."

"I usually send tortillas and cheese for dinner, instant oatmeal and a hard-boiled egg for breakfast, Ramen noodles for lunch. Gorp to snack. Sound good?"

"Works for me." Sugar turns in my direction. "That work for you?"

A few things are occurring to me at the same time. For starters, I can't cook for Flint if I'm already on the trail with Sugar. And secondly, Sugar only ordered for two when he assured me there'd be four. Maybe the other pair will take care of their own meals?

"You're going camping? Tomorrow?" Flint's brows come together.

"I forgot when we were leaving." I pull my list of ingredients back toward me and frown. "Raincheck?"

Flints looks at Sugar. "What time do you want it ready?"

"Three should be good."

"You'll be able to pick it up by two thirty."

"Awesome, man. Thanks." Sugar takes a large bite out of the green apple he's been holding and doesn't quite finish chewing before adding, "I booked us Teklanika. Supposed to be gorgeous. Nice little valley creek to follow into the mountains."

Flint asks, "Only you two going?" and I sink my forehead to the table. I cannot look at him during this conversation. I want to disappear. Apparate *Harry*

Potter style, far, far away to my high school soccer field, where I can run and run and run and forget these boys and my stupid bumbling around them. And Chris would be waiting in the stands to drive me home. There'd be no guesswork or awkwardness when Chris slung his arm around me as we walked to his car. Everything about us was easy. Is easy! Chris is easy and my current boyfriend. And he is in Texas waiting for me.

Meanwhile, the boys in Alaska are still talking about food.

"Jake and Lauren from housekeeping are coming if Lauren can switch her schedule around. He said he'd order his food from you once he knows for sure."

"By breakfast would be good."

"For sure. They'll figure it out tonight." I raise my head as Sugar sinks his teeth in for a second apple bite, grinning while he chews, then plops it right back down again. I want Sugar to leave, so I can attempt an apology for Flint, get a sense of whether or not he's mad or indifferent. But there's no slide of the chair as it backs away from the table, only the steady munching of an apple and the soft scrape of Flint's fork against his dinner tray. Awkward. Awkward. Awkward.

Flint drops the fork. "You two probably have to go through your gear and pack for tomorrow if you plan to head out around three."

"Sure do. Dawn? You taking a nap or you want to come on? I got Dylan's pack for you. Let's get it fitted."

In spite of my best mental efforts at magical disappearance, I'm still here, so no use putting things off. I scoot from the table. "Let's go."

CHAPTER FIFTEEN

Sugar leads me to the second floor of the building next to mine, to the room he shares with Dylan who lays sleeping on one of the beds.

"Hey." Sugar turns the light on and kicks Dylan's foot. "Did Jake tell you if Lauren got her shift changed?"

In muffled pillow-speak it sounds as though Dylan says, "Pickled pork snout," but I'm able to rework that into, "Didn't work out."

My breath constricts in a squeeze of panic. My mind goes to what my sisters would say in this situation. Dolly, God bless her nurturing nurse's heart, came up to my room the day I got my ETBU acceptance letter, shut the door behind her, and handed me a brochure about campus rape.

"You will not be the first Wilkes sister to become a statistic. One in five girls, Dawn. And don't think because it's a Christian campus, you'll be fine."

"God, Dolly! Acceptance letter days are supposed to be all congrats and hugs. Couldn't this have waited a few weeks?"

She'd sunk onto my bed, her eyes blooming with tears. "I know. I'm sorry. But we had this lecture at nursing school today on detecting and reporting abuse. You know how I internalize that stuff." I wrapped my arms around her in comfort, but eventually, she started up again. "I can't imagine anything happening to my baby sister. At least you'll be close by where everyone can keep an eye on you."

For all the twins' enthusiasm toward cute boys, they are Team Chris for sure. And even if they weren't, I'm not sure how they'd feel about me overnight camping with a mid-twenties guy I've only known about a week. Not without a Daddy interview, complete with shot gun demonstrations, finished by his low grumbled threat, "I'd go to jail for any one of my daughters. You understand me, boy?"

Chris, always trusted in the Wilkes household, had been spared the ordeal, but the fact that one of Daisy's would-be homecoming dates had gone to the doctor with a stomach ulcer after a talk with Daddy has long become family legend.

My mind races with possible excuses to get out of going with Sugar. I'm too healthy right now to fake a sudden cold. If I invent a migraine issue, I could fall back on it all summer. But then I'll also have to fake riding out migraines alone in my dark room. Not worth it. "How about Kendra?"

Sugar looks confused, and Dylan doesn't budge.

"My suite-mate, Kendra. If Lauren can't go, how about I ask Kendra?"

"Ja-ke," Sugar hollers into the air. Dylan fumbles for a second pillow lying beside him and holds it over his head. "Jake? You over there?"

A door opens, and Jake, wearing only low-slung athletic shorts, stands on the bathroom side. "What?" Then, when he notices me, "Oh hey, Dawn."

"If Dawn gets Kendra to come backpacking, you still in?"

"Is she one of the new Florida girls?"

"Yeah, she's the White one who's not the cupcake one." Leave it to Sugar to already have all the new girls pegged.

Jakes stretches, his hands wrapped around the door frame and leans his taut bare chest into the room. "Sure. You packing now?" He nods to a pack beside

CHAPTER FIFTEEN

Dylan's bed and winks at me. "Don't let him give you all the weight."

"Wouldn't dream of it." Sugar holds up the pack, and I slip my arms through the straps. He snaps the waist belt, does something to the straps to make everything lift, and considers the fit. "It should be on your hips."

I twist and wiggle. "Seems right."

"You'll know better once it's weighted up." He unsnaps me and pulls it off my back then takes a sleeping bag from off his bed and begins stuffing it into a bottom compartment. "You'll have this sack, your own clothes, the tent foot, and the cook stove inside. Then strap this Therm-a-Rest on the outside," Sugar hands me a rolled piece of foam, thicker than a yoga mat but narrower, "plus two water bottles here." He indicates toward the mesh pockets. "I'll have the food, the tent and poles, and my stuff. And get your own toilet paper and plastic trash bag. Everything gets packed back out. Everything. Even..."

My mind fills in both tampons and condoms at the same time, neither of which I want to hear him say. "Everything. No trash left behind. Got it."

He shoves down the cook stove and a piece of plastic that I'm guessing is my part of the tent weight. "Rearrange how you want."

I take the pack and yank it over my shoulders again. It's still light. "I'll go find Kendra and let you know what she says."

Kendra and Shelby are sitting across from each other on their beds wearing green facial masks, holding their own copies of the same wedding book, reading aloud to each other.

It's vaguely similar to my sleepover experiences except not at all.

Shelby turns her head the slightest fraction in my direction. "We're reading vows, so I can get ideas. I think they have to be read out loud to feel their impact."

"You both have the same book?"

"I bought copies for all my bridesmaids. I want them fully engaged in our wedding process." She says it as though there's a whole team of bridesmaids beyond those assigned Alaska companion duty.

"As they should be." I don't have a strategy for Shelby responses yet, but this comes off more sarcastically than I'd intended. Time to change the subject. "Kendra, when's your start date at the restaurant?"

Kendra closes her eyes to think on this, and the book falls to her lap. "I'm on call tomorrow night if it gets busy. On the schedule for sure Sunday."

"Any chance you could start Monday night and come camping with me, Sugar, and Jake?" I don't know the restaurant manager, but it sounds stupid even as I'm asking it. How can someone ask off their very first shifts?

Her eyes flutter open. "Is this twin Jake we're talking about?"

"Yup."

"I'm in. Shelby, can I use the tent?"

Shelby has gone back to reading vows and pronounces her fiancé's love an anchor, but she nods toward Kendra.

I don't care how Kendra plans to get out of work. Her eye-sparkle reaction to twin Jake is enough to convince me she will. "I'll go tell him," I say.

CHAPTER FIFTEEN

"Ooooo. Me too." Kendra uncrosses her legs and scoots off the bed.

"Your face is green."

Kendra laughs and sits back down. "Good call. You go tell him."

I turn for the door, Shelby's smooth promise to "love who you are now and who you are yet to become," floating behind me.

A now-awake and uniformed Dylan stands beside a still-shirtless Jake, leaning over the banister of the second-floor walkway. Sugar and Josh emerge from the twins' room, a glass bottle half-full of golden liquid in Sugar's hands, shot glasses in Josh's.

Sugar holds up the bottle. "Dawn from East Texas! You made it for whiskey night cap."

Nope. Not getting in the middle of that. I holler my news from the ground. "Kendra's in, and she has all her gear. Tent too."

"Good," smiles Jake while elbowing his brother in the ribs. "Our tent smells like ass."

I roll my eyes. "Aren't you cold?"

Jake takes a glass and downs it before answering, "Not a bit."

"Good night then." I turn for my room but pause, scanning the doors for where Flint's room might be. I'm still mad at myself for backing out on dinner.

"Hey!" Sugar calls. "You haven't used today's guess. What's my name?"

A door opens below them and Gabby steps out, tapping a cigarette into her hands. "His name's Rodney, but Sugar used to get crap for it, people telling him it's a Black boy's name. He's racist as fuck so started going by Sugar." It's a mumble meant for me, not the Bama boys above us.

I study her face, trying to decide if she's being serious, then consider the name Rodney. Rodney King—Black. Rodney Dangerfield—White. Rodney Hudson, my brother Dale's best friend and the only Rodney I know in real life—Black.

"Go on, guess it," she says.

"First name Brock. Middle name Lee," I holler. All the Bama boys are already buzzed enough to laugh.

Gabby leans against the building and pulls out her lighter. "Fine then. Keep playing his game, but don't come crying to me when he changes the rules."

I step nearer, under the walkway, while also doing my best to steer away from the smoke cloud she exhales.

"Is there something you need to tell me about Sugar?" I ask.

Gabby flicks an ash toward my feet. "Don't be surprised when he gets what he wants and moves on."

"I don't like him like that. He's not getting anything."

"If you say so."

"Do you know where Flint's room is?"

"Keeping those options open. Maybe you're the one playing the best game."

"Maybe I am."

Gabby smiles. "Feisty. That's why Flint likes you. And you're safe. He likes the Sugar distance and the Zeke distance and the flirty Jake distance. He's licking his wounds from the last girl to break his heart, so even though he likes you, he likes you distanced."

"Psychology major?"

CHAPTER FIFTEEN

"Maybe I am." Gabby throws my own line back at me. "Or maybe some of us have to work our way through a few years of community college before we can even think about declaring a major at a fancy private university."

"Who said I was going to a school like that?"

Gabby points with her cigarette at what I'm wearing, the long-sleeve ETBU shirt Mama sent in her package.

"This is my mama's school. I haven't figured out what I want to do." It's a lie, but it's a truth too.

"If you say so."

Above us the Bama boys whoop for some unknown reason and a second later Dylan pounds down the steps. He doesn't notice us as he jogs around the building and off to his night shift.

"Flint's in the one-story dorm. Room eight," Gabby says as we watch Dylan go.

It's almost ten, and I'm desperate for sleep after last night's late gab fest, but I want to talk to Flint. "Thanks," I say to Gabby and set off in the direction of Flint's building.

Even though I know I've found the right room, after knocking and waiting, knocking again and waiting some more, there's no Flint.

I slink off to my own room, unsettled by what I've left undone and by what I've committed to do.

First Backcountry Eve

(oh what am I doing?!)

Teklanika means...
    water   amulet.

Do I need a protector river?
From what evil must I be saved?
It really means changing clothes in a tent and peeing I don't know where.
It means mosquitoes, valleys that stretch 91 miles, and a Nenana tributary, another water cousin.
    Part of Denali
        Part of the Stampede Trail
            home of "the bus"

She has been a choker, a taker, a watery grave.
        For _me_ she means:

First. Risk. Brave.
            (I hope.)

CHAPTER SIXTEEN

Teklanika is closed due to bear activity in that section of the park, the weather's dipped to freezing for some inexplicable reason, and I slept in such a tight coil of stress ball, my neck is a kinked, angry mass of pain.

Nobody's in a good mood.

Jake and Sugar flank a park ranger, the three of them crowding over a map, trying to figure out if there's a section of Denali we can still get for two nights. Kendra's run off to the bathroom. I'm across the table, pretending I can make sense of the map from my upside-down vantage point, but it's a topographic wavy mess I can barely read right side up.

My neck's a little better. Wanda massaged it out as best she could at the start of our shift and ran to get me a hot and cold medicine patch during her first break. I smell like an old lady, but the knot's eased enough I can turn my head without wincing.

DENALI SUMMER

Flint didn't work breakfast or lunch, and it feels like my first day all over again—like he should be here, but he isn't. It's hard to believe that wasn't even a week ago. Harder to believe that last Saturday I graduated high school. My toenail polish from my graduation pedicure, shoved in work shoes and hiking boots all week, is no worse the wear.

"Savage River it is," Jake says.

"There's nothing else open. Unless you want to do Cathedral Mountain tonight, come back out, and do only one night in Savage tomorrow," says the ranger.

They've been saying some version of this for fifteen minutes. "Great," I say, determined to end the cycle. "Let's hike Savage River. Two nights. Off we go."

The ranger blinks at me as though realizing, for the first time, I'm here. "I'll get your new permit and your BRFCs."

"Bear-resistant food containers," Jakes explains before I can even ask.

When the ranger returns with two hard black plastic cylinders, we set to work removing all our food and toiletries from our packs, anything scented, to stuff inside the containers. Sugar schooled us before we left the lodge about the limited space in BRFCs, so we have one toothpaste for the four of us, one travel-sized contact solution bottle for Kendra and Sugar, the contact lens wearers of our group, and Kendra and I opted to share lotion and deodorant. Sugar and Jake don't appear to have brought deodorant.

As Jake and Sugar strap the BRFCs to the outside of their packs, the ranger reminds us about the one-hundred-yard triangle rule: cooking, food storage,

CHAPTER SIXTEEN

and tent set up should all be about one hundred yards apart, three distanced points, with the cooking point and the food container points both downwind of the tent.

So many regulations related to bears. We haven't even set foot on a trail, and already I feel like we don't stand a chance.

No. I'm brave. I'm strong. And I'm an adventurer. If I live out these things enough, even in the potential face of a bear encounter, they will be true anywhere.

There's a shuttle devoted to the Savage River campground, so we don't have to wait on a bus. The four of us and our packs take up half the van, but the only other passengers are a young, German-speaking couple. They give us wide smiles and thumbs up.

The hiking area is crowded with tourists, but Sugar and Jake promise the day hikers will stick to the trail that follows the river, and we'll be rising above them on the ridge-line shortly after the bridge.

Wanda and Red's bridge.

At the quiet of sunrise on a bright, clear day this stretch could be majesty and miracles, but on this cold afternoon, it's a half-dozen British-sounding hikers taking pictures under a cloud-heavy sky. The river clips beneath at a hungry pace, funneled tightly by the narrowness of the valley in this section. We wait for the bridge to clear, so we can cross then veer away from the main path onto a sliver of a land scar, a single footfall wide, that ascends steeply. Jake climbs in the lead with purpose.

"Have you hiked here before?" I call after a few minutes from my position at the end, raspy, breath already missing from my lungs.

"Josh and I did a day hike. Three miles in, ate lunch with a McKinley view, then back out. You have to go that far before the park road disappears, and you really know it's you and the bears."

Enough with the bears. I'd seen Dall sheep and a moose. Heard rumors of caribou and wolves. Why did bears get all the attention?

The wind surges and gusts, sweeping a sudden release of icy snowflakes against our bodies. It's sleet-like but with enough full white powder in the air that I'm going to call it snow. I tilt my head back and see it's not a fluke; there's a steady intensity to this squall.

"It's the beginning of June. How can it be snowing?" Kendra's question is more awe than annoyance.

"Alaska plays by her own rules," says Sugar.

Hunching forward, I lower my head to shield my face from the weather. I'm missing the view as I concentrate on Sugar's footfalls, planting mine a beat behind. My thin gloves are no longer doing enough to keep my fingers warm, so I reach into an upper jacket pocket for a packet of hand warmers to crack open and slide inside.

We continue our lateral climb toward the peak of the ridge long enough for my mind to empty of everything but the sound of our four pairs of boots trudging in the tundra, dulled by the spongy layer before the permafrost a few inches below.

I'm all absences. Of air in my lungs. Of heat through my body. Of myself. Dawn from East Texas is way outside of her wheelhouse. My body is in charge—one foot in front of the other. For at least a mile, that's all I know.

CHAPTER SIXTEEN

Then come new presences. Chaffing at my hip as the pack belt rubs my pants against my skin. Pressure as the straps compact my layers of clothing and dig into my shoulders. Burning and tingling at the tips of my ears because I don't want to ask the group to stop so I can find my flannel head wrap. The bear on the ridge at the other side of the valley.

Wait. Is that really what Jake just said?

"Check him out," Jake stops and points at the brown mass. From this distance, it could be a boulder, but it's moving, so we can all tell that it's a bear.

Kendra takes the large camera hanging from around her neck and adjusts the lens to its highest zoom. She snaps three times before checking her screen. Her fingers fly over the buttons, and she snaps three more, checks again, and holds out the camera so I can see. The bear's snout hovers inches from the ground, and his limbs lumber mid-stride. His coat is thick and fat, and the mossy greens of the terrain sparkle in front of him where a patch of sun pushes through the cloud cover. It's an image of cozy bedtime-story picture books and real-life nightmares rolled into a single frame.

"I wish he'd lift his head. Give me a good shot of his face." Kendra looks over my shoulder at the image.

Jake continues ahead, uninterested in giving the grizzly time for a better pose, so we're off before I ever get a chance to ask Kendra to pull out my head wrap for me.

"Didn't realize we were in such a hurry," I mumble to myself, but I fall in line and keep pace. The delay at the ranger station put us behind an hour, and I know Sugar and Jake want to get five or six miles in before we set up camp and cook dinner. We're all likely to get hungry sooner than later, but the guys won't unpack everything twice. No eating till we set up camp. No setting up camp till we've hiked the right distance. I get it.

We hit a dense patch of shrubbery and entangled trees, but rather than turn and follow the lower border of the tree line, Jake pushes up and through.

"It's bush-whacking time," says Sugar, holding a limb for me to take so it doesn't thwack back into my face.

"I hit this part before," Jake calls back from the lead. "It's about a half-mile thick, and then it's clear all the way to the top of the ridge. That's where Josh and I stopped."

At least in the thick of the skinny interlocking branches, we're protected from the snow. We high step and pull limbs and crouch beneath or twist around branches. After enough yoga-like maneuvering, I'm warmed and sweaty.

Jake and Kendra clear the last few trees and wait. Sugar stumbles over a low branch but catches himself and joins them, and finally, I free myself from the grip of a limb pushed through a mesh pocket on my pack and make it into the clearing. The three of them stand in a semi-circle, and I can hear Kendra's camera clicking again.

"What are we looking at?" I whisper, stepping beside Sugar.

"Mouse," says Sugar.

"Pika," corrects Jake.

"It's like a bunny mouse," Kendra says, inspecting the shot she's taken. The little critter sits hunched,

CHAPTER SIXTEEN

nose tilted to the air, frozen as though trying to blend into his gray rock perch. By the time Kendra lifts her camera again, he's scrambling off the rock, skipping forward so quickly I can't distinguish the moment he disappears.

We've been hiking for an hour straight, so I'm relieved when Jake unsnaps his pack and lets it slide to the ground. "Water break?"

Sugar notices when I pull out my head wrap before my water bottle.

"Your ears are so red," he says and cups his hands over them. My face is at the base of his neck, and I inhale the minty scent of his aftershave.

I want to push away, but his hands are warm, and my ears are already burning now that we've stepped into a windy, cold-again clearing. A moment of closeness doesn't mean anything.

"Thanks," I say before finally stepping back and slipping the wrap over my head, stretching it wide so it fully covers my ears. "They'll be good under this." It also helps that the snow has slowed to almost nothing. The ground looks dusty, not snowed on. There won't be any accumulation.

"Can you hear anything?"

It's muffled, but I think he's speaking low to give me a hard time. "What? Did you say something. Your lips moved, but nothing came out."

He responds by mouthing something wordlessly. It looks as though he's said, "You're really cute, Dawn from East Texas," but I'll let that go. I reach for one of my water bottles and chug down a few gulps.

"Another hour. Then we scout for a spot to set up camp." Jake hoists his pack off the ground and tugs it on again.

"Group selfie first!" Kendra holds up her phone for this picture. We scrunch together, the boys bent at the knees so they can get their faces closer to mine and Kendra's, and she clicks. We're well out of range, but I make her promise to text it to me when she can. Denali backcountry with a whole new set of friends— a shot I want to send on to Daisy, who last night texted me, "Miss you. Come home early!"

True to his word, Jakes leads us another hour, ridgeline hiking where we pick up the pace and travel, according to Sugar's estimation, another three miles. The guys choose a flat space to pitch the tents about thirty feet from a cliff's edge overlooking the river.

We toss down our packs and take in the view of the valley below. It's widened, leaving the Savage room to twist and braid around silt mounds. A few boulders break up the now-green mountainsides. It did not take Denali long to shed the brown and come to life. A tangle of tall blue lupine flowers dance along the ridgeline where we stand framing the scene below in more spring color.

"Tomorrow, we'll push a few miles deeper, then hike down into the valley to camp. On our morning out we can follow the river home," says Jake.

"Yes, sir, Ranger Jake!" I further tease him by adding a salute.

But he takes this as a compliment and quirks a smile. "Damn straight."

While the boys tackle tent poles, Kendra and I scout our cooking spot and food container drop off

CHAPTER SIXTEEN

spot, sticking to the one-hundred-meter triangle method we'd been taught this afternoon. I unpack the foil-wrapped quesadillas already lined with cheese. By Flint. I'm cooking supper but Flint prepared it. I sigh. I want to be here and there, so I'm both happy and sad. A lot to be reminded of by a flat disc of wheat stuffed with yellow cheddar.

The wind picks up while we're eating, and I'm grateful for the swiftness and distance it will pull the scent of our smelly food. Once we've eaten, cleaned our cook stove, and repacked the food containers, it's back to the tents where Kendra and I veto a game of Never Have I Ever. These boys have not earned our confessions.

"I have Uno cards. How about that?" Kendra asks.

Since no one has a better idea, we crowd into the tent Kendra borrowed from Shelby. Both tents are two-man's, but it's a touch bigger. Jake and Kendra's packs are inside, so that answers how the boys expect us to divide up tonight.

Kendra shuffles the thick deck with the mastery of a casino dealer, and Jake whistles his praise.

"Good thing we aren't putting any money on this. Girl brings her own deck and knows how to handle it," he says.

She laughs and snaps her final shuffle bridge like a pro. "It's Uno, people. Just Uno."

But it isn't. At least not the way I remember playing with the neighbor kid I sometimes babysit. Kendra passes out more cards than I'm used to and establishes new rules for playing exact matches out of turn and multiple cards of the same number in one turn.

"Makes it more fun," she says, drawing a yellow five for the first card in play.

We're like little kids, trying to beat each other to get our cards down, squawking "Uno!" with the excitement of a lottery winner, and groaning when the next player sticks us with a Draw Four.

It goes on for at least an hour, the cards favoring Kendra, Jake and I evenly but somehow never working out for Sugar who doesn't win a single game. I'm grateful for each passing minute we're all together. The later we stay up embroiled in card battles, the more feasible for me to claim being exhausted to make sure Sugar leaves me alone later tonight.

"Let's go outside and check the glow," Sugar says after another loss.

"The what?" I ask.

"The alpenglow. Cool lighting thing that happens on the mountains at sunset. If the clouds have lifted enough to see it."

We file out one at a time through the small tent opening into an evening that has cleared and brightened. And there she is, the high one, Denali in plain sight, set aflame by the lowering sun reflecting reds and oranges everywhere. Fire on ice. The hot swirls of an opal cracked into multiple peaks. Rocks and snow at such majestic height and magnitude they're rendered regal. I have never seen anything like her.

Nature isn't done showing off by displaying the mountain. A trio of caribou break out of the shrubbery on a balcony of land below us, grazing through the moss, oblivious to our presence.

"This is my favorite time to be out here." Jake's words are a reverent whisper.

CHAPTER SIXTEEN

I'm off-trail, standing at the top of a Denali ridgeline—as far as I've ever been from the road and the buses that can bring us back to electricity and hot water and Flint-cooked meals. Far from the reach of Mama packages or sibling texts or boyfriend letters. Everything in me knows this is the right place to be—held by vast, endless, empty spaces that are filled with freedom. This is the paradox my soul needs.

The higher the view and the harder the terrain—all the better as I continue to prove my right to be here, my ability to keep up. I'll be re-rutted in East Texas soon enough, but look at me now.

I don't realize that Kendra isn't beside me until she's returned, camera in hand. She shoots the caribou first, then the mountain, and then she makes us pose. Every bit of me wants to remember this moment forever that I'm not about to protest being in the photos. Finally, she finds a rock to prop her camera and takes a timer picture of the four of us together with the mountain behind us.

The caribou descend, and we sit on the ledge until they've made their way down to the river. We're so quiet we can hear their raspy huffs, the clomping of their footwork, and finally their splashing, as they select a shallow fray of the river braid for their path. We sit in silence until the animals disappear beyond a bend, back into the mountains that hold us all together in this stunning and intimidating world.

CHAPTER SEVENTEEN

I enter the tent first, strip off my hiking pants, but leave on my long underwear which look like leggings. I change into a clean sports bra and shirt before giving Sugar the all clear to enter.

He steps in and dives onto his sleeping bag, scrunching the fleece he'd left there into a pillow-ish ball.

Good. Stay right there and go to sleep, I think.

I unzip my own sleeping bag a third of the way and slip inside.

Sugar turns onto his side so that he's facing me. His face relaxes into a lazy smile.

"What?" I say. I can't read his expression.

"It's been a good day. I'm happy."

"It has been a good day." An amazing day, and now it needs to end. "Good night." I reach for my own fleece and tuck it under my head. "Sweet, bear-free dreams, Sugar."

CHAPTER SEVENTEEN

"I promised I'd give my first initial on our camping trip. I'm a man of my word."

"All right. Out with it," I say but close my eyes. I'm bored with this name game.

"My real name starts with *R*."

I can hear Gabby in my mind telling me to guess Rodney, but it feels wrong. Like I don't want to give her that power. Like I don't really want to know this about Sugar. "Ricardo," I say.

Sugar laughs. "You have some funny guesses, Dawn from East Texas. I'll toss in a second clue for free—it's not Hispanic."

"Good to know. You saved me from guessing Roberto tomorrow."

"Tomorrow then." He leans over and kisses my forehead lightly. It's friendly. I'm okay with friendly peck kisses. But it's probably also a test-the-waters kiss, so I'm keeping my eyes closed, laying very still, and revealing the waters to be very, very frigid.

Sugar rustles around. A quick, squinty peek shows me he's taking off his shirt before moving on to his pants. I don't need to see if he's a boxer, brief, or long underwear guy. I turn to face the wall of the tent. Somehow my body adjusts to the thin mat, and my mind, heightened to the potential of animal noise, relaxes anyway. I drift off to sleep.

In the morning we trek to the cook site together, and Sugar prepares our oatmeal breakfast. I'm not usually a fan, but I wake up hungry and eat every bite. Kendra offers to clean up, and I stay behind with her while Sugar and Jake return to the tents to break them down.

DENALI SUMMER

As soon as the guys are a safe distance away, Kendra asks, "How'd it go last night? Did you two go right to sleep or..." Her voice trails off, but I get where she's going with this.

"Right to sleep. I'm trying not to give Sugar the wrong idea." I fold up our trash tightly and pack it into the plastic ziplock bag we've been using for waste.

"Yeah? I thought you were into each other. He has the hottest arms." Kendra wipes down the cook stove and then works to take it apart.

"I'm not into anyone. I have a guy back home."

"What happens in Alaska stays in Alaska."

"Kendra!"

"I know. That's bad, but this guy back home can't be serious. It's not like you ever mention him. And if it's not serious, and it's not serious with the guy here—you know, just kissing—that's not so bad."

I'm not sure Sugar's the kind of guy who's into just kissing. Besides... Flint. If I'm going to apply Kendra's logic, and I'm not saying I am, I'd rather be kissing Flint. I consider whether or not I'm ready to entrust my crush with Kendra. A Kendra share is probably a Shelby and a Vanessa share too. But they are my roommates, and I don't have my sisters or Charlet here to talk to.

"If I picked a guy up here, it'd be Flint." There. I said it. Admitted it out loud to Kendra and any eavesdropping pika or marmots or whatever else could be denned or burrowed in earshot.

"Flint? The cafeteria guy?"

I nod.

CHAPTER SEVENTEEN

"You sure he's not hooking up with housekeeper Lauren?" Everything's packed up, and Kendra stands, ready to retrieve the bear-resistant food container.

My heart jumps, but I calm my voice. "Why do you think that?"

"Shelby and I went for a run yesterday morning. We saw him leaving her room, looking like... well, like he'd been there all night."

Not in his room in the evening when I knocked. Leaving Lauren's room in the morning. Oh. My heart sinks. Oh no. Kendra evaluates my silence. "Sorry."

I'll process this later. "How about you? You into Jake, or did ya'll go right to sleep last night?"

"Not right to sleep, no." She smirks and turns the cook stove in her hands. "Some talking, some snuggling, some first-base-level goodnight kisses."

All of that sounds nice. I reimagine an evening where I'd reciprocated Sugar's goodnight peck and where else it could have led.

"There's still tonight," Kendra adds. "And if Flint's into Lauren, why not let a little something happen with Sugar? Maybe that will help you figure out whether you still want your guy back home."

We hike for an hour before we stop for water, and Jake guesses we've trekked almost three miles. The clouds have settled in around Denali again, but above our ridge line it's fully clear and blue. Yesterday's cold snap lingers, and I'm thankful for our pace, brisk enough to keep me warm.

DENALI SUMMER

We pass caribou antlers and stray bones here and there but no live animals. The waist belt on this pack is chaffing my hip bone worse than ever. The blisters on my heels woke up again yesterday. Today they are fully angry. I'd bought moleskin in the gift shop, but it isn't doing the trick on my left foot.

I unsnap myself from the pack and let it fall to the ground. After choosing a large flat rock for my bench, I pull off my left boot and peel down my gray wool sock. The moleskin has scrunched and shifted, leaving my heel exposed and newly chaffed. I pull off the strip and tuck it into my pocket then unzip my pack so I can cut myself a fresh, much wider piece.

"How far are we going?" I ask, peeling the back away from my new strip and gingerly pressing it over my seeping blister. I inhale and shudder and try to think about something else until the burn of touching it subsides.

"We have all day," Jakes says, recapping his water and tucking it into his pack.

"But then the hiking we've done over two days we'll have to cover in one day tomorrow and I don't want to be exhausted when we hike out. I work Tuesday. Early." My blister's made me grumbly.

"We all do," says Sugar.

"Not me," interrupts Kendra. "I don't work till the lunch shift."

"Okay," Sugar tries again, "three of us do, so we won't hike too deep. Maybe another hour, stop for lunch, then we descend and come back along the valley, camp down there tonight."

"That sounds good," I agree. I hope we're in a descendible section in the next few miles. Since we

CHAPTER SEVENTEEN

left our tent site, the terrain has grown rockier and drops off more sharply, jagged edges of harsher land and not the smooth, rolling hill-into-mountain where we began.

I'm tender and slow as I tug my sock back on and sink my foot into its boot. I flex so that there's pressure at the heel, and the moleskin does its work cushioning and protecting my raw skin. I can do this. I can keep pace with Jake, and I won't be the one who makes us stop.

I'm equally gentle with my waist clip, and the skin there is fine until I move. At least as we hike I'm concentrating on my footing or signs of animals, so my mind isn't on my hip bone. Much. When I have to step up or twist around, it's worse. And more rocks means twistier steps. But I'm not going to complain. I came to Alaska, so this is what I do. Hike, hike, hiker girl. Hikety, hike, hike. And maybe turn my brain off entirely because my own sing-song thoughts are annoying.

We haven't gone very far when Kendra, in a whisper-shout, demands we stop. She points below us to the river where a grizzly and her cub are approaching the lip of the widest part of river.

"Plan revision. How about we not sleep down by the river tonight?" I say.

"They'll be miles away by this evening," says Jake.

"*Or* they're in charge of grizzly bear party setup and are soon expecting the rest of their grizzly friends who will then all be waiting on us to show up like the pizza delivery."

"Maybe," Jake smiles, "but probably not."

DENALI SUMMER

Kendra's snapping pictures, and I'm annoyed I don't have my own good camera. It felt bulky hanging in front of me and like unnecessary weight when I knew Kendra would have hers. "I want all these pictures. You know that right?" I say.

"Of course," she says and shows me the shot she's taken of only the cub who looks about the height Dale's girlfriend's five-year-old daughter. But in a really fluffy coat.

The bears lap at the water's edge, and the cub tumbles around his mama. They don't appear to be in any hurry to go anywhere else.

Jakes senses what I'm thinking. "If we do decide to descend into the valley, and there's fresh signs of bears, we'll climb up the other side or keep going till we're past it. The thing is, with four of us talking and carrying on, we're scaring off the bears nearest us. They don't want anything to do with a group as big and noisy as ours."

We haven't been so noisy, not noisy enough to keep that mama from leading her cub to the water right below us. Hundreds of feet below us, but still. I'd guess it's a short distance to cover for a running bear. "Let's amp up the noise to be safe."

"Ninety-nine bottles of beer on the wall," Sugar bellows. "Ninety-nine bottles of—"

"By talking," I cut him off. "More talking."

"Hey, bears! Stay away bears!" Jake shouts up the ridge line.

"Yes, more of that," I say.

Kendra clicks the lens cap back on her camera. "I've gotten plenty of bear shots so that works for me."

CHAPTER SEVENTEEN

We only hike a half hour when the ridge descends in a wide and grassy ramp-like section that leads into another area of heavy brush. Jakes suggests we stop for lunch a little early before starting in on the bush whacking, so we can follow the slope down into the valley.

I didn't realize I'd been so hungry but when my portion of Ramen noodles is gone, I look around for something else. Sugar seems to be thinking the same thing as he pulls the bag of gorp out of the BRFC.

"Who needs more?" he asks, and we all take a handful.

Sugar downs his all at once. "Hamburgers better be on the lunch menu when we get back. I need meat."

"If not, we go to the snack shack and get one anyway," Jakes says.

"Amen to that," Sugar agrees.

While I'm not feeling their cravings for red meat, I am looking forward to larger portions and a shower. One or two nights at a time in the back country seems plenty. Nothing in me is thinking I want to take off for weeks or months at a time and hike the Pacific Crest Trail or the Appalachian. No, thank you. Wilderness immersions buffeted by comfort. On my first trip in the backcountry, I can already tell that's what I'm about.

Once in the valley, I heighten my vigilance, searching for signs of recent bear activity—digs or scat, but I don't see anything. I maintain a constant stream of chatter, convincing the group to play Twenty Questions, so we don't accidentally fall quiet. There is no way Dale is going to win the sibling group text bet.

DENALI SUMMER

This trip has pushed me further than even my moose encounter hike, but I'm doing it. Chaffed hips, blisters and all.

By five p.m., we're back at a section of the river valley that's so wide the river bed gravel gives way to mossy, grassy patches that grow fuller toward the slope of the ascent at each side. Nearer the water, the greener areas are overgrown with shrubs so it's not flat enough for a campsite. We select a spot where the slope mostly flattens out before the striated gravel and rocks of the riverbed. The center river braid flows as a quick pace, but some of the outer threads calmly reflect back the billowy clouds above.

We agree there's no use pushing on as this is probably the best section to set up camp unless we want to risk having to hike up again.

My hips are on fire, and my pack is on the ground before it's been officially decided. I need a full twelve hours, preferably fifteen, of being pack-free.

We set up our camp triangle and start in on dinner, finishing off all our food except four measly oatmeal packets and four protein bars.

"If we get up early enough, we can be back at the lodge by lunchtime," Jake promises.

And in keeping with the early start plan, Jake and Kendra push for an earlier retirement to our tents, vetoing my suggestion we bring the Uno cards out again.

"I'm too tired," Kendra says, but she's smiling. Tired my hiney. She wants to hurry up and begin making out with Jake.

My stomach knots and jumps because I'm thinking through the possibility of the same. Sugar gives me a

CHAPTER SEVENTEEN

head start into the tent as he did the night before. I pull on a clean pair of long underwear, sports bra, and shirt, and shout out that he can come in. I've decided that if Sugar doesn't try and kiss me goodnight, that's fine. I friend-zoned him, and if he chooses to stay in that zone, that's what is right. But if he does kiss me goodnight, well, I'll figure it out if that happens.

But of course I start thinking about Chris. All my tender, steamy, and even sad kisses have belonged to Chris. I'm kidding myself if I think I have any idea what to do with much older, much bolder Sugar.

I yank up the tent zipper. "Decent!" I call outside.

Sugar ducks down so that he's right in my face, our noses a paper-thin distance. "That's too bad," he says.

I fall back on my sleeping bag and groan, my attempt at silly and casual, but my heart is thumping in my ears. I will it to calm down. *I don't even like him*, I tell myself. *Nothing's going to happen.*

Sugar thuds down on his own sleeping bag, peels off his shirt, and lies on his side to face me.

"I'm not really all that tired yet," he says.

I prop myself on my side too. "Oh really, Ronald. What's that supposed to mean?" I inhale the mossy, sweaty scent of him and will my heart to slow. It's hard to think this through when distracted by the heavy, steady thumping of a nervous heartbeat. If I let Sugar close to me now, he'd feel my chest chaos and think I'm having a heart attack.

"Not Ronald," he says and scoots closer. Reaching for my hair, he tucks a long strand behind my ear and then rests his hand on my shoulder.

Our faces are inches apart, and I'm still deciding if I want this when he leans in and kisses me—a hard, decisive kiss on the mouth this time. His forcefulness makes it clear this is a make-out kiss, not a quick and simple goodnight.

I stop thinking and kiss him back.

It doesn't take long for Sugar's hand to leave my shoulder, glide down my arm and onto my thigh. He moves it to my ass, then up my back on the inside of my shirt. The sports bra should be a good block, but his roaming hand is not deterred. He pushes under the tight elastic at my back and slides his hand forward to cup my breast.

"Hey now." I reach for Sugar's hand and pull it away. He took all of twenty seconds to go the distance it took Chris almost a year. Clearly I am not dealing with a church-raised, guilt-ridden son of a deacon anymore.

"Just kissing," I say and then, in a renewed effort to keep things light, "you didn't even buy me dinner."

"Carrying the weight of our food is the backcountry version of buying you dinner." He barely finishes the sentence before he's kissing me again, hands in my hair now. He rolls me back to lay over me.

I rest my own hands on his upper back but keep them there. No massaging, no shoulder rubs. Certainly no butt grabs. We've only just started, and I'm considering how I can shut this make-out session down. Abort. Jump ship. Sugar is too much, too soon for this girl.

I arch backward and push against his shoulder. "Okay, okay. Let a girl breathe."

Sugar humphs. "What? I'm feeling a little teased here, East Texas."

Now I'm mad.

CHAPTER SEVENTEEN

Daddy says it's like a switch with me. And Sugar's gone and flipped it.

A girl should be able to kiss a guy without that guy assuming her lips have given the go-ahead for every other part of her body.

"You're all gropy and grindy. That's not what I want."

He laughs, a cold ripple of a chuckle that's not jovial but mean. "You're a virgin, aren't you?"

That isn't any of Sugar's damn business. "What's it matter?"

"All right, high school girl, we can go slower. I can do just kissing." He kisses my nose. "I like kissing here." He kisses my lips, a quick peck this time. "And I like kissing..." He bends his head down like he's going to kiss my boob.

I push him again. "Good night, Sugar. Go take a dip in the river if you need to because it's time to cool down."

"I thought you were more fun than that, East Texas."

I am not a place. The location of my birth and home is not a notch for Sugar's belt so he can say, "I hooked up with a girl from that part of Texas once."

"My name is Dawn, and I'm plenty fun. Just not for pushy assholes." I flip over and yank my sleeping bag up to my neck.

Sugar humphs again then says, "Dawn, come back."

I do not turn over.

"Dawn, what the hell?"

I seal my eyes shut and will myself anywhere but here. I'm mad at him, but I'm mad at myself too. I know Sugar isn't right for me. I knew it before we came on this backcountry trip. Kissing him didn't teach me anything about my relationship with Chris other than the fact that I'm a big cheat.

Sugar is like beer at a party. It's seems okay in the moment, but it's not something you want your mama to know about. And when you get home hiding your buzz, heavy-limbed and stupid enough to mess up your story and get grounded... It's not worth it.

Meanwhile Flint—he's like a spicy, mulled cider that makes you feel warm inside anytime outside life leaves you cold.

I'm not supposed to be thinking that about Flint. He's got Lauren. I've got Chris. And Sugar is a mistake no matter what.

A few minutes pass. I hear the terse yank of the tent zipper, feel a cool snatch of air, the shake of the tent, and the dissolve of anger as Sugar stomps across the tundra to get away or take a piss or whatever.

I will myself not to cry. Chris understood what it meant to be a gentleman in a way Sugar never will. My experiences so far have been so slow and so mutual and so respectful that I'm scared to think what would happen if I ended that and opened myself up to a world of the opportunistic and pushy.

Bears, not boys, were supposed to be my biggest Alaska threat. Tonight, being in Alaska is showing me how good I have it at home.

CHAPTER EIGHTEEN

The next day, about an hour into the hike out, a weird step sends a shriek of pain through my knee, and I go down.

Kendra rushes beside me. "Oh my gosh! What happened?" She unsnaps the belt on my pack, then unsnaps the top clip and guides the whole thing off my shoulders while I writhe and clutch my knee.

I gasp. In my years playing soccer, nothing like this has ever happened to me before. Freakin' Darlene's guess in the sibling text jinxed me.

Jake kneels beside me. "Did you twist it? Is it a sprain?"

"I'm not sure yet." I'm huffing the words. I need air to filter the throbs pulsing through my leg. When I look back at my knee it looks dislocated. I rest my hand on the small bulge of my kneecap that now floats on the outside of my knee instead of in the middle of it.

Jakes watches me, wide-eyed. "That's doesn't look good."

DENALI SUMMER

Sugar stands arms crossed above us looking curious but isn't budging to see how he can help. We haven't spoken a word to each other today.

This happened to a teammate in practice once, and I know what I have to do. I count to three in my mind, grab the knee cap and wrench it back into place. Then I continue long pulls of air and extended exhales. After a few more rounds of this I ask, "Did anybody bring ibuprofen?"

Kendra reaches for the top compartment of her pack which got dropped to the ground at some point during my agonizing. She pulls out a packet, rips it open, and sets two pills in my hand. At the same time Jake unscrews the top from my water and hands it to me.

"Those are supposed to be in the bear containers." Sugar says it under his breath, but Kendra hears him.

She waves the empty packet. "How is this scented?"

Sugar shrugs. "Ranger said all medicine."

"Whatever." Kendra's been terse with Sugar ever since breakfast when I'd taken advantage of a moment alone with her to explain my frustration over Sugar's rushed, gropy make-out technique. I'd worried she'd treat me like a baby, ask me what I thought was going to happen. But no, Kendra was fully on my side, assuring me, "If a guy goes past what a girl says, he gets iced out. What a creep."

Jake ignores both of them. "How bad is the pain? And how did you know how to put it back in?"

"Do you need to be airlifted out of here or something?" Kendra asks.

Last night, Sugar. Today, this. But I'm not giving up.

CHAPTER EIGHTEEN

"No, I'll hobble out. I might need a shoulder. And I might need to take out some weight from my pack. Then it's ice and elevation for a few days. And more ibuprofen."

"You're not carrying any weight." Jake is already unzipping my pack and pulling out its contents. It's impossible to think that my things can be divided by a third and stuffed into already stuffed sacks, but they manage it, leaving me with only my sleeping bag.

Jake helps pull me into a standing position, Kendra working to steady me from the other side. I drape one arm around Jake, and we hobble forward one hesitant limping step at a time.

After another half hour we break for our protein bars. At my new pace, we're not going to make it back at lunch time. Sugar's stomach grumbles loud enough for all of us to hear.

"I can carry her. She could hold her pack on top," Sugar says, stuffing our wrappers into the food container.

"I'm right here. Don't talk about me like I'm not right here." I'm still seated, and even though I've snapped at him, I'm considering Sugar's offer.

"You want to try it or not?"

It's a testament to the amount of pain I'm in that I nod. Sugar crouches over me, and I reach my arm around his neck. He extends an arm under my knees and gently pulls me off the ground.

"Damn, East Texas. I thought I could get in an arms workout, but you don't weigh a thing."

Kendra sets my pack on top of me. "There. Have a little more weight," she says, but her facial expression is asking me if I'm okay with this.

DENALI SUMMER

Even though it's Sugar, even if he doesn't make it far, I'm very okay with moving forward without having to walk.

Jake checks the clock on his phone. "Bet you can't make it fifteen minutes."

"Set your timer. I'll bet you a snack shack burger I can."

Jake punches a few buttons. "I set it for fourteen, since you've already been holding her a minute."

Sugar shakes his head and presses forward. I do my best to hold on without slipping or moving to make this as easy as possible. I doubt he'll make it fifteen minutes, but I'm going to do my best to help him try.

Kendra skirts around Sugar to take the lead, and Jake slips behind us as we continue along the river valley toward a connecting point with the Savage River Loop Trail, the most direct route to the shuttle and cooked meals and showers and beds.

Sugar's arms don't quiver, but I know from his deepening intensity of concentration that this is an effort for him. He doesn't glance down at me but appears to be focusing on the back of Kendra's head. I want to tell him that I'll buy him a burger no matter what, he can put me down when he needs to, but I can't bring myself to break the trance he's put himself in.

A rippling trill sounds behind us, and Jake yells, "Time."

"Not yet," Sugar mumbles and keeps going. I'm guessing he's holding out for that last minute. I count to sixty in my mind, but Sugar still doesn't stop. It's only when we reach a large boulder, both flat and wide enough for me, that Sugar eases me down.

CHAPTER EIGHTEEN

"I saw this up ahead. Figured it'd be a good stopping point," he says and turns to Jake. "You owe me a burger."

"I do. You're a beast, Sugar." Jakes slaps his shoulder.

Sugar entwines his fingers to stretch out his arms in front of him, then rolls his shoulders a few times. "Give me a ten-minute break, and I bet I can carry her another ten."

I slip off the rock but take care to keep all my weight on my good leg. "I think the ibuprofen is helping a little. I can limp on my own for a while." My knee's still a throbbing mess, but I don't want to complain. I slip my pack on, and inch forward a few steps.

Kendra cocks her head. "That's bull. Jake? You up for a turn?"

"I can maybe do ten minutes."

"I'm not betting you," Sugar says, "I want my free burger."

"I'm not sure I'd bet on that anyway." Jake turns to me, "I'm sure you're light, but I'm no gym rat like Sugar."

"It's fine. I can walk—" But Kendra's removing my backpack again, and Jake's pulling my arm around his shoulder. He counts to three and scoops me into his arms, not as gently as Sugar, but it does the trick.

By the time Jakes carries me ten minutes, and Sugar goes another twelve, we make it to the trail, and I convince them I can walk some. Limping along, sometimes on my own, sometimes using Kendra or Jake as a crutch, we get to the shuttle stop two hours behind what we'd originally hoped.

I hoist myself inside and take the first seat.

DENALI SUMMER

Sugar sits down across from me. "I've never been so excited about a burger in my life." His stomach rumbles again further making his point.

"Sorry I delayed us. Stupid knee," I say.

Sugar ignores this, but Kendra adds, "Not your fault." She reaches over from her seat behind him and swats Sugar's arm. "Is it?"

"Whatever. This is what I get for taking a kid on the trail. I should have known better."

Ouch. Now I'm a kid. Because I didn't want to be groped. Because my knee betrayed me, proving me the weakest link of our team. I can't wait to get away from this jerk. I try to focus on being angry so my eyes won't register the hurt that's there too, but they grow watery in spite of my efforts. I slump down, hoping no one can see my face.

Jake and Sugar choose food as their priority, but Kendra and I want to return to our rooms to shower and change first. We're about to part ways in front of the lodge when Gabby comes bounding out the front door, and before I know what's going on, Sugar's lifting me back into the air.

"East Texas," Sugar says, "how about I bring you to your room?"

Part of me wonders what this is about—if Sugar's being nice to me because he somehow thinks it will bother Gabby. But I don't care enough to ask. My knee pain overpowers my pride, and I feel stupid. I'm tired, sore, dirty and hungry.

"Wow." Gabby stops and looks us both up and down. "What'd you do? Elope? Carrying your bride over the threshold of the lodge?"

CHAPTER EIGHTEEN

"Yup," Sugar says at the same time I say, "I sprained my knee."

"That sucks," Gabby says and keeps going. It's a response that answers both of us.

"Hey, Jake," Kendra's tone has immediately gone into purr mode. That's what my sisters and I call the change in a girl's voice when she gets flirty right before asking for a favor. "Will you go with them and take my pack? I'm going to run to The Zoo and get some ice for Dawn."

Jake agrees, and I close my eyes as I bump along in Sugar's arms.

Sugar sets me on the bed, Jake goes through the bathroom to deposit Kendra's pack next to her bed, and then they both take a second to pull out the things of mine that ended up in their packs. Jake asks if I need anything else, but I assure him I'm fine. Shelby and Vanessa aren't here, and I'm ready for the guys to leave, so I can have a minute of quiet.

"Just ice, and Kendra will be here any second."

"Take it easy." Jake winks, and they both leave—Sugar not bothering with any kind of goodbye.

A few more minutes pass before there's a tap on the door and a voice hollers, "Room service!" Not Kendra's voice. Flint's.

"It's not locked," I call back.

"Hi there," he says. He's holding a bag of ice in one hand and a bowl of something in the other.

"Hi back," I say.

"Kendra sent me with this." He holds up the ice. "And I brought watermelon because I knew you'd be hungry."

"I am hungry, and I love watermelon."

"Good. Once this gets set out at dinner it'll be gone in three minutes. Fresh fruit over the canned crap is gold around here, and I wanted you to have first dibs."

The youngest of six never gets first dibs, but here's Flint feeding me again because that's what he does. Flint in my room, adorably talking about food, mutes everything I'd been feeling moments ago. He steps toward the bed and hands me the bowl then eases the ice pack onto my pillow-propped knee.

"Kendra changed her mind. She's grabbing food first which is why you get me."

"You'll do," I say, trying to keep my grin small, not manic.

"She also wanted me to tell you Housekeeper Lauren and Bus Washer Ben were holding hands outside The Zoo. She said that was important, and I couldn't forget." He studies my expression. "Why is it important for you to know that Housekeeper Lauren and Bus Washer Ben were holding hands?"

I've already stuffed my face with watermelon, so I hold up my finger while I chew, indicating he should wait. It's important because Kendra is awesomely mindful of my Flint crush, but I won't say that. "Because Kendra knows I really want Bus Washer Ben to be happy."

"Girl-speak for you're not going to tell me." His hand is still on the bag, holding it in place even though it's well balanced, and he doesn't need to. He looks from my knee to my face. "But smile-speak says you like this news."

Not succeeding in keeping off the manic.

CHAPTER EIGHTEEN

"It's good news." How do I say more without saying too much? "Because if Lauren is with Ben that means Lauren is not with someone else."

"Probably."

I pause from taking another bite. "What do you mean probably?"

"Minutes ago, you were in Sugar's arms, and now you're alone in a room with another guy whose hand is on your knee. Plus there's some technicality in Texas if I recall? Maybe Lauren's holding hands with Bus Washer Ben this afternoon, and later today, she'll be cuddling with Bus Washer Bob."

"We have a Bus Washer Bob?"

"No."

I laugh. "Then Bus Washer Ben has nothing to worry about it. The point is," I want to turn this back to us. "Lauren's not with..." Fine. I'll say more, maybe too much, but... "you. I thought maybe she was with you."

Flint looks confused. "Why would you think that?"

"Because I went to your room the night before we left, and you weren't there, and then someone said they saw you leaving Lauren's early the next morning."

"Nothing like an early delivery of toast and cold medicine to get the walk-of-shame rumors flying."

"Taking care of Lauren, and now you're here taking care of me. You're like the food nurse." He readjusts my ice but doesn't respond to this, so I keep talking. "And I may have been carried by Sugar, but I'm not interested in him."

"No more canceling our dinner dates to go camping with Sugar?"

"I am never ever never," I hope I'm emphasizing this enough, "as in absolutely not ever going camping with Sugar again."

"Good," Flint says, and maybe I'm projecting, but there could be a little mania in the smile he's now flashing at me.

CHAPTER NINETEEN

By mid-June, my Chris letter count stands at seven—averaging two a week, with a postcard thrown in from Schlitterbahn when his family spent a long weekend in San Antonio. He's sent more than my three sisters combined. From them I've gotten nada from Darlene, one camp postcard from Daisy, a pretty card from Dolly at the beginning of the summer and a longer letter that came the day before solstice including the juicy family gossip that Dale officially proposed to Jesslyn, and the family is now in shot-gun wedding planning mode because Dale Jr., (He swears it's a boy, but they don't really know yet.) is on his way. Mama hasn't said anything to me since that one text at the beginning of the summer, so it can't be moving that fast.

The letters from Chris are brief accounts of who's always at the movie theater where he works or who's going out on the lake, who leaves where for vacation, who's off for summer sessions at college. Most of the time it seems like he wants to tell me something, but he has nothing to say. One letter contained a good story about Charlet successfully getting this guy Jackson from the baseball team to take them all out on his daddy's pontoon boat—its hard top perfect for hours of crazy dives and backflips into the water. That one made me homesick.

When he gets whiny that I'm not writing enough (I've sent three post cards.) or writes that he'd love it if I'd start texting him more—I want to ball up the letter in the trash. It's not Sugar groping me in a tent, but it still feels pushy.

I've saved the letters though—lined up beside my knickknack basket on my nightstand, untouched after their first read except for once when I noticed Flint shuffle through them. We were sifting through gear, our one-night permit for Toklat already dangling from Flint's pack. When I returned from Shelby and Kendra's side of the quad with Kendra's sleeping bag, he was returning them to the nightstand.

Because also by mid-June, not only have I cooked Flint dinner, but we've been camping. In Toklat we were joined by river rats Jonelle and Elijah. We scaled sweeping grassy slopes with gradual inclines, enjoyed caribou sightings galore, and we didn't pick up even a whiff of bear scat much less a bear. No moose either, but we did find one, old sun-bleached antler and took turns taking pictures holding it over our heads while making silly faces.

Easy, beautiful sprain-free hiking. We planned on a single night trip in case my knee, a little under two weeks out from my sprain, couldn't take more. They were sure to keep my pack light as well.

CHAPTER NINETEEN

That night the four of us talked and laughed till two in the morning when the almost-dark backdrop magnified a full, strawberry June moon. I'd told them the superstition Charlet had always held—get pregnant under a full, strawberry moon, give birth to a red-head.

"Pretty sure that doesn't work for Black people," Jonelle had said, and I giggled so hard it was clear I'd hit slaphappy-level tired. Flint declared me overdue for bed and ushered me back to the tent where I promptly fell asleep.

And Flint is a gentleman—the sum total of my physical contact with Flint on the trip came in the morning when he rubbed my shoulders for a minute before I put on my pack (also borrowed from Kendra).

We're camping together again for the solstice party.

The solstice party is a longstanding employee tradition, with at least one repeat hotel worker bringing everyone back to the same pullout off the highway, to the same field with logs and rocks circled up around the obvious bonfire spot. The party has to be in a field off the highway because we can't have a bonfire inside the park. This year about twenty of us including Jonelle and Elijah, Zeke and his brother, Kendra and Jake, Sugar and Housekeeper Alisha, Gabby and a gift shop co-worker, and the rest of the bus washers and housekeepers I don't really know will be celebrating.

Flint and I are ready to head out the same time as Kendra, Jake, Gabby, and her tent-mate, so we finagle a ride from one of the shuttle drivers, convincing him to go off his route and run us up to the site. This is especially helpful since Flint's packed an entire cooler full of who-knows-what from the kitchen.

Before we've even loaded, four bus washers rush toward the closing doors. Once they're seated and the doors shut again, we hear a booming, "Wait!" and I look up to see Shelby skip on board, Vanessa huffing behind her carrying a large bakery box. With packs taking up some of the seats, there's only one seat available. Shelby insists Vanessa take it while plopping herself on Kendra's lap.

"Do we have everybody this time?" the shuttle driver asks, watching us in his mirror.

Jakes hollers out, "We're full. Let's get a move on!" At the same time Kendra, Shelby, and Vanessa hoot, "Solstice party!" Somehow Vanessa already has a beer in hand and holds it up to toast the cans of sparkling flavored water Shelby pulls out for herself and Kendra.

"No food or drink on the shuttle, so I'm not seeing that," says the shuttle driver.

Shelby sing-songs, "No, you're no-ot," and takes another sip.

I catch Vanessa's attention. "When did ya'll decide to come? I thought you didn't like tent-camping?"

She holds up her beer. "But I like a good party."

I bump my shoulder into Flint's. "How about you? Do you like a good party?"

"With this company, I'd say so."

He threads his fingers into mine, and a thrill runs up my arm and down my spine. But at the same moment as I'm inwardly questioning what this means, he lets go, sliding his hands along the tops of his rust-colored jeans as though drying sweaty palms. Except his palms weren't sweaty and neither were mine.

"What kind of trips did you take growing up?" he asks.

CHAPTER NINETEEN

I'm still trying to decide why the mind-change on the hand-hold that I don't answer. He adds, "Ever go camping with your family?"

"Ha!" It's hard to imagine the twins tent camping. "Not my sisters. No way. Besides, if my whole family went together we'd need a circus-sized tent."

"Really? None of you camped?"

"Daddy took my brothers a few times to a hunting cabin and maybe to a state park for a trip here or there, but they weren't Boy Scouts or anything."

His eyes widen. "Is Denali the first time you've camped?"

"I tent-camped at a KOA once for a church retreat. Not with my family though."

"Oh yeah? Who got you camping on a church retreat?"

"My high school boyfriend. The youth pastor at his church was all about that kind of thing."

"The Texas technicality," Flint mumbles then goes silent and stares out the window. Vanessa hollers for me, so I let it go.

"Roomie! Beverage? She holds up a beer and a sparkling water. I point to the water which then comes hurtling over Kendra's head directly toward my face. I react quickly enough to catch it and spare my nose the pounding.

Wanting to save our clothes from fancy water spray, I settle the shaken can on my lap and wait. In front of me Sugar calls for the beer, but Vanessa smirks and says, "Doghouse boys don't get free beer."

I tuck my chin and smile downward, then nudge Flint to come back to our conversation.

"How about you? Did your family camp?"

DENALI SUMMER

"I camped a bunch with my dad and brother. When we were on the East Coast, we did sections of the Appalachian Trail a few summers. After we moved to Texas, Dad took a few weeks before he started his new job, and we went all around Yellowstone."

"Sounds amazing."

"I wanted them up in Denali at the end of this summer, but Dad says work-wise he needs to wait. I think we'll manage a good trip when my brother graduates. If not Denali, then Montana somewhere."

"My family never vacations like that. Too many of us. Plus, since my dad owns his shop, he doesn't like to be gone more than a few days at a time. I don't know what he thinks will happen, but that's how he is.

"Anybody in your family taking advantage of your employee discount and coming to see you up here?"

I never told my family about the room discount. The point of this summer is to be away. Far away. "Postcards are good enough for them."

"If you could have one visitor from home up here for a few days, who would you want to come?"

There are definitely moments when I've wanted my trio of sisters, but so far my trio of roomies have worked as good stand-ins. Pulling their supportive weight after the "Sugar Incident" confirmed their qualifications. I think about the rest of my family. Of Chris. Of Charlet. I'll have Charlet every day all day as my roommate, so I'm good with not breaking up this break from her. And Chris. No part of me wants Chris here when I'm having this much fun with Flint.

"No one."

"No one? Really?"

CHAPTER NINETEEN

I don't understand why this is so hard to believe. Do I sound mean because I'm okay with being away from my loved ones for all of ten weeks? "My college is close to my house. My high school best friend is going to be my roommate. This is my only shot at doing something totally different, meeting people who are totally different. I don't need to see anyone from home until I get back."

"Oh."

I'm going to need more than this single syllable. I search his face. There are worry creases in his forehead. He runs his fingers through his hair, tussling what had been lying straight.

"You were supposed to say something else, and then I was supposed to feel smug because I know something you don't know. Now I feel like I should warn you." His eyes flicker to the window then appear to be concentrating on the seat ahead of us. "You can't tell anyone."

Not knowing what I don't know, I'm not ready to promise anything, so I nod slightly. Nods are easily misconstrued. They are most definitely not binding promises.

"Promise you won't," Flint insists.

"I'm not going to spit and shake, but I'm not going to run my mouth either." This is the best I can offer. It appears good enough because Flint continues.

"There's a reservation in the books that Wanda's been keeping a surprise, but she told Red who told me, and—"

He pauses a little too long. "And?" I prompt.

DENALI SUMMER

"And it seems Red doesn't like surprises, so he thought you might appreciate being warned." He rubs his pants again. This boy sure can stall.

"Out with it."

"Your family has two rooms for four nights starting July 30th."

"Oh." He finally got to the Band-Aid rip, and I'm okay.

July 30th is my eighteenth birthday.

For my eighteenth birthday, Mama's gonna chase me all the way up to Alaska. God bless her and dammit. Positive feelings are coating over my annoyance, and I might get teary.

"Are you furious? Neutral? I know you're not happy, but say something."

I swallow back the emotion and will my voice steady. "That's my birthday. I guess I have family coming for my birthday. It's sweet." In spite of my efforts, my voice cracks on "sweet." No girl wants her birthday forgotten, and I'm too touched to hide what it means to me that mine was special enough for this.

I wonder if it will be Mama and my sisters or Mama and Daddy and some other combination of siblings. I rethink Flint's question along the lines of—since you know people in your family are coming, who do you want to come? I'd love it to be just the girls, but it's on account of Daddy I even got to come to Alaska. I know he'd be proud if I led him out on a hike, showed him what I've learned. I envision Dustin and Dale coming up the trail behind us, discovering with every tangled scrub tree bushwhacked out of the way that their baby sister managed to grow up after all. Just like that, I'm wishing there were three rooms under the reservation, so I could be sure they were all coming.

CHAPTER NINETEEN

The shuttle rattles me back to reality as the driver pulls off the road onto an area where the shoulder has widened to a pothole-riddled pull-off.

"Welcome to nowhere," he says, opening the door. "I suppose I can swing back up here tomorrow morning. 'Bout eight. Be ready or plan to hitchhike."

We thank him and gather our gear. Shelby punctuates the exodus by occasionally shouting, "Solstice party!" which Kendra and Vanessa answer with squeals. Gabby's bitchiness has met its match in my quad-mates unrelenting merriment. She shoots eye daggers in rapid succession, but they all go ignored.

Vanessa leaves the driver with a cupcake from her bakery box and a beer chirping, "For later!" before exiting the bus.

It's not long before we've all erected a semi-circle of tents, and we're around a fire, stuffing our faces with Vanessa's cupcakes. Jake and Sugar get the fire started and won't leave it alone, poking and prodding the logs into maximum flame position. Flint and I each choose a chocolate cupcake with cookies and cream filling and frosting. For a common flavor, it's still supernaturally good—the chocolate cake moist, the cream sweet and thick and delicately chunky with the perfect ratio of cookie crumbles. Vanessa is my hero. I pop the last bite into my mouth and moan, "So rich," then rub my stomach, "no more food."

Flint laughs. "That's only the beginning." He taps the side of the cooler which we're using as a seat. "I scored strawberries. I'm making quesadillas. Not lame backcountry, nothing-but-cheese quesadillas. Fire-roasted chicken and green pepper quesadillas with my homemade salsa. We're solstice feasting."

DENALI SUMMER

"You have a homemade salsa?" Of course he does.

"Had a study group freshmen year that couldn't function without nachos. I've had plenty of practice."

"Nacho clubs disguised as study groups. College is looking better and better."

"Can't speak for ETBU, but if you were at UNT..."

The idea crackles as alive as the fire in front of us. If only I could. Taking a summer off from Mama's expectations is one thing, bringing that back to Texas? Unimaginable.

Someone busts out a Bluetooth speaker and blasts Janis Joplin from their phone. What kind of person keeps Janis Joplin on their phone? But soon enough we're joyfully shout-singing along.

The string of classic rock and country that follows brings me home— *The Joker*, *Wagon Wheel*, and all the old Martina songs I came out of the womb knowing—they're songs Mama has played from scratched-up CDs on a won't-ever-die boombox that's been in our kitchen since the beginning of time. Many, many Christmases ago, when I was just a little kid, my sisters and I went in together for an iPod with a quality speaker-docking station. Darlene made sure to put all Mama's music on it before we even gave it to her. Mama made a show of using it Christmas day, but it never made it onto the kitchen counter. Sometime later I noticed it in Dale's auto shop because, as the oldest boy, he's got Mama wrapped tight around his finger. Thieving asshole.

"You know all the words," Flint says, watching me.

"Grew up on this stuff."

CHAPTER NINETEEN

"Feeling homesick?" It's not a tease; he's studying my face as though he really wants to know how I'm feeling.

"Not really." It's the truth. Listening to these songs in Alaska reminds me I can take parts of home anywhere. It's comforting more than anything.

Flint gets started on his quesadillas, and now I fully understand the nickname I learned back at the airport. Everyone should try Flint's fire-roasted chicken quesadillas. Thank goodness he brought enough to make three large ones. My roomies, drawn by the smell, cozy up to us.

I don't want to share a single bite. Nicer-than-me Flint divides the spare quesadilla into thirds for them and then, when Gabby shows up, cuts off a part of his own.

"Delicious. Another sliver would really do the trick." Gabby looks at me.

I pull my foil-wrapped quesadilla in tighter. "Don't even think about it."

The party continues closer to sunrise which is supposed to be around three thirty. It's an unspoken goal, but we all seem determined to watch the sun both leave and return. Sugar's tent-mate, Housekeeper Alisha, is the first one who clearly won't make it. At three a.m. her drunken stumble almost lands her in the bonfire, so Sugar announces it's time for them to tuck in. A sharp stab of worry freezes me in place. Sugar's bad enough alone with sober girls.

Kendra and Shelby are on it before I can even stand—Kendra steadying Alisha but also tugging her to step away from Sugar.

DENALI SUMMER

Shelby gets right up in Sugar's face and jabs him in the chest with a long, manicured nail. "Sugar, honey. You do not have the reputation of a gentleman. Alisha will be sleeping it off in my tent."

"That so?" Sugar looks too amused to realize what he's up against in the always-gets-her-way bridezilla that is Shelby.

Shelby purses her whole face and nods, standing her ground, but Sugar takes her hand and removes it from his chest to step toward Alisha.

"You ladies are sweet, but you're out of line. How about you go back to the party and let me take care of mine."

Kendra exchanges a look with Jake who steps forward. "Let her go, bro. It's not a big deal where she sleeps."

"Their tent fits two, and they already have two. This is stupid." Sugar's grip on Alisha's arm tightens.

But Kendra's hand tightens on Alisha's other arm. "She either crowds in with Shelby and Vanessa or she comes in with me, and Jake goes in with you. That's it. Those are the choices."

Jake's eyes widen, and he looks at Kendra to see if she's being serious. Her steady gaze on Sugar indicates that, in fact, she is.

Hot damn. South Florida girls showing Don't-Mess-with-Texas-level fight. Imagine that.

"You crazy bitches can have her." Sugar discards Alisha's arm with so much anger, the entire side of her body slumps, and Kendra looks as though she's about to drop her until Jake rushes to steady her as well. They help Alisha into Shelby's tent while Sugar stomps off on his own.

CHAPTER NINETEEN

"Jackass? Is that your real name?" I call across the bonfire before he disappears.

He turns and locks his eyes on mine. "That doesn't start with R." One side of his mouth slides up to a cocky smile. "Always were a bad guesser, East Texas."

"It fits though," I say and hold the stare until he turns away.

When he's zipped up in his tent, Gabby raises a beer and shouts over the music, "A toast to crazy bitches."

I lift my glass. Whatever it takes to keep a sister safe. I'll drink to that.

Flint and I settle back on the cooler and stare into the dying fire.

"Tell me something else about college," I say. "What's the best part?"

"The course catalog."

"What?" Not the answer I'd been expecting.

"The course catalog is page after page of passions you don't know you have. Learn Chinese, study Mayan culture, or explore the realities of global aging in the gerontology department. You can study anything."

He's even more enthusiastic than the guidance counselor from ETBU.

"Gerontology? Seriously?"

"Don't knock it. Amazing class."

"Endless opportunities. Got it. What's the worst part?"

"When the girl you think you're falling in love with comes back from spring break and tells you she's getting back together with her high school boyfriend."

Ouch. Flint doesn't wait for my response but motions for me to hop off the cooler. He pulls out a root beer, and I grab one too.

DENALI SUMMER

"I probably won't be in danger of that," I say after we sit back down.

"Probably not."

We stare into the fire and sip our drinks. The cold brown bottle of root beer in my hands makes me more aware of the chill in the air around me.

I shiver, and Flint scoots closer.

"Did you take any of the poetry classes offered up in that course catalog?" I ask. Poetry doesn't fit in with any of the majors I'm considering, but an elective that's all words—swirling, swimming, deliberate, head-exploring words. I could fill a lot of journals with such words.

"No poetry. No writing classes of any kind. I took a psych class in the fall that had so many papers—I couldn't have handled any more writing." Flint stares into the fire and takes another swig before speaking toward the flames. "Distinguishing Fact from Fallacy in Psychology. It's where I met the girlfriend. I passed the class but failed the life application of the concept."

I drop my head onto his shoulder. "I won't be that girl."

"You sure?" It's a whisper into my hair, but I hear him.

I want to answer him so that he'll believe me. I need to answer him in a way that convinces my own heart I'm being honest. That this new adventurer, risk-taker me will be stronger than the part of me who could go back to the comforts and familiarity of Chris when the summer ends.

Solstice, the longest day of the year, is the day which marks when the throb of summer grabs Texas and begins its slow strangle of heat. I know what

CHAPTER NINETEEN

happens there. In Alaska, solstice is not the beginning but the mid-point. As daylight wanes and slips toward full-time darkness, my Alaska calendar days remaining will grow smaller than those I've already had. I need every moment of these days. This trip is about moving forward so far that even when I have to physically return home, I'm not going back to how things were. I can't. I won't.

When I get back to the hotel—I'm letting Chris know we're done.

"I'm sure." I tilt my head back and stare into Flint's golden-flecked eyes, willing my resolve to transfer through these two little words. I brush my hands down his cheek and say it again. The third time I begin to repeat myself, I'm cut off, his lips finding mine. And we seal my promise with our first kiss, the bonfire renewed and blazing its strength behind us—light upon light upon light.

♪ Cantwell Bluegrass Festival ♫

Mama would not have a good time dancing barefoot to the Denali Cooks

Cantwell swells. Festival everything sneaks past the tracks & tents creep beyond designated borders, sweeping the town* into musical frenzy.

It's a happy chaos. ☺

★ (small but still a town. There's a school and a post office and an RV park - definitely a town)

An old lady pushes a petition my way. Her long braids scrape the words "... initiative to extend LGBTQ protections beyond the workplace..."

The Cooks strike up another chorus, and I grab the pen.

♡ is ♡ is ♡ is ♡ is ♡ is ♡!

CHAPTER TWENTY

After our first kiss on solstice night, Flint and I didn't do anything else. When we finally got into the tent, we both collapsed into sleep—not surprising on account of the fact we'd stayed up till four a.m. Since then, it's been nothing but hand-holding and good-night cheek-pecks. Going slow is nice, but part of my brain has got to wondering if he's pulling back again, guarding himself from the girl he knows got two more letters from another Texas boy this week.

But we're spending more time together. Flint and I sync our work schedules so we both get Thursdays and Fridays off. Our next weekend coincides with a music festival in Cantwell. It's another event that most all the employees work into their schedule even if only for the afternoon after a shift. Flint and I plan to camp it for two nights. Kendra and Jake will join us the first, Jonelle and Elijah the second.

In my mind, I've broken up with Chris. But I'm putting off telling him because it feels like something

I should do in person. The roommates are divided on this point.

Kendra says it would be fine to wait and do it face to face.

Shelby says I have to call him. Until we've broken up, it's cheating. If I'm to have any sort of future with Flint, it should not be on a foundation of cheating.

Vanessa says... either way, she gets that it's hard, and she's happy to make me cupcakes if I need to drown my confusion in chocolate.

But it's like a cloud looming over me, and when I'm honest with myself, I agree with Shelby.

But this can't just be about Flint because no matter what happens with Flint, I've moved on from wanting Chris. This has to be about me and what I want now and what I think I'll want when I get back to Texas.

I'm finally ready to do what I should have done on graduation eve when Chris first pulled out that ring. I make up my mind to call Chris. Tuesday after my shift, I walk straight to my room and sit on the bed, phone in hand, and on his contact picture—a close-up of his face he took himself and left for me to find.

"A call is even better than a text!" He answers with so much enthusiasm, it's a punch to my gut. Oh Chris, I'm so, so sorry. I establish that he's got a minute and ask if he's alone and this line of questioning gets him serious pretty quick.

"What's the matter? What do you need to tell me?"

"Chris, you know I've loved you for a long time."

"And still do, I hope."

I let that go. I wrote down what I want to say, and I have to get through it. "But I don't see our future

CHAPTER TWENTY

together the way you do. I've got so much still to figure out—"

"We'll figure it all out together, Dawn-baby. We've talked about all that."

I cringe. "No. I want to figure it out alone. I want to break up." I still had three more lines written before I was supposed to say that, but "Dawn-baby" helped me skip to the point.

He laughs, actually laughs. "It's a little early to be getting cold feet."

"It's not cold feet."

"We can't break up. We're meant to be together. I gave you your space this summer, but when you get back here, I think everything will fall right back into place. Maybe we can even talk to your Mama about you transferring at Christmas. I bet if I proposed for real, she'd allow it."

I'm breaking up with him, and he's pushing up our wedding date.

"What if I don't want to transfer? What if I love ETBU? What if I've decided to stay on in Alaska and go to college up here?"

"But you don't know, do you? You don't much care, so I make the decisions. That's one of the reasons we work so well together."

I want to strangle him through the phone.

"I made the decision to come to Alaska, didn't I? And I'm telling you right now, I've made the decision to break up."

"Let's talk about this some more when we can do it in person. Nothing has to be decided right now."

"I've decided."

"And I want to leave things till we can talk face to face. You're going through something. Okay, but I'm not giving up on us."

It's infuriating. I've changed, but no one at home has. They still don't listen to me.

Even so, I've done my part, and I feel pretty good telling Flint that night at dinner, "No more technicality. We've fully and most definitely broken up."

His eyebrows raise, "Is that so?" I nod, and he reaches for my hand. "That's good news."

The next day after our shifts we leave for Cantwell where we dance to band after band and kiss between songs. The cloud is gone. This is the summer I'm meant to be living.

I spend every cent I'd brought with me on vendor food and ulu knives to take back as present souvenirs. A homeless mutt decides he's our responsibility, sleeping beside our tent and whining for food. Flint spends his money on a bag of dog food at the town's only convenience store. It's one third of the size and ten times the cost of what I know we buy for Rusty back home. If I ever decide to live in Alaska, remind me never to get a dog.

By the morning of our third day, we have two dollars and a quarter between us and two granola bars left in the food cooler, but it's fine because everyone shares. When we ride back to the hotel later that evening, it's with bellies full, and our mutt responsibilities and dog food passed on to a couple who pitched their tent as soon as Jonelle and Elijah broke down theirs.

I could get used to this life.

Work life at the hotel falls into its own steady, happy rhythm. After work, I go one day a week to the

CHAPTER TWENTY

kennels with Wanda. The rest of the days I hike, usually with Flint sometimes with Kendra or Shelby if Flint works dinner. A second attempt at Horseshoe Lake with Kendra turns up four beavers and zero moose. Now that's what I'm talking about.

On days when no one is available, I have a Dawn-sized, flat river rock just beyond the Savage River campsite. I have to cross about eight feet of mid-calf-high Savage stream to get there. The frigid waters catch my breath, and then my toasty rock is the best exhale. It's the perfect spot for sunning and journaling and naps but just below a railroad bridge. I wonder what the tourists looking for wildlife think of the Dawn-in-the-wild instead of the caribou they're scanning for.

At the rock I have to remind myself I'm following through with the ETBU plan, that the weather will turn colder and the dark will settle in. But on that sun-heated, smooth surface, it's easy to dream away reality and imagine a life stood-still on summer.

♪ Cantwell Day 2 ♪

My pre-college study abroad education!

Teachers:
- Dancing crowd
- Vendors selling Ulu Knives, burritoes, brownies...
- Bands!

Lessons:

1. Don't hold food low enough for stray dog to snatch.

2. Keep dancing

Seriously. Worry less. Dance more. You can keep dancing longer than you think!

CHAPTER TWENTY-ONE

My roommates, who announced a Christmas in July celebration to take place on July 25th, are not as entrenched in forever-summer as me. Shelby, with too much of her wedding planned, clearly needs more to do. I'd been gung-ho on the idea right up until I drew Gabby's name in the employee-wide Secret Santa exchange Shelby organized. Definite fake-Christmas buzzkill.

Needing presents and supplies from the lower forty-eight has increased my communication with Mama. Determined to solve the puzzle of who in my family is coming for my birthday, I'm prodding and poking for any hints she might drop. I'm also curious how Mama's feeling about Dale and Jesslyn making her a grandma. On the phone I tease, "Should I be calling you Granny now?" But she tells me to hush, so I drop it, wondering if maybe Mama is against rushing this wedding.

DENALI SUMMER

I expect her to complain when I warn her she'll see charges on the Amazon Prime account since the shipping doesn't cover Alaska, but she just agrees. Agrees without ever mentioning that our arbitrary holiday could be held a few days later, and then she could bring everything with her for free. She even wastes more money on shipping by sending up another care package with leftover blank Christmas cards and Christmasy paper plates and napkins she bought last year on sale after the holidays. No "see you soon!" on the included note. No jokes about how close to Christmas my birthday is this year. No mention of my birthday at all.

I don't tell her I broke up with Chris, either. No point in getting into that over the phone.

By the middle of July, I break down and call Charlet, begging for her to come clean if she knows or to find out if she doesn't.

"Dawn Everly Wilkes! Are you kidding me? Your Mama planned the surprise of the century and your stupid co-workers couldn't keep it a secret?"

Stupid? I've swapped spit with this person she's calling stupid. I exhale loudly into the phone. "The people I work with are my friends. They were looking out for me."

Charlet doesn't seem to believe my break-up with Chris will stick either, so I haven't bothered to explain that the "friend" is something more.

"They shouldn't have said a thing. I'm your friend who's known you the longest, and I'm not about to say anything except that I know who's coming, and I think it's awesome."

"Charlet, will you please tell me?"

CHAPTER TWENTY-ONE

"No."

"Charlet Rae Dawson."

"No."

"When we're at school, I'll fart on your face in your sleep."

"I have a big brother too. Not afraid of that."

"Fine. Don't tell me, but I'll tell you that my best guess is Mama, Daddy, Darlene, and Dolly. I want Daisy here, but I don't see how she'd be able to get out of summer camp counseling. Am I Hot? Cold? Give me a clue."

"You're right, and you're wrong, and I'm not saying any more than that." Her tone is so annoyed, I know I'm close. She must mean that Daisy did get off, and I'm getting all my sisters after all. Maybe I'm wrong about Daddy too. Maybe it's just a girls trip. I squeal. Bringing in eighteen, my adult life, with my sisters in Alaska. It's going to be so amazing.

"Oh hey, do you know anything about Dale and Jesslyn? Dolly wrote that she's pregnant, and he proposed, and back a long time ago Mama mentioned a summer wedding, but I haven't heard anything since, so maybe not?"

"I ran into Jesslyn at the craft store. She's not showing or anything, but she did have a buttload of light pink ribbon in her cart and fifty zillion sheets of craft paper."

"She making wedding invitations?"

"She said the paper's for origami flowers for her bouquet. Something she saw on Pinterest and wanted to try because her daughter has allergies."

"Have they set a date?" I can't believe they have. Surely, I'd have gotten at least five texts, if that had happened: one from Mama, one each from my sisters, and one from Jesslyn herself.

"I don't know anything about that." She says it so rushed, my bullshit radar pings.

"Charlet. What aren't you telling me?"

"I haven't told you that Parker and I broke up, and Jackson from the baseball team has taken me to the movies three times, and tomorrow he's coming over to hang out."

Hang out means make out, and I have duties as the best friend to ask her about the new boy. She and Parker had been together since right before Valentines, and Charlet usually moves on after a month or two, so they'd set a record, but her moving on isn't really a surprise either. It's good to have her boy news to focus on, especially since I feel a touch guilty for not telling her about Flint.

But something's definitely up with Dale and this wedding. Thank goodness I'm too far away to get rolled into that drama.

We're not supposed to shop for anyone other than who we drew for Secret Santa, but whatever. It's Wilkes girl standard practice to do more than assigned at the holidays. The siblings always draw names instead of shopping for everyone, but only Dale and Dustin stick to that plan. They get their one required sibling gift, or probably ask Mama to buy them their one required sibling gift, but we girls shop for everyone—a

CHAPTER TWENTY-ONE

main gift for who we pulled and a little something for everyone else.

For Denali Christmas, I've got the "everyone else" covered. I've ordered a dozen mini red stockings and green glitter-glue pens to write names on the fluffy white border top. I'm doing one for Wanda and Red, one for each of the River Rats, my roomies, and Flint. I ordered candy canes and flashing reindeer noses for all of them, plus a few extras for some. The roomies each get a bottle of nail polish called "Meet Me at the Altar." Jonelle gets the bonus gift of a Denali National Park sticker for her Nalgene water bottle. She keeps saying she wants to decorate it but never makes it over to the gift shop. In Flint's, I've included a recipe card I wrote up with Mama's chocolate chip oatmeal squares recipe. On the other side, I've made it out to look like a coupon and written: *Good for one dessert date night*.

But I have no idea what to get Gabby. I had Flint ask her for me while I was picking out Jonelle's sticker and absolutely eavesdropping, but all she said was, "I can always use cigarettes."

"That's it?" said Flint.

"What I really need is a roommate for when I leave this place. My cousin and I were supposed to get an apartment, but she's ditching me for her trash boyfriend. You think my Santa could swing me a new roommate?"

No, she cannot, and I may not be the most churched girl in the south, but I'm not going to celebrate baby Jesus in the manger's fake birthday with a pack of cancer sticks either.

So yeah. I got nothing beyond a leftover stocking with a candy cane and flashing reindeer nose I don't expect Gabby would wear long enough to snap a silly selfie.

Shelby orders ample Christmas loot as well—a four-foot fake tree, and to decorate it, a gold sequined tree skirt, a gold foil star tree topper, white pearl garland, and two strands of small white globe lights. On the day it all arrives, Shelby, Kendra, Vanessa, and I set it up together in the rec room.

Now that it's up, people are supposed to leave Santa surprises through the week leading up to Christmas and then reveal who they are with a final something on Christmas day. I return to the table and pull out one of the Christmas cards Mama sent from my bag. After scrawling "Gabby" on the envelope in a tall, skinny cursive meant to disguise my own handwriting, I find I have nothing I want to write in the card.

The outside of the card features a looping strand of brightly colored lights, and the inside reads, "May your Christmas be merry and bright!" Writing "Merry Christmas" feels redundant.

Kendra holds up my envelope. "You pulled Gabby, huh? What are you getting her?"

"I don't kno-ow." I stretch out the "know" in a whiny way. "Any ideas?"

"I've been in her room. She likes the Houston Rockets."

"A Texas basketball team, really?"

"She's from the Houston area. Didn't you know that?"

I did not. "Notice anything else?"

"She had a jar candle that looked low. I teased her about it since we're not supposed to have candles in our rooms."

"Did you happen to look at the scent?"

CHAPTER TWENTY-ONE

"It was yellow, so lemon maybe?"

Lemon scented candles and Rockets gear. Now we are getting somewhere.

"Why were you in her room?" I ask.

Kendra shrugs. "We're friends."

"How did that happen?" A preppy, polished Kendra and rough-around-the-edges smoker Gabby friendship is hard to picture.

"You and Vanessa always work in mornings, and Shelby sleeps too late. Gabby and I eat breakfast together. She's super nice."

Kendra probably thinks everyone is "super nice," and no one likes to eat alone. Friendship of convenience. I have those.

I tap my pen on the table a few times before writing, *Happy Christmas in July! I'm busy planning your holiday surprises.* I then draw a sloppy heart and sign it, *Secret Santa*.

When I return to my room, I do a final order, filling my cart with Rockets metallic armband tattoos, a Rockets poncho that comes stuffed in a small basketball container, one soy lemon candle, and a long sleeve Rockets tee for her main Christmas Day present. Then again, with only ten days till our Christmas, if my package doesn't get here fast it will all be her Christmas Day present.

Aside from delivery, work as a Secret Santa is done. Now to discover who drew me.

Merry July Christmas!

Gifting:
- July 21 — Poncho
- July 22 — candle
- July 23 — armbands
- July 24 — stockings × a lot

✱ July 25 ✱ long sleeve Tee

Getting:

July 18: text with meme
"It says Xmas Party... but I think we all know what that's code for." (ha!)

who has my number and would send that?

July 20: pack of moleskin (Flint?)

July 22: cupcake (Vanessa?)

July 24: Denali ornament from gift shop (anyone!)

July 25: T.B.D. :)

Fa la la la la la ...

CHAPTER TWENTY-TWO

On July Christmas I'm woken not by my usual soft alarm music but to the sound of Shelby hollering, "It's Christmas! It's Christmas!" Kendra, in tow, blares *Joy to the World*.

I prop myself on my arm and try to focus. They were kind enough not to flip the main light, but the room is aglow in a strand of colorful Christmas lights strewn across the window that were not there when I fell asleep. My phone alarm reads 4:38—only two minutes before it should be going off. Front desk clerks are needed for the early shift even on fake Christmas.

Vanessa, who gets up at the same time because she goes in early to bake, is not giving up her two minutes. She's pulled her unicorn blanket completely over her head. Its horn is now her horn. Shelby sinks onto Vanessa's bed and grabs what may be her shoulders.

"It's Christmas!" she says again, and Kendra increases the volume on the music.

"Is that my speaker?" I ask.

DENALI SUMMER

Kendra nods. "I grabbed it last night when we came in to put up the lights. Here," she tosses a plastic bag at me, "this is your final Secret Santa gift."

"Are you my Santa?" I ask and rip into the bag. Inside there's a soft red shirt. On the front, in white letters, the slogan "Don't Mess with Texas" is configured in such a way that it makes the shape of my state.

Kendra sets the speaker on my nightstand table and settles onto my bed. I flip the volume down to almost nothing. "Nope. I had HR Angie," she says.

"Then who had me?"

She shakes the bag, and a sheet of folded notebook paper flutters into my lap. It reads, *Good thing Kendra stepped in to help. I'd have just sent you memes. Roll Tide. Merry Christmas. Love, Jake.*

Kendra answers questions before I ask them. "It was his money. I picked things out and made him buy them because he totally would have just texted you stupid Christmas memes and stopped at that."

"I had Vanessa." Shelby has now pulled down Vanessa's blanket and is swaying a stuffed tote back and forth in front of her face. "Don't you want your present?"

Vanessa squirms to sit and takes the bag. "It's so," she stops to yawn, "cute."

Shelby bats her on the arm. "Don't sound so excited."

"This is as excited as it gets at five a.m. without coffee." Vanessa turns the bag to me revealing a picture printed of the four of us taken the night of the solstice party. Beneath the picture Denali Summer and the year are scrawled in a bold cursive font.

"So cute," I agree. And I mean it. I'm a little jealous of that bag.

CHAPTER TWENTY-TWO

"Good," Shelby says, "because I got us all one, but only Vanessa's is filled with loot. Dig in there."

Vanessa pulls out an assortment of cute kitchen gadgets: cookie cutters and stamps, a Santa-shaped timer, a metal trivet shaped like a snowflake, and a neon-green apron with Vanessa's initials monogrammed in cherry red.

"Not my colors, but I thought you'd like it," Shelby says while Vanessa holds up the apron.

"I'm going to ignore that thinly veiled insult because I do like it even if you think my color tastes are tacky. I will wear it today with pride as I bake my Christmas-themed treats. Now shoo. I have to get ready for work."

"But we haven't sung any Christmas carols." The mock shock is clear in Shelby's voice, but both Vanessa and I fall back onto our beds and groan. This incites Shelby to jump up, drape her arm around Kendra, and shout-sing, "Deck the halls with boughs of holly!"

In spite of ourselves, we all join in with the fa la la las as they leave to go to their room. Their Christmas morning ruckus achieved, those two get to go back to sleep.

Denali would be one of the most likely places for Christmas in July snow, but I step outside to a bright clear morning which, according to my phone, is a crisp fifty degrees. There's a current of magic in this day that has begun with lighted windows, presents, and songs. I can't help but hum *Deck the Halls* and skip every few steps as I walk to the main lobby.

DENALI SUMMER

Wanda wears the red nose from my stocking. Yesterday after work, I strung red velvet ribbon on the wall behind Shelby's rec room tree and clipped on the dozen stockings. When I checked before bed last night, only Gabby hadn't plucked hers down. Her gift from the day before lay under the tree as well. Part of me is paranoid she's guessed her presents were coming from me and didn't want them anymore. The other part figures Gabby isn't that into our fake Christmas.

"Merry Christmas, Rudolph," I say, glad someone appreciated my present.

Wanda pulls a small green bag from behind her and holds it out for me. "Merry Christmas."

I take the bag and pull out the tissue paper. Inside there's a magnet that reads, "Wag more. Bark less," as well as a jar of fireweed honey.

"I don't know if you like tea," Wanda says, "but that's the honey I use to sweeten mine. You can taste the Alaska."

I wrap Wanda into a hug, inhaling the sharp scent of her shirt's detergent along with a softer lavender smell coming from her neck. "These are so perfect. I'm saving every drop of honey for when I'm home but want to be back here."

Wanda laughs. "Then you might want to pick up a few more bottles."

The morning runs smoothly and quickly with a steady stream of in-person guest questions and calls about check-in. I'm surprised when Wanda lets me know it's already time for my break. Flint will be working breakfast, and Gabby usually eats around this time. Under the front desk I've stashed her final present as well as a set of red baking spatulas I bought

CHAPTER TWENTY-TWO

for Flint as a follow-up gift. I grab the presents—Gabby's wrapped in red foil paper, Flint's simply tied together with curling ribbon—and wave goodbye to Wanda.

Flint wears a Santa hat while working the breakfast line.

"Hey there, Santa's helper." I hold the cluster of spatulas in front of my face. "One more little thing for you." I extend them forward, and he reaches for the spatulas over the glass.

"I'll use these when I redeem my coupon. Thank you." His eyes are twinkling and happy. If he weren't so tall, he'd make an excellent elf.

"And when might that be?" There aren't many nights before my family comes, so I want to get this decided. No one's behind me in the line, so now's as good a time as any.

"I was thinking on your birthday eve."

"That works. And I ordered all the ingredients. No pilfering from the kitchen needed."

"Everything? You have eggs?"

"Ummm. We'll have to pilfer a few eggs."

"What about butter?"

"Right. So. I have all the dry ingredients plus some fancy vanilla Shelby made me order, but we'll need eggs and butter."

He laughs. "I will have the eggs and butter." The hazel in his eyes fires more brightly with yellow today. "And I have a Christmas present for you. Any chance I can lure you to my room this afternoon?"

"Absolutely." I would very much like to be lured. "But you didn't have to..." I don't finish my half-hearted protest because at that moment Gabby bumps up beside me. "What's a girl got to do to get some pancakes around here?"

Flint makes her a plate with two pancakes, scooping a spoonful of eggs beside them. "For everyone else today they have to sing a carol for their food, but gift shop employees get a pass. I've heard you're all terrible singers."

"Good because I don't sing." Gabby takes her plate and sets it on her tray.

I place the lumpy, wrapped tee there as well. "Secret Santa. Final delivery. Hope I was a half-way okay elf."

"Really, you? After the poncho, I thought maybe Kendra because she knows I like the Rockets."

"I did know that, so I told Dawn," Kendra says, joining us in line.

"Thank you," Gabby says, elbowing her lightly then turns back to me, "And you were more than half-way okay. I got my armbands and stocking thing this morning. It's all been great."

After Gabby walks away, I give Flint and Kendra my best, what-the-hell face. "Was that Gabby being nice?"

"I told you," Kendra says.

Flint nods. "She appears to be softening toward you. Time and presents have done the trick."

"More like a Christmas miracle," I say.

After my shift, I shower and change into a red sweater dress, black tights, and black ballerina flats—an outfit I had no business packing but am happy to have for

CHAPTER TWENTY-TWO

today. Cozy, festive, and fitted in a way that makes me feel curvy not stumpy. Until I'm sure Flint will be in his room, I attempt to read but can't get into my book. I flick through music on my phone and play a few games before I decide he'll be ready for me.

His hair, wet from his own shower, is a darker shade of red and matches his rust-colored corduroys. The shirt he's changed into features a Texas-grown band. He's worn it before, and I've already told him I like them. The punctuated bluesy beat of my favorite song from their first album floats from somewhere behind him. Flint lets me in and stretches toward his dresser for a small box wrapped in brown paper. Scratched across the top in red marker it says, *Merry Christmas, Dawn. Love, Flint.*

My breath catches. It's jewelry small. I don't want jewelry small. Been there, done that at the beginning of the summer. But when he lets go, and I have the full weight of the box in my hand, it's weightless as though empty. A quick shake makes a tapping noise sans jingles or jangles. Promising.

I tear into the paper, and it drops to the ground. Inside the box are two concert tickets for the band on his shirt. A glance at the details—Dallas in September. My stomach flutters at the sight of a September date. September. I could be meeting up with Flint in September. The banjo picking slows as the song winds down, and the lead singers dip into their signature harmony, stretching out their final word as I scramble to find words of my own.

"These are... amazing. Best present ever. I mean it, Flint. Holy wow times a billion."

DENALI SUMMER

"And they're both your tickets. It's a no-strings ticket gift."

"What do you mean no strings?" I'd be okay with some strings connecting me and Flint.

"You don't have to take me, and if you don't want to take me, you won't see me there."

"But of course I want to take you."

"Then I'm there, but I don't want you to decide now. Decide in September. Go to school. Meet new people. Then decide."

The bubbling in my stomach deadens. "What are you really saying?"

His eyes lock into mine. He's scrambling for how to answer. "What do you mean?"

Stalling with a question—fine. I'll spell it out: "It sounds like you don't expect me to take you, like you expect me to bail on you once we're back in Texas."

"I don't expect anything," he grabs my hands, "that's my point."

"But I expect something! I expect that if what we're doing here stays this good all summer, we'll try to keep it going once we're back in Texas."

Flint plops on the bed and sighs. "I'm screwing this up." He lays back, folding his hands under his head and looks up at the ceiling. "I want that, but..."

"No buts." As soon as I say it, I hear Chris in my head, how he didn't listen to me. How he expected to make all the decisions until it finally drove me away. "No, I'm sorry. Finish what you were going to say." I sit down next to him and motion for him to scoot to make more room. He props himself up on his side, his back to the wall, and I lay on my side facing him.

CHAPTER TWENTY-TWO

Flint takes his free hand and rests it on my hip. "I like you, and I'd love to keep seeing you in Texas, but—" he pauses as if to see if I'll let him continue. I wait. "I also want you to experience college however you want to. At ETBU or anywhere you might want to transfer, and I can't be the deciding factor in any of these big decisions you have coming up."

I have to figure out me before I get too serious about another us. *The best thing that ever happened to you should be you.*

"Okay."

"That's it?"

"Sorta. I still want you to come to the concert with me." I brush my fingers along his clean-shaven face.

"Okay," he says finally, his breath warm against my hand.

I lean forward pressing my forehead to his. "Anything can happen, but a September concert date *will* happen."

"Anything?" A very flirty Flint grin accompanies this single word, a grin that makes me shift so that our lower bodies are touching, aligned, and I feel him get hard.

That was fast.

"What should happen before September?" he says it straight into my lips, so there is only one way to answer him. Every part of me presses against him. His hands go to my hair, against my face, over my body. My hands do the same. His lips are on my lips and my neck then return to my lips. We roll so that his body covers mine, and I inhale the spice of his after shave, the musky scent growing beneath it as he starts to get sweaty.

DENALI SUMMER

Dates roll through my head. It's July 25th. I leave Denali August 12th. Five of those days will be taken up with my family's visit. We don't have enough time, which makes me want to stop kissing him. It also makes me want take off my dress to speed things up in the time we have. Both. Neither. I don't know.

I never did go off the pill.

More dates—Tiger Camp Move-In and soccer camp starts August 14th. Classes start the 22nd. We keep kissing, and I wonder if I can skip move-in activities and a few days of camp, stay in Denali longer. We'll have September. I can work and get a car, and then we can have any weekend or school break we want.

Flint exhales, kisses the top of my nose, and pushes himself away, propped so he can look at me.

"What?" I ask.

He sinks forward again but presses his face into the covers beside me. "I want you."

"And I want you back," I say into his shoulder.

We lay there like that for a while, both caught in our own emotional conflicts until I wiggle an arm free and nudge for him to give me space. I scoot my body so that I'm sitting up, my back to his pillow. My dress scoots with me and Flint lays his head on my leg.

I thread my fingers into his hair and comb through it again and again. I don't care about ETBU in the fall. I definitely want this now. That's as much as I know.

Chocolate Chip Oatmeal Bars with Flint How-To:

1) Gift Flint recipe card on July Christmas Eve in his stocking. Watch him read over it while wearing flashing Rudolph nose.

2) Give Flint new red cookie spatula set and ingredients (I can't steal from kitchen) on July Christmas Day.

3) Set baking date (my bday eve)

4) pre-heat oven to 350°
   pre-heat Flint with initial kissing

5) beat butter, sugars, add eggs one at a time, add vanilla

6) Kissing break

7) mix in salt, baking powder, flour, rolled oats, one cup choc. chips

8) spread ½ of batter in a buttered pan

CHAPTER TWENTY-THREE

Oatmeal Bars...
(not done yet!)

9) ~~feed each other 2nd cup of choc chips~~

Yeah... no. We have self control. (Sometimes.)

9) Sprinkle 3/4 cup choc chips in pan (we had to eat some!)

10) Spread on the rest of the battar

11) Bake 30 min.

12) Find something to do while we wait (Ahem)

Birthday Eve = perfect

Can't wait for what's to come!

(18!!!)

CHAPTER TWENTY-FOUR

My brothers Dale and Dustin, along with Dale's best buddy since grade school, Rodney Hudson are approaching the front desk. Oh hell no. I don't know what this is, but it's not the crew of my eighteenth birthday guest list.

I don't rush out from behind the check-in desk to give a single hug. I cross my arms, stare into my oldest brother's brown eyes and say, "What are you doing here? Where are the girls?"

Wanda's taken the day off to be with her own family visitors, and her substitute is on break. I don't have to pretend to be nice.

"No girls. This is a Denali bachelor party trip," Rodney answers and slaps Dale on the back. "Dale's getting married."

I return my death stare to my oldest brother, "Yeah, I heard from Dolly. Thanks so much for bothering to spread the news yourself."

DENALI SUMMER

Not a birthday surprise but a bachelor trip invasion. I'm hot-pepper-judge-at-the-county-fair level on fire. Damn it all to hell, back, and then down to hell again but deeper where it's hotter to inflict more pain.

"Jesslyn was supposed to send you something."

"Well, she didn't," I say. The steam lifting off my body is about to combust and burn this whole place down to the damn ground.

Dustin, God bless him, looks confused. "Didn't you know we were coming?"

"No."

"You're about to be really ticked-off then."

It is not possible for me to be more ticked-off until it is. He looks back to the entrance, and I follow his gaze. This is beyond Mama's usual meddling. Between Mama and Daddy, smiling like a fool, walks Chris.

Dustin tries to excuse the site of Chris walking toward us. "I've been so busy with my project, I didn't know he was coming till this morning. I should have texted you then, but I didn't think, I mean I assumed...." Dustin wisely stops talking. He studies the expression on my face for another second before moving to a couch and picking up the closest magazine to hide in.

My head explodes. I'm seeing through the wave of fire, and I'm hearing Dale through the crackles. "It's my bachelor trip, and he's my friend, and I figured you'd be excited to see your boyfriend."

"We broke up," I say.

Dale lets out a low whistle. "Oops."

The only thing holding me even a teensy bit together at the moment is that the Bama twins are working, coming up behind my family with carts of

CHAPTER TWENTY-FOUR

luggage. These two are my friends. These two will help me right now.

"Josh, can you manage both carts? They go to rooms 104 and 106." Josh nods and turns around in the same instant. My, must-be-visible-to-all, ignited head has let on that this is not the place to be.

"Jake, will you find Amy? I need her to come in early to cover my last hour. And if you see Jonelle or Kendra, tell them to wait for me in my room."

I will gather my girls. I will den up and roll out with them tomorrow on the girl-trip backcountry night I planned for us. It will be minus my sisters as I'd hoped, but it will most definitely not be plus any of these conniving, manipulating...

"Happy Birthday, Dawn." Mama sets a large gift bag on the counter. I ignore it.

I turn to Daddy and hand him two hotel keys. "You're in 104 and 106. Go down that hallway where you saw your luggage disappear." I search the computer for further details of my family's reservation, details I'd sworn to Wanda I wouldn't look over until they checked in, but of course I'd peeked. "You've prebooked a dinner reservation for a party of seven in the hotel restaurant at six." (I'd assumed this was for five of them, me, and maybe a friend of MY choice, it being MY birthday and all.) "You have a reservation for two on the bus tour tomorrow morning at eight," (I still assume this is for Mama and Daddy which is why I felt safe planning a backcountry trip for my sisters.) "and a reservation for four to go rafting on your final day at ten in the morning." (Thought this was going to be for me and my sisters, and I'd already decided to lie and pretend as though I hadn't yet been.) "There's plenty of room in your schedule if you'd like to book more excursions. I haven't done it yet, but the helicopter ride to a glacier is supposed to be worth every penny of the price. They can take up to seven in one tour provided your combined weights don't go over—"

"Dawn Everly Wilkes." Mama's voice is tight and her face matches. "That is no way to greet your family and our guests."

That's it. I'm done. I step from behind the desk and stomp out of the lobby. As I pass the gift shop I holler in its direction, "Send someone to cover the front," then I pick up my pace jogging to the back exit where I slam open the door before sprinting all the way to my room.

I left my lanyard with my keys at the desk, so thankfully Kendra is already on my side of the quad to let me in. But as I'm about to pass through the door to unload my frustrations, she points behind me.

Chris followed.

"I'll be next door if you need me," Kendra says.

I'm not inviting Chris inside. Instead, I press my back to the wall beside my door and slide to a squat, pushing my hands to my face, so I don't have to look at him. The pressure releases some tension, and I move my hands across my forehead, kneading two fingers on each side at my temples, keeping my eyes closed all the while.

"I'm sorry," Chris begins, then he lowers himself to the ground beside me, sitting so his knees are at his chin. "I was going for the grand gesture. I thought you'd be happy."

"I guess you should have thought for two seconds that if I called to break up with you, that if I wasn't

CHAPTER TWENTY-FOUR

writing you back or texting you, then maybe I didn't want a grand gesture. Maybe, just maybe, I would not be happy."

"Maybe so, but..."

"No buts, Chris. How could you keep this from me when I called?"

"I had to. This trip was meant to be a surprise."

"But I broke up with you. Didn't you think you should have told my family and bowed out?"

"I talked to Charlet, and she said you hadn't mentioned anyone new, and when Dale asked me to be part of the wedding and told me about the trip, it felt like fate or something."

Or something. I sigh. I roll my eyes. "What's it matter if I'm with someone else or not, and why's Dale even here? How in a million years did Mama think to ruin my birthday with Dale's bachelor crap?"

"Ruin?" There is definitely a wounded puppy thing going on in Chris's expression when he repeats this word.

"Fact is," I say, "the surprise got a little spoiled. I knew someone was coming, but I didn't know who. I expected it was a girl's thing. Maybe Daddy, but mostly that Mama was truly doing something for me, for my birthday."

"Your mama thought bringing me here was doing something for you."

"But we broke up!"

His hair's grown since graduation, and maybe he's been eating too much of that movie theater popcorn, but his face has already filled out with the first few pounds of his freshman fifteen. It's been two months, and he's already changing.

DENALI SUMMER

I need him to see that we both get to change.

I slide and shift so that I'm fully seated, but we're not touching.

Chris goes on, "And it was supposed to be a girl's trip, but Daisy couldn't get off work, and Darlene made some last-minute bonus that qualified her for a reward trip this same week. At first, Mama suggested Dolly still come, and Charlet could take a ticket, but Dale got fussy saying it should be family—that he and Dustin should come before Charlet. Not a week later he convinced Dolly to give up her spot, so he could have a bachelor trip. At first Rodney couldn't get off work, so Dale asked me. I'm not technically a groomsman, more like an usher or an extra helper. Then Rodney was able to come, and you know your Mama never says no to Dale. So she bought another plane ticket. She put her foot down on another room though, said we could double up or alternate on the floor. I never cared about that, kinda hoped I'd be crashing with you."

I jerk my head. "You're not."

He throws up his hands. "Okay. Got it."

Chris brushes aside my bangs and touches the side of my face. "Aren't you even a little glad to see me?"

If Chris had been waiting for me the day I got back from camping with Sugar, my knee screwed up, my hope in the decency of the male species strongly wounded, I would have sunk into his arms and taken all the familiar comfort he had to give. Hell, I might have cut my summer short and gone home with him.

But not now. Now I have a favorite husky named Timber who whimpers for me the instant I'm in sight. Now I have co-worker turned friend in Wanda who

CHAPTER TWENTY-FOUR

relaxes around me as though I'm the non-bitchy daughter she never had. Now I have my circle of gals— Jonelle's girls-can-do-anything strength, Vanessa's vibrancy and never-ending abilities, Shelby's over-the-topness that works because it often manifests as generosity, and Kendra who's an all-around awesome friend—supportive and fun, never assumptive or bossy. Even Gabby—who's rough at times, but I think she'd have my back.

Now I have Flint.

And there's all that I've done and decided and experienced that has altered how I see things, what I think I can do. I've gotten on trails again in the backcountry without re-screwing up my knee. I've danced in Cantwell. I've melted the exterior of bad-ass Gabby with my solid Christmas effort. I didn't let Sugar get to me. I stood up to him, and I carried on with the summer I wanted. Needed.

But if I say no again, I'll break Chris's heart.

"I'm not ready to see you. I wanted a whole summer off."

"I waited and did everything I was told for most of the summer, two-thirds of the summer really. Can't we compromise a little?"

"Way to force the compromise."

He smiles the smile of a boy who's used to getting his way. "Come to dinner, Dawn. Hear your Mama out. Open up your gift. Let tonight be about you."

I'll cut Dustin some slack, but unless I can ditch Dale, Rodney, and Chris from the birthday dinner, it's not at all about me. Youngest child. Deal with sharing. Story of my life. I've got the same two choices I've always had: pitch a fit or keep the peace.

It's only five days. It's only five days. It's only five days. And this day is half-way over. I can play along. I'll keep the peace for this trip.

I ignore the next thought that comes to my brain as an exasperated question—but can you keep it up for another whole year after that?

"Tell my mama and daddy I'll be at supper," I say.

"Can we go for a hike or something till then?"

"Go on and tell them. I started my shift at five a.m., and I usually nap in the afternoon." Taking the easy route with a little lie, oh yes I am. "I'll see you at the restaurant."

I stand up with Chris and let him hug me goodbye which would be fine if it weren't for the fact that Flint comes around the side of the rec center and sees us, his face pulling to a pronounced frown before continuing on to his room.

As soon as Chris is out of sight, I go after Flint. He's left his door open like he knew I'd be coming.

"Was that one of your brothers?" he asks. He's sitting on his bed, his pack upside down between his legs. Camping gear lays haphazardly around him on the blanket and the floor. He's stuffing his sleeping bag into the lowest compartment of the pack with short angry punches, making it clear he already knows the answer to his question.

I lift a cook stove from the bed and sit next to him. "No, but they're here too plus another friend of Dale's."

"Why?"

I tell him what Chris told me, making clear at every chance I didn't know, didn't ask for this, and certainly didn't want it. As I talk he continues packing, sometimes pacing because he can't find something,

CHAPTER TWENTY-FOUR

but it's always right under his nose. He's blind with frustration.

When I decided to plan a girl's camping trip for my sisters which included Jonelle—he cooked up a trip to go to the bus with Elijah. As good a time as any for him to go because I'd long since decided the twenty-mile Stampede Trail with its sketchy river crossings was not on my summer musts. I've been nervous about Flint wanting to go, but after fussing the way I did when he worried about me on Horseshoe Lake solo, I wasn't about to ask him not to do it.

"At least I won't be around much while they're here," he says.

"Me neither. I made my trip a one-nighter because I knew my sisters wouldn't do more, but if Jonelle and Kendra are game, I'll extend it. Seriously. I'm not hanging around to entertain them. Dale's bachelor trip is more important than my birthday or what I want—that message is clear, so they can enjoy their vacation without me."

"You really going to say that to them?"

"Something like it."

"Good luck."

I expect him to come over and kiss me, but he doesn't. The Flint of last night's kitchen date is not the same Flint here with me now. He yanks the drawstring at the top of his pack, mashes down the extra fabric, and snaps it shut.

"I'm supposed to be meeting Elijah to catch our ride to the trail head," he looks at his phone, "now."

"Come find me as soon as you're back. I want you to tell me everything."

"Yeah, see you then."

DENALI SUMMER

He steps toward the door, but I grab his arm. "Hey."
In response he gives my cheek a quick, perfunctory peck, sans a final reassuring squeeze.
He's gone without even wishing me a happy birthday.

CHAPTER TWENTY-FIVE

I enter the hotel restaurant through the back entrance, stepping first into the kitchen then through a small area where the servers hang out. Shelby grabs me by the shoulders and looks me straight in the eyes.

"Kendra told me what's going on. I'll be your server tonight, so if you need me to spill water on anyone, a subtle point to my victim, and I'm on it."

The peacekeeper in me ebbs away as I think about how I can use Shelby's willingness to retaliate against my oldest brother. A freezing cold dump into Dale's lap might get me feeling better. Because what the hell? Talking Dolly out of coming and inviting Chris on this trip? He can fix all my cracked phone screens and repair any car I ever hope to own, but from here on out he's first and foremost an ass.

"Do we have to stop at one glass of water?"

Shelby grins. "Oh, girl. What do you have in mind?"

Dale and Dustin have the same dusty brown hair and deep-brown eyes as me, but Dale's shorter and thicker than Dustin, and he's got some old acne scars on his cheeks, so I'm pretty sure Shelby understands her target. We go through possibilities but overall, the plan is excellent service for everyone but Dale. Plain and simple.

By the time I step into the dining room, my family has been seated. The only remaining chair is beside Chris and across from Mama. I'd hoped to beat them and claim a seat on the end so as not to be next to anyone, but I took too long with Shelby. It'll be worth it though.

"You going to open your present now?" Mama asks instead of a greeting. At my spot sits the gift I'd ignored this morning—a tall navy bag overflowing with gold tissue paper. I guess ETBU colors are the default from here on out.

I stand behind my chair and pull each tuft of paper, letting them fall to the floor beside me. This lasts six sheets before I reach a soft clump wrapped in tissue paper which, once torn away, reveals a blush-colored pink dress. I hold it out in front of me. It's strapless and knee length and looks like it'll fit, but it's not something I need.

"Keep at it," Mama bosses.

At the bottom of the bag is a shoe-box. Inside a pair of gold strappy heals shimmer in the restaurant's overhead lights, around them is a pair of dangly gold earrings, and a small gold clutch purse. I check inside and find fifty dollars.

My first thought—prom's passed. My next thought—oh hell, this has to do with Dale's wedding. I silently gather the paper around my feet and re-stuff it in the

CHAPTER TWENTY-FIVE

bag. After taking the bag off the table and setting it beside my chair, I sit down. Peace be damned.

"Lemme guess. Darlene, Dolly, and Daisy got the same bag, and they didn't have to turn eighteen to get it."

"Their purses didn't have fifty dollars," Daddy says at the same time Mama kicks me, literally kicks me, under the table. I crouch over to rub my shin, thankful I'd worn jeans, and Mama always wears rounded leather flats and not something pointier.

"Does this mean we're all in the wedding?" I turn to Dale, "Isn't that something Jesslyn is supposed to ask me?" And shouldn't have usurped my eighteenth birthday present. The twins got a car when they turned eighteen—one to share—but still, a car.

"Mama, you explain it. I never can keep straight what all Jesslyn has going on," Dale says.

Mama goes into the whole spiel of who's doing what. Apparently, Darlene's a bridesmaid, the twins are singing, and I'm a greeter that gets to stand by the guestbook.

"When's all this happening?" I ask.

"August 7th," Mama and Dale say together.

"That's," I calculate it out. "That's a week from tomorrow."

"Getting married on a Sunday afternoon cause it's cheaper."

"I'm not leaving here till the 12th. I can't come."

"Wedding has to be then. It's got to be before school starts, or we wait till winter. She doesn't want to be big for the pictures, and I don't want her to be big for the honeymoon." Jesslyn teaches pre-k, so I get their schedule, but that still shouldn't mean I have to change my plans.

Shelby chooses this moment to show up with our drink orders. She delivers everyone their coke, no one bothered to get tea since it's unsweetened here, and has a water for Dale this time. She sets it right at the edge of the table and lets go so it falls, splashing onto Dale's crotch.

Dale jumps backward, glass thudding to the floor, the light blue denim of his jeans splashed dark across his whole lap.

"Sorry!" Shelby squeaks. "Let me get you some napkins."

Dale wipes the water on his chair with the one large cloth napkin he has and sits back down. "Crap that's cold."

"You could go change," Mama says.

"I'll be fine," he mumbles toward his lap as though he's unsure.

Mama hands her napkin to Dale, but she's looking from me to Daddy and back to me. Daddy clears his throat. "What we'd hoped," he starts, "is that you'd cut this trip a little short."

"There's no way I'm—" I have been ganged up on. Again.

"Here us out, baby. If you changed your ticket so you came back with us, you could be a real help. We'd match what you're making here if you'd babysit Jesslyn's girl while she's running around doing the final wedding touches, and then when they're off on the honeymoon, she'll stay with us, and you'll be in charge of taking care of her, earning money for that too." Daddy is using his everybody-settle-down voice,

CHAPTER TWENTY-FIVE

but it's not working on me this time. Maybe because I'm tired of Daddy siding with Mama instead of me. Maybe because Chris is rubbing on my leg in his own effort to soothe. I swat his hand and turn toward Daddy.

"This isn't fair to me. This trip is how I chose to spend my graduation money—"

This time Mama cuts me off. "Being home early would give you time to shop and get everything you need for your dorm room without being so rushed."

"I already told you. It doesn't matter—"

But I don't get to finish sentences anymore. Mama continues, "It's your first sibling to get married, Dawn. Our first family wedding. We all need to be there, and Daddy and I are serious about paying you whatever you're getting here for the babysitting. You are needed at home."

That is meant to be the end of the discussion.

Welcome to adulthood, Dawn. Your Mama plans your life here too.

I do my best to dead-leg Chris under the table and hiss, "You could have warned me."

Shelby's antics with Dale are my only reprieve at this meal. She never does bring Dale any more napkins or another glass of water. Shortly after our food arrives, Shelby adds another salt and pepper shaker to the table, but loosens the salt lid and drops it onto Dale's plate, dousing his dinner, rendering it inedible.

She whisks the plate away and smiles. "It's just not your night, is it?"

The rest of us are finished before Shelby even comes back to tell Dale his meal will be a few more minutes. He grumbles that he may as well have it boxed to go.

DENALI SUMMER

"Sure thing!" Shelby says without bothering to apologize again. When she returns, she doesn't have Dale's box but a huge brownie a la mode topped with a candle. Three other servers join in with Shelby to sing the birthday song and clap when I blow out the candle—my first true birthday moment of the day.

As soon as they leave, Mama says to Daddy, "Did you order that?" And when Daddy shakes his head no, she says low, but not low enough for me to miss, "Make sure it's not on the bill." And just like that, happy birthday moment over.

As we wait to pay, Dustin and Rodney want to know about back country permits, and I find myself agreeing to take them even though it'll mean delaying my own trip.

It's not until we're standing up to leave that Shelby gives Dale his box. He pops the lid to peak at his food, but everything's wrapped tightly in foil.

Daddy tries to talk me into taking him and Mama on a nearby trail after their bus tour. I think he feels bad about how Mama steamrolled me. I'm vague about my plans and tell him I'm not sure how long we'll be getting the permit, and after that I'm needed at the husky kennel, and then we'll have to see how late it is.

"It's not like it gets dark around here," he says.

"I'll let you know tomorrow, Dad." My tone and the fact that I didn't call him Daddy registers on his face.

In my room, a much better party is assembled: Jonelle, Gabby, Kendra, Vanessa, and Shelby, who clocked out right after we paid. Vanessa has cupcakes which I can't even look at after refusing to share

CHAPTER TWENTY-FIVE

my over-sized restaurant dessert, but the rest of the girls dig in.

As they eat, Shelby explains her final Dale prank of the night. "When he unwraps that foil, all he'll find are those napkins I never brought him."

"Will you get in trouble if he comes back into the restaurant?" I ask.

"I explained it all to the manager. She's on our side. I told her, if he came back to complain, she should say that his ruined night was our birthday gift to you. It's not like his dinner was on the bill or anything. We don't owe him a thing."

"Did my Dad even leave you a tip?"

"Ten percent—more than I expected."

I'd offer to make up the difference, but I know Shelby doesn't care about the money, and like she said, that was her birthday gift to me. A damn fine one too. Much better than an outfit for a wedding that's ruining the end of my summer.

When I show and explain the contents of my birthday bag, they're torn on what I should I do.

Jonelle and Shelby think a sibling's wedding, a family event of that importance, should push up my plans. Kendra, Vanessa, and Gabby agree that the conflict blows, but I've got to stop letting my family push me around.

"Would Dale cancel his plans for your wedding?" Vanessa asks.

"If Mama told him he had to, yeah, probably."

"Does anybody in your family go against your mom?" Gabby asks.

I think on this. "Dustin missed the twin's high school graduation ceremony. He had to be at school to finish up some research grant. Mama didn't like that much, but she got over it. Last year Dale missed Christmas to go on a trip with Jesslyn's family, but that's about it."

"There are six of you!" Vanessa says. "It's not reasonable to think you'll all be at all the family things from here on through eternity. That's ridiculous." A girl with blue hair wearing shimmery lime-green tights and a yellow dress, sitting on a unicorn blanket under an emoji towel used as wall art is calling my family ridiculous. And she is so right.

"It's awful. And it's worse since Flint will be on the Stampede Trail tomorrow and into the next day, and I'll have all of one day with him if I leave with my family."

"Wait, so Flint's a consideration? He's more than a summer fling?" Kendra asks.

"Before today I was thinking about pushing *back* my travel date and missing move-in week activities. He lives in Texas. We have plans to go to a concert in Dallas in September." In other words, yes.

Jonelle is not swayed. "If it's meant to be with Flint you can hook up in Texas, but you can't miss your brother's wedding. It sucks big time, but it's still your family."

"Weddings are important," Shelby agrees.

"Gee, Shelby, I'm shocked to hear *you* say that."

We go around and around, but the vote remains at two for the wedding, three against, and me stuck in undecided land as usual.

omg chris wtf even for you.

At Riley Creek

<u>My</u> flat rock. <u>My</u> sunning spot.

Taken! ☹

A woman sits like Buddha
fat rolling over tan cut-offs
short strings long enough
to mingle with her leg hair
shirt, a split strata
of earth tones, merely
a scarf pressing breasts
to chest.
Fireweed tiara crowns
sandy hair

Is my rock her enlightenment tree?
How many more days till her awakening?

Because my days are running out.

I want it back!

this birthday sucks.

CHAPTER TWENTY-SIX

I help my brothers, Rodney, and Chris with a permit in the Savage River section for the night, tell them what I know about the area, and part ways with them at the door of the information center. Then I turn right back around for my own permit so Jonelle, Kendra, and I can get going as well. We'll hike Polychrome as planned, just for three instead of six. Then I head back to the hotel.

I find Kendra in the dark of her room, curled into a ball on her bed. "Migraine," she whispers. "Give me four hours, and I can get up. Promise."

On my side of the room there's a note from Jonelle saying she had to cover Zeke's ten a.m. raft tour, but she's still good to go after lunch.

I grab my journal and take off for my sunning rock only to find it's already occupied by some hippy from Healy. Fine. I'll cancel all out-in-nature plans for the morning. Point taken, universe.

But the universe isn't done. On my way back to

CHAPTER TWENTY-SIX

the hotel, the sky opens up with the heaviest downpour we've had all summer. By the time I reach my room, my hair and clothes are soaked through, my feet and hands are tight with cold, and all I want to do is strip naked and crawl into my bed and cry.

I take a hot shower instead, doing my best to keep quiet for Kendra who still hasn't moved.

I'm angry. I'm bored. I can't even offer to work because I'm trying to avoid my parents. Flint's out in this mess, and that has me worried.

After dressing in jeans and a sweater, I crawl into my bed, but I don't cry. I pull out a color sheet and let my mind go numb.

Jonelle taps on my door a little after one o'clock.

"Thirty minutes into the raft ride, and the rain came. Thought we were all going to drown. I'm so wiped." In other words, please don't tell me you want to camp in this rain, Dawn. She has nothing to worry about; I don't.

"Today's a wash. It happens." This is a kinder, more accepting take on the day than I'm feeling inside, but what else is there to say?

Jonelle lifts a wad of cash out of her pocket. "The good news is tourists who think you've saved their lives are really good tippers. Want to go into town for lunch? I'll treat."

"Not hungry." As I say this, I realize I haven't eaten anything today, but I don't care. I'm not up for leaving my room.

"Maybe we can still get in a day hike tomorrow."
"Maybe."

Jonelle looks confused, like she's not sure what to do with mopey Dawn.

"I'll come by in the morning then?" she asks.

"Sure. See you then."

I close the door and get back in bed and don't move until Vanessa comes in hours later. She jostles my shoulder and waves a sheet of hotel stationary in front of my face. "Your mom left this at the front desk, and Wanda asked me to bring it to you."

The note reads:

Is your cell phone off, or am I not getting reception? You dad and I are attending the Cabin Nite Dinner Theater. We made a reservation for three for the 5:00 meal. Please meet us in the lobby at 4:45.

Flint and I had planned on going to this on my last night. No, I do not want to attend with my parents. I check my phone and see that it's only a few minutes after four, and that I have five texts from my mom starting with,

Loved the bus tour. We saw two moose on the way out. Coming back, the rain made it hard to spot animals. Going to relax in our room for a while. What should we do for dinner tonight?

And then,

We had lunch at the snack shack and met your roommate Vanessa. Her cupcakes are truly the best I've had. Fun girl. Also spoke to Wanda who said the nicest things about working with you. She recommended the Cabin Nite Dinner Theater. We want you to come. Is 5:00 or 7:30 better?

And,

We're going on a walk on the Oxbow Trail now that the rain has stopped. Join us?

And,

CHAPTER TWENTY-SIX

We made a reservation for three for the 5pm. Please meet us in the lobby.

And finally,

Are you getting my texts?!?

I reply with a sick-faced emoji and add,

Not feeling well. Came back to bed after helping the guys get their permit. Phone was off—sorry. Go on to dinner without me. Have fun. Haven't been yet but hear it's great.

She sends back a sad face and nothing else. Finally—no Mama push back.

I'm ready for dinner but The Zoo doesn't start serving till five.

"Do we have any cupcakes left?" I ask Vanessa, who's already on her bed, nose in a book.

"One—the one you didn't eat last night." She points to the box across the room on our dresser.

They've left me a lemon drop cupcake. Thank goodness for roommates who don't go in for a second cupcake. I haven't tried this one yet, but the hint of lemon in the buttercream and the tangy lemon filling are the pick-me-up flavors my tongue didn't know it wanted.

Kendra and Vanessa are both ready for dinner at five. Kendra apologizes for being out all day, "My meds work, but then they knock me out dead tired."

"Same here on the dead tired. But no migraine and no meds."

"You're stressed." She hugs me. "You decide anything about your brother's wedding?"

"No. I've avoided Mamma and Daddy all day, so I didn't have to."

"Good plan. And we can go on a day hike tomorrow and keep avoiding decisions and parents."

But at dinner the restaurant manager pushes Kendra to take a lunch shift to cover for servers who are out, and Jonelle finds me to say Zeke's still sick. With Elijah gone, she has to cover him all day. There's a bug going around the staff that's left me on my own again. I've got two options to avoid my parents—use work or go into the back country alone.

CHAPTER TWENTY-SEVEN

I'm on the earliest bus, a must since I've picked a section more than three hours into the park. The camping plan had been for Polychrome, but the ranger warned us of steep inclines and loose rocks—a section best not to go alone in case of falls. For a solo day-hike, I switched to Stony Dome for its smooth and gradual inclines.

The early morning is too wrapped in fog for tourists to be calling out animal sightings. While it's quiet, I'm in and out of sleep on the bumpy road. When the gray haze lifts about a half-hour out from my stop, the colors, coming to life across the ridge lines, excite the tourists around me. I snap a few pictures on my phone and attempt to text one to Flint.

I'm here. Where are you?

But the message fails as I expect it to.

At my stop the driver opens the door and says, "Have fun in the food chain." I think this is a joke, but he doesn't smile. A middle-aged woman in the first seat protests that I shouldn't be hiking alone. I smile and wave to both as though I didn't hear.

Standing by the side of the road, I wait until the bus grows small in the distance, and disappears around a curve.

I'm alone. In the backcountry. Of Denali.

"Bears, go on and get. Dawn's coming!" I holler into the breeze and step further away from the road.

I hike for an hour, first through a tundra meadow spotted in a yellow flower Wanda calls silverweed then up a gradual slope threaded over with blueberry bushes. Bear food. At the first land bench I'll stop for water and pull out my bear spray. I pluck a purplish berry and pop it into my mouth then wince at the sour flavor. Or maybe the bears are smart enough to know they should wait another week or so, and I have nothing to worry about.

A ptarmigan followed by a clutch of chicks erupts from a bush before me, and I laugh as they scurry ahead, indignant over my disruption. The laughter feels good, and I give into it—let it grow against the fear gnawing my nerves. I'm standing in the depths of Denali all alone. Jagged brown peaks of the Alaska Range loom beside and beyond, and the alpine meadow where I began my incline after turning out of the stream drainage I'd used to get beyond the road is far enough away that I'm impressed with my own pace. In this landscape of the magnanimous, I am a passing, insignificant speck. Worries over an earlier Alaska departure or disappointing my family or college or Flint... what's it matter when, at the moment, I'm just another member of the food chain?

CHAPTER TWENTY-SEVEN

It's a slow ascent, but I'm shivering by the time I reach a flat stopping point, so I pull out my gloves with the bear spray then gulp down a quarter of the water in one of the two Nalgenes I packed. I have my eye on a saddle of tundra between two peaks and aim to get there, so I can settle in to snack on my gorp and pull out my journal.

At the next smoother land bench, a pile of bear scat gives me pause. I'm no expert, but this does not look dusty with time, and a nudge with my boot confirms its give and freshness. I scan the upper ridgeline for bears, but all I notice is a wooden sign post uprooted and face-down on the ground. In a few quick steps I'm at the sign, kicking it over, confirming the suspicion that has risen within me: *Closed due to bear activity.* My heart quickens and my brain tingles in recalling a story about a photographer killed by a bear a few years back. When exactly had that been? What section of the park? And what happened to the bear?

I spin around to begin my trek downward but after scanning the area, I freeze. There's a large grizzly below me. As he came down, I'd been behind, too concentrated on my footfalls to realize what had probably passed only a hundred yards ahead on the mountain. He's facing away, but he's stalled, so I stall. I can't decide if I should continue my climb away from this bear even though it puts me deeper into the closed section, or if I should wait here and pray the bear moves on down the mountain, so I can hustle back to the road.

The bear turns his head in my direction, making the decision for me—stay put.

Please don't kill me. Please don't kill me.

DENALI SUMMER

My mind races through bear safety training, and though my whole body feels weighted, I manage to lift my arms and wave them over my head, hoping they make my short self appear taller, more threatening. "Hey, bear! Go away, bear!" Fear cracks the words as I attempt to speak them.

As I make the motion, I realize the stupidity of this. I'm just too damn short. The bear, as if to prove my point, raises to a standing position. Even from this distance, he looks the size of three-of-me-tall.

Okay, bear. Get a good look at me and move on.

I attempt more power as I yell, "Go on, bear. You go on your way, and I'll go on mine."

Not happening. He continues watching me, then tilts his nose to the air.

"Get, you. Leave me alone. Outta here. You need to—" The sentence freezes in my throat.

The bear drops and charges.

This can't be happening. Turns out a bear can cross the distance of a football field faster than any kickoff returner I've ever seen. My brain scrambles as I'm trying to remember what I'm supposed to do. My bear spray shaking in my hand, I know I'm not supposed to run, but do I stand and face him or get down and play dead? I can't imagine standing up to this bear, so I thud to the ground. Curling my legs beneath me and tucking my nose between my knees, I press my forehead to the tundra while folding my hands over my hair. Somehow in this process, I drop my bear spray. A quick calculation of my backpack's contents to determine how many layers stand between the bear's claws and my spine does not make me feel better. Damn my morning's determination to pack lightly.

CHAPTER TWENTY-SEVEN

This grizzly does not believe in false charges, and he pounds his way to me. I brace for the weight, about as much as Daddy's pickup, to crush me into the ground, but the bear slows at the last second and stops beside my body.

He snorts, rank breath invading my tiny air space. I will myself not to quiver or shudder, hiccup or flinch. If I flinch, he'll eat my fingers. And I can't cry. If I cry, he'll eat my face. Mama will not have the same sense of satisfaction fussing, "I told you not to go to Alaska," toward a closed casket.

The bear sniffs and grunts, whipping rough fur across my hands. Low rumbles like little earthquakes rattle through me. I imagine his thoughts—how did that barking tree turn into this here rock? Weirdest rock I ever saw, but will it taste good?—then plead with my brain to go numb.

A nudge jostles me sideways, but I lock in, refusing to expose my face. A second of nothing before a huff and a pounce. Paws crashing onto my back leave me breathless. His weight on my body deepens my imprint on the spongy earth. Piercing pain attacks my forehead as a rock rips into my skin like shrapnel. The bear lifts and circles then digs near my shoulder. One claw slip, and I'm sliced open. He bats at my hands, and the skin on my hands up onto my forearm stings in protest.

I don't want to die here. I want my life. Mine. Where I make decisions for myself. I don't want to go to ETBU, and I'm desperate to keep living for whatever else is out there for me instead.

And I do want to see my family again. I want to tear up as Jesslyn walks down the aisle and agrees to spend the rest of her life with my asshole brother. I want to be with Flint, and I want to make that clear to Chris. If I ever get to leave this spot alive, I'll be damned sure to make all that happen.

The bears huffs again near my face, the foul odor of his breath stilling my thoughts. I picture his every step, calculate every noise according to its proximity to my body.

How much time passes? A minute, an hour? The bear backs off but not away—the kicking and pawing sounds as though he's still in striking range. I remain hunched, egg-like, at the mercy of a bear who, in a flash, could crack me open.

Another stretch of silence, and I'm less certain where he looms. A thud makes me think he's flipped the sign as I did, putting him about ten feet away. I dare to hope.

I'll live. I'll face Mama. I'll say every bottled up thing to her face. After today, I can do anything.

More silence before a more distant thud, a full snort, then finally the most beautiful rhythmic thumping of heavy paws fades softer and softer, lengthening the distance between deathly grizzly and too-young-to-die me.

I remain frozen on the ground, wanting to make sure the bear doesn't double back around. I count, slipping Mississippis through numbers to guarantee I don't rush, all the way up to five hundred before I unlock my hands, set palms to the ground, and turn my head. A cluster of baby-blue forget-me-nots blurs in the foreground. Torn earth and an uprooted shrub are all that remain of the bear. Tingles pierce through my sleeping legs as I stretch and stand while the grizzly

CHAPTER TWENTY-SEVEN

slides at an angle up the mountainside, small as a tuft of Texas tumbleweed.

Food chain, my ass. Nothing out here wants to eat sassy, scrawny me. I feel for my forehead and my fingers come away sticky with blood, its rusty scent wrinkles my nose. I kick at the offending rock, uprooting it from its spongy surroundings. Another kick bounces it forward. A third kick sends it tumbling ahead down the mountain side. Teach that rock to bite at me. My shoulder stings, and a glance back shows my fleece is torn through, and there's an angry red scratch running from the base of my right thumb halfway to my elbow. I'll be needing a little patching up. Time to get back to the road.

As I trek to the park highway to wait for a ride, I edit and re-edit what parts of my hike to include when I have to face my family. That ptarmigan and her line of chicks bumbling ahead once I'd flushed them from their bush. Those forget-me-nots—their small beauty, their flash of color an immediate apology.

But I have to report this to a ranger, the details of the bear, our location in the park, it's proximity to the sign. My family will find out. When I reach the level meadow, I pull the straps of my backpack so it's tighter against my body and jog all the way to the road. Once stopped, I drink the rest of the water from the bottle I'd started then re-inspect my arms. The red slash on my arm seems to be glowing brighter, probably fed by the increase of blood pumping from my jog. Now that I'm still, I'm aware again of the throb in my forehead and shoulder. I don't have a mirror, but I can feel the small dent at the start of my hairline where my face had been pressed against that stupid rock. The blood is still wet where I'd hoped it would have become dried and flaky.

Before long, the truck of a patrol ranger rumbles into sight from the direction of the Eielson Center.

"Need a lift?" he asks.

"I do, and—" I exhale. Here goes nothing. "I have to report a bear issue. An attack I guess, but I'm fine." I hold up my arm. "He did give me this scratch though."

I can't look too pitiful because instead of climbing out to help me, he reaches across and pushes open the door from the inside. "Got a cut on your forehead too."

I toss my backpack onto the floorboard and hoist myself onto the seat. "That was a rock. I did the whole crouch-and-play-dead thing."

This ranger is young but thorough. He walks me through the whole story twice, nodding as he listens, releasing low whistles of surprise both times I describe the bear's pounce against my backpack.

"You might have dropped too soon. That's why he sniffed you out. Curious was all. There's a good chance if you'd held your ground he'd have veered off. This is the first report of bear contact at Stony Dome."

"Sir. With all due respect, I'm right at five foot three. My standing height isn't much taller than me crouched over in a ball on the ground."

This makes him laugh, but then he notices my leg bouncing, and his expression gets serious. "You feeling agitated?"

"Wouldn't you be?"

"How about nauseas or dizzy?"

I consider for a second before telling him no.

CHAPTER TWENTY-SEVEN

He looks into my eyes, taking his own off the road long enough for me to be uncomfortable. I didn't survive a bear attack only to die in a car wreck.

"Your pupils look all right," he says, "but you could still be in shock from the trauma. We should get you to the hospital in Anchorage."

"I don't want to go to Anchorage." If I go to Anchorage there's a good chance I'll never make it back to Denali to say goodbye to anyone. It'll be out of the hospital and straight to the airport.

"You probably need to."

I will my leg to stop bouncing. "See? No bounce. Keep me under surveillance while we drive, but you'll see. I'm fine." And I'm going to keep telling myself that until it's true.

He radios in the bear report, and I peer out the window but don't lean my head against the glass. I don't want to smear blood on it. I spot three caribou after a few miles, their heads bowed low as they graze. A few more miles after that, a fox slinks out from behind a bolder that's only a few feet off the road. Why couldn't these have been my hiking partners? The mountains that held promise this morning are no longer filling me with any sense of awe. I just want them to leave me alone.

He settles the mic piece back on its hanger and looks over to me. "Bear attacks draw press, you up for giving any interviews?"

"Not a chance. The article can say, 'Victim declined to comment.'"

"No hospital, no reporters. You want to get on with your day, don't you?"

I nod.

DENALI SUMMER

"I can't make you go to Anchorage, but I am taking you to the clinic in Healy. That forehead might need a few stitches."

I agree to go to the Healy clinic. The rest of the drive I drink water and munch my gorp while answering questions about my summer, my other hikes in the park. He seems both impressed and bewildered by what I've done.

"No camping experience to speak of, and you think Denali backcountry—that's as good a place as any to start?" He shakes his head and laughs. "We don't usually draw the inexperienced hikers. I'm glad you lived to tell today's story."

It occurs to me when we pass through Healy that Flint and Elijah said they'd get in around this time. I text Flint.

You back? I'm in Healy. Can we meet up?

But I haven't gotten a reply by the time we're parked at the clinic. The ranger asks if I want him to come in with me or if there's someone he should call. He looks as though he expects me to expect more from him—like I should be a higher maintenance bear attack case. I assure him I'll be fine. My phone is at almost full charge, and I'll be able to get a ride. I only have to insist on this three more times before he leaves me with his number, and he takes mine in case he has follow-up questions. I jump down from his truck and wave my final goodbye at the entrance of the clinic.

They clean up my arm and forehead. My shoulder is fine, bear didn't get all the way through my clothes. They apply a topical antibiotic to my arm and give me three stitches in the forehead. There's no wait, and I'm back out the door in less than an hour, proud of myself

CHAPTER TWENTY-SEVEN

for having my insurance information in my wallet and paying the co-pay with cash instead of sticking it to Daddy on the emergencies-only credit card he makes me and the twins carry. Eighteen-year-old me pays for her own stitches.

I step outside and get my bearings. There's a coffee shop, The Black Bear, where I figure I can wait on Wanda. The café name isn't my favorite right now, but their food is delicious, so I'll let it go.

In the parking lot, I stop and wonder if my head injury is more serious than I or that Healy clinic doctor suspected. I have zero recollections of calling Wanda, but there, in the parking lot, sits the shared employee jalopy.

I step inside, wondering if it's Wanda, HR Angie, Red or even the big boss himself who's come, but the place is empty except for Gabby who's tucked into a back corner, earbuds in, empty mug indicating she's been here awhile.

I wave, but she's too in her own headspace to notice me. I go to her table before ordering.

"Hey," I say and settle into the chair across from her.

She pulls out her earbuds. "What are you doing here? What happened to your forehead?"

I'm going to be answering this question a lot until I can fix my hair so that the stitches don't show.

"It happened on my solo hike, so a ranger brought me to the clinic. Now I'm trying to get back to the hotel. What are you doing here?" I'll tell Gabby my bear story but not yet.

"Waiting on Flint and Elijah. Red was supposed to drive them, but he's backed up on projects, so I offered to come."

"When will they get in?"

"They were supposed to text when they got into cell range. When he left, Flint said that would be today after lunch sometime."

"So he texted?"

"No, but once it got to dinner time, I thought I'd come into town to eat and wait here."

"Shit."

"No kidding."

"Have you talked to Jonelle?"

"She won't be done with her last river tour for another hour."

I pull out my phone again and text Flint,

Please text me as soon as you're in range. I'm starting to freak out.

"Can I wait with you?" I ask.

"If you tell me how you really got busted up."

"Let me order food first."

I'm famished as I'm choosing a chicken salad wrap and fruit bowl, but when it comes, all I can do is pick at a few grapes. I'm either nauseous over some lingering trauma issue, or I'm nauseous with worry for Flint, but either way I can't eat.

It had been easy to tell the ranger my bear story, but reliving it now is like telling a story I heard about someone else, not something that happened to me. Well, when I relate the facts: hiking in Stony Dome for about an hour, saw restricted area bear danger sign, saw bear, felt bear, bear left, I lived. That's no problem to tick quickly through all that. If I linger on the details I can still feel the breath at my neck, the dizzying fear. So I don't linger on the details.

CHAPTER TWENTY-SEVEN

"Why didn't you call someone when you were at the clinic? Isn't your family here? You could have had them with you."

"I wanted to save my parents the heart attack until I knew I was fine." And myself the scolding for going out solo. "And I am fine. I didn't need anyone there."

"What will you tell them when you see them?"

"I'm going to tell them that I was attacked by a bear, and when I was crouched in a ball, and I thought I might really die," my voice cracks, but I push through, "that I knew I wanted to be with my family. Which means I also want to be there for Dale's wedding."

Gabby frowns.

"Don't get all frowny disappointed. I'm not done. It's not like I went to them straight from the park. I love them, but I also love being away from them. So family wedding—yes. All the other stuff—no."

"What other stuff?"

"I'm going to tell Mamma I'm not going to ETBU." That feels good to say out loud. "I'm calling Charlet and telling her to find a new roommate. I'm calling the school and letting them know I won't be using my spot."

"What are you going to do instead?"

"Get an apartment somewhere, work, take a few community college classes until I get it figured out."

"Somewhere by Flint?"

I laugh. "I haven't thought it through that far."

"You want a roommate?"

"I'll need one, I'd imagine." But not Gabby. Surely not Gabby. Is she suggesting that?

"My cousin and I were living together in Houston, but her boyfriend moved in this summer. Forget that. I'm not moving back in with him there."

"My brother Dusty is in Houston. Not the one getting married—the other one."

I imagine myself in Houston. It's farther away from where Flint's in school, but this isn't about Flint. This is about me.

"You like Houston?"

"Houston's amazing. Stressful traffic, but I love it."

"I could see myself in Houston." I could. A big city. A new adventure.

"Keep talking." Gabby picks a strawberry off my plate.

I consider if I want our conversation to keep going in this direction. Flint and Kendra like this girl, and we have been getting along lately. We do both need roommates…

"I banked pretty much all my summer pay. I have enough in savings for safety deposits and first month's rent and all that," I say.

"If you want a roommate, and you want to come to Houston—I'm in. You'd be helping me out a lot."

"Why? I thought you didn't like me."

"I was pissed about Sugar moving on so quickly, especially to a spoiled thing like you, but I got over all that forever ago. You were the one who stayed weird. You'd come to the kennels and not talk to me."

I thought Gabby was bitchy, but she'd thought the same of me. Typical.

She adds, "And are you being serious about Houston, or are you the type to back out when you talk to your mom?"

Bear attacks make a girl serious. And decisive. And up for new things because if a bear didn't kill me then… Anything. I can do anything. "I'm serious."

CHAPTER TWENTY-SEVEN

"And you won't change your mind again?"

I don't answer right away, not because I'm going to change my mind about ETBU, but Houston? Gabby? Can I really make that work?

"No smoking in the apartment," I say.

"No guests for more than two nights in row," she counters.

"Utilities, cable, internet—all that split 50/50."

"And I want a place where we each have our own bathroom."

"We're getting a dog, right?" This is it, I think. This could be the deal-breaker.

She stabs her fork into my abandoned fruit bowl, takes another strawberry, and grins. "We are abso-fuckinglutely getting a big-ass dog."

CHAPTER TWENTY-EIGHT

After another hour of waiting with Gabby at The Black Bear, HR Angie calls because she needs the car. We have no choice but to return to the hotel, putting ourselves miles away from where Flint and Elijah should make it back out to the road.

It's now seven hours past when Flint said they'd be back. Even if they stopped the whole time it rained yesterday, that was only about three hours. They're both experienced hikers. They both had the right gear. Did a flash flood surge the river to trap them? Or worse, did they misjudge the water and...

I've been texting Jonelle, ignoring texts from Mama, and my leg has bounced away every calorie of the few bites of chicken salad wrap I managed to eat.

We pull up to the hotel at the same time a shuttle lets off my brothers, Rodney, and Chris back from their overnight at Savage.

"Let me out here," I say to Gabby. "I'm going to deal with my family. It'll help me stop thinking about Flint."

CHAPTER TWENTY-EIGHT

"Baby sister needs a hug!" Dale says when he sees me.

"Get your sweaty paws away from me." I point to my forehead. "I guarantee I've had a wilder time in the back country today than you did, and I'm not putting up with your crap."

Dale looks surprised, but lets his arms drop, and follows me into the lobby. Sugar is standing at the door as we all pass, so I point to Rodney and say to him, "Rodney meet Rodney," enjoying the look of surprise on Sugar's face. He doesn't congratulate me for guessing correctly, but he doesn't deny the name either.

"Are you on your way to dinner?" I ask the boys.

"Shower then restaurant. That's the plan," Dustin says.

"But please tell me your friend ain't working tonight. I'd like to be able to get something other than water in my lap," Dale says.

"If she is, Shelby will be nice. I promise."

I text Mama that I'm in the lobby, and I'm about to call Wanda to ask her about reporting Flint and Elijah missing when I see her. She steps out from the behind the front desk and grabs me into a tight squeeze. As she lets go, she sweeps away my bangs, "Just had to go and tangle with a bear didn't you?"

"That ranger has a big mouth."

"It has to be reported. The bus drivers all get updated about not letting people into the section. Fairbanks newspaper even sent someone down already. All the tourists are buzzing about the dangerous bear and the poor girl he practically swallowed whole. The gossip mill has you missing an arm and an eye."

DENALI SUMMER

I show her my scratch. "This is it. Sorry to disappoint. Now how do we re-direct all that attention into a man hunt for Flint? I'm losing my mind."

"Red's already talked to the rangers, but the boys aren't in the park—"

"Can we call the police? Some non-Denali rangers?"

"State troopers went in with a helicopter when that Swiss woman drowned a few years back."

"Please don't say the word drowned."

"Sorry." She squeezes me again. "Fact is—they usually say to give it one extra day, and yesterday's rain was bound to hold them up."

"You think it made the river too high, and they got stuck on the other side?"

"That's exactly what I was thinking, and it's better they wait. Elijah and Flint are smart. I'm sure they've got enough food and water for another day or two."

Mama enters the lobby, Daddy at her heels, and she doesn't look happy.

"I'll call the state troopers, see what they have to say, and let you be with your family," Wanda says, returning to the desk.

"Dawn Everly Wilkes. Where have you been all day?"

"Can we wait for the boys, so I can tell it all at once?"

"I think it best you tell me right now."

"Have your heard any rumors about a bear attack in the park today?"

"That's not funny, Dawn."

My phone buzzes, but Mama stays my hand when I reach for it. "You don't answer my texts, you don't need to answer that either. Let's get us a table and wait on the boys. Your Daddy and I ate supper hours

CHAPTER TWENTY-EIGHT

ago, but we were going to get coffee and split a dessert while they tell us about their camping trip."

The host leads Mama and Daddy to the same table where they sat the other night and pulls together more tables, tripling the space.

Kendra's working and rushes toward me before I can follow them. She's either heard about the bear or Flint or both because her first reaction when she sees me is to hug me as tight as Wanda did, and she's crying when she lets go.

"I'm fine," I say.

"I know, but you almost weren't, and now Flint and Elijah. Alaska's being too much."

"Sun won't set till eleven. They've still got a few hours of hiking in daylight left. They might still make it out today."

She nods, but her eyes are brimming, and I know she doubts this possibility as much as I do.

Chris, Rodney, and my brothers enter the restaurant in a noisy herd. I follow them to the table, but I don't sit. I can't sit. Instead, I pace back and forth the length of the pulled-together tables. I don't want coffee or dessert. I want to say what I need to say and get back to Wanda to find out what and when the troopers are going to do something for Flint and Elijah.

"Dawn, stop it already. Your pacing is making me nervous," Mama says, "and explain to me what that girl was carrying on about."

I circle around and lean on the back of my chair, but before I can start, Chris butts in.

"Did you hear about the bear attack in the park today? Shuttle driver told us all about it. Some poor girl took a beating, but they say she's all right."

DENALI SUMMER

"Yeah—" I hold up my arm. "I heard she got her arm scratched and," I make sure my bangs are out of the way, "her head pounded into a rock, so she had to get a few stitches."

Mama hops up to inspect my wound. "You weren't kidding? Dawn..." Her eyes widen and fill with tears, and she grabs me.

"I'm fine, Mama. Promise."

Daddy's next, taking my hand to inspect the cut. He's teary too when his eyes move to the stitches on my forehead.

I explain the whole thing again. And bless him, even Chris is teary-eyed by the time I'm done.

"Ya'll are pitiful," I say, looking around the table. "The bottom line is, I went one round with a bear, and he gave up. Best hiking story ever."

Mama, who's had her arm around my shoulder while I talk, pulls away and swats me. "Dawn Everly. This will never be funny. You are definitely coming home with us now."

I take her hand and look her in the eye. "Oh no, Mama. I'm not." She starts to object, but I cut her off, "You might want to sit back down. I have a lot more to say."

I turn to Dale. "First thing is that, yes, I'm coming to your wedding, but I'll get in on the last possible flight on Saturday and not a second earlier. That gives me two more days in Alaska, and I'm not giving them up."

Dale shrugs. I know none of this is as important to him as it is to Mama.

I add, "I'm still mad at you for taking over this trip because I'd rather have had Charlet and Dolly here,

CHAPTER TWENTY-EIGHT

so there is no way I'm getting you a wedding present, but I'm coming."

Mama nods as though I've struck a fair compromise.

"I've made another big decision." I can't look at my mama as I continue, "And this one you're not going to like." I will myself to keep going, gush it all out and be done. Emotion hits my eyes and threatens to crumble my voice, but I suck in a deep breath determined to stay steady and clear.

"End of senior year I didn't really know what I wanted, but I started to get a sense of what I didn't want. I didn't want everything to stay the same. I didn't want to keep on with Chris." I turn to Mama. "We broke up officially a few weeks ago." And then to Chris, "And I'll get you that ring back because we are not getting back together." I glance over all their faces. Poor Rodney, mixed up in this mess. He's probably wondering if he can sneak back to the room and order food there. Too bad. I'm not done. "And I didn't want ETBU except I didn't have any other options. But if there's one thing a girl learns when she's crouched on the ground hoping a grizzly doesn't eat her," my voice cracks on that, "is that she does, in fact, have options. And maybe it doesn't make sense. Okay, financially it makes zero sense, but Mama, I decline your offer to pay for ETBU."

"Of course I'm still paying for you to go to ETBU," she interrupts.

"No, you're not because I'm not going to ETBU."

My brother Dustin claps and calls out, "Good for you," but Mama shuts that down with her don't-you-dare glare.

"That's ridiculous," she says.

DENALI SUMMER

"Maybe so, but it's my choice. I'm eighteen now, and I'm not starting my adult life letting everybody make my choices. I may be the baby of our family, but I'm not a baby. I don't even have a plan yet, but I know what I'm not doing and that's enough for now."

Neither Mama nor Daddy gets to react again. And if I had more to say it doesn't matter. A very muddy Flint and Elijah have tossed down their packs at the entrance of the restaurant.

I shriek and run toward them.

"You're alive! You're alive! You're alive!" It's my turn to do the relieved hugging. I'm laughing and crying and swaying with Flint back and forth. My face rests right in the middle of his chest, and I want to stay here forever. He kisses the top of my head and murmurs, "Remind me to be half a day late every time I come back from hiking without you."

I stomp on his foot. "Don't you dare."

Jonelle rushes into the restaurant and gives Elijah the same treatment as the host hauls the packs back outside and rests them by the lobby desk. "Those need to stay outside," he says, but no one is paying any attention.

Except my family. I can see them from where my head is pressed against Flint. They're all sitting quietly, watching the commotion of our reunion. They're probably shell-shocked from my ETBU announcement, and now I'm hugging on a boy they don't know. At least Dustin's smiling. He's on my side. But Chris flushes red. He looks like he's about to choke or throw-up. Maybe both if that's physically possible.

CHAPTER TWENTY-EIGHT

I may as well get all my announcements over with at once, so I take Flint's hand. "Want to go meet my family?"

His look questions whether or not I'm sure then he sees my stitches. "What happened here?"

"You weren't the only one with an interesting hiking day."

His eyes widen, and I squeeze him again. "I survived a bear. You survived a river. Now let's go survive," I wave my hand in the direction of my family, "that."

CHAPTER TWENTY-NINE

Right up until I see them onto their shuttle Mama asks why I insisted on two more days in the park when the easiest thing would be to travel all together.

"Easy's not my priority," I say with finality as I kiss her on the cheek. "See you Saturday night."

Chris has not so much as made eye contact since my Flint hug-tackle in the restaurant the other night. Not even yesterday when I joined the boys for their raft ride. At the first rapid, Razor Back, Chris bounced into the water. When I quickly stretched out my paddle to pull him back to the raft, he took it, and when I assisted Zeke with yanking his wet ass back on the boat, he let me. But did I get a thank you for either? No, I did not. What I did get at the end of the ride when I hugged Zeke was a snide mumble of, "Did you date him too?" behind our backs.

So I am not surprised when Chris takes his seat in the shuttle without saying goodbye. I'm glad I've

CHAPTER TWENTY-NINE

shoved him out of denial and into the anger stage of dealing with our break up. 'Bout damn time.

I'm helicopter riding to a glacier and dinner theatering it with Flint today then Polychrome hiking and husky visiting one final time tomorrow. There is a lot of Alaska to pack in yet, and I'm not wasting one more minute on my visitors. I'm inside the lobby before the driver even rumbles their shuttle to life.

The night after we left my family in the restaurant, and I told Flint the entire bear story, he kicked out his roommate and made me stay with him, acting like he thought the bear might return and finish me off in my sleep. This afternoon after our helicopter ride when we're out on the ice, he won't let go of my arm as though a slip might be another way to meet my Alaska doom. It's not until we're seated before our plates heaped with meat (salmon for me, ribs for him), corn, potatoes, and biscuits, that he finally seems at ease and understands that I'm not suddenly fragile or, in this environment, at risk of choking, so he claps along and even stomps merrily when a banjo emerges.

The next day, as we near our bus stop at Polychrome, he asks me if I'm sure I want to go.

"You don't have to prove anything. If it's too much too soon, we can ride the bus back. No big deal." His eyes go to my forehead where my stitches shouldn't be visible if my hair is how I arranged it this morning but who knows.

"I want to get out there. Back on the horse or whatever." I smile and reach for his hand. "Really. I'm not letting my last hike be the bear encounter hike."

Once we're off the bus and a few yards beyond the road, Flint motions for me to walk first perhaps so he can catch me if I lose my footing once we're higher up. As we climb and the prairie grasses of the valley get farther below, my rock scrambles are surer and faster than his. I can see the stress of his worry for me dissolve with each step. We choose a route that's a quick ascent, but after a summer of regular hikes, my thighs are ready. We choose a rocky patch to spread out our lunch picnic, and we're high enough that I feel as though I could reach out and grab a handful of cloud.

I take out my water bottle and the bag of gorp I carried. Flint lays out the package of tortillas and his own water, but then reaches back into his day pack for something else.

"Happy belated birthday," he says and hands me a ball cap. The back is white mesh and the front section is navy and has Denali embroidered on it under a graphic of a bear in front of a mountain. He pulls out a second, identical hat and pulls it on his own head. "I thought it would be funny to match. I meant for them to be birthday hats or whatever, but then I got stupidly jealous and forgot about them." He exhales and looks toward the next ridge. "I never apologized about how I was that day, but I've been sorry ever since I stepped foot on the trail. Then by the time I went to text you, I was out of range, and—"

"And it's been a bit hectic ever since," I finish.

"But I am sorry," he says again.

CHAPTER TWENTY-NINE

I run my fingers along the word Denali. "Apology accepted," I say, putting on my hat, and then I kiss him on the cheek. We take pictures in our matching hats, some selfies, a few with the timer setting, and I don't stop to look and criticize myself and delete the ones I don't like. Any true depiction of this last day on a mountain with Flint is a picture I'll want. I have no doubt about that.

That evening with the huskies, I can't tell Timber goodbye, but after I finish rubbing him down the final time, I press my freshly tear-stained face into the soft, thick rumple of fur at his neck. He jerks his head around and laps at my salty face. His wide-eyed expression emits understanding. These pups are used to end-of-summer goodbyes.

Wanda and I ride back from the kennels in mostly silence, but once the hotel comes into view she gets misty-eyed too. "Who knows what this year will bring, but if it brings you back to Alaska next summer, I sure would be glad."

"If Gabby and I don't kill each other, there's an excellent chance of that."

"Not holding you to it, but if you do come back, you can skip the application formalities because your old job will be yours again. You know how to get ahold of me, and if you do, HR will send you your acceptance packet, simple as that."

"You're the best."

DENALI SUMMER

But Wanda's not done, "And you know you can use me as a reference once you settle wherever you're going."

"I will. Thank you."

She eases the car next to the boss's trailer, turns off the ignition, and lets it rumble down to quiet. The trees sway in the woods beyond, and a moose emerges from the small pines. Behind her follows a steady but still gangly calf.

"Told you you'd see them sometime this summer," Wanda says.

I watch the pair, one confident and knowing, the other trusting and learning. "You sure did," I say. We watch in silence as Mama Moose grabs a mouth-level branch and munches at its leaves. The baby calf, a young bull by the looks of small protrusions on his head where antlers will grow, nudges into the deep brown fur of his mom and partakes of the limb below hers. A few months old and this baby is already three times as tall as my dog at home and outweighs Rusty by hundreds of pounds. These two are just snacking along, but they're breathtaking. Their mundane is another small summer miracle for me. We stay in the car watching until the pair disappears again into the woods.

For my departure day, Flint finagles another day off and the keys to the employee car to drive me to the Anchorage airport.

CHAPTER TWENTY-NINE

"Here comes the moving pod," Flint says as I struggle to wedge my suitcase out the door of my room. He's pulled the car right up to my building, and I'm glad. I've thrown out my ripped fleece, and I sent my Dolly bag filled with the Ulu knife gifts and some other things I knew I wouldn't need back with Mama, but I still have an embarrassing amount of stuff.

We chatter non-stop the first hour of the four-hour drive. I recount the story about how I broke the ETBU news to my family, the look on Mama's face. The deepening of that look when it became apparent I could not be swayed.

"You think she's over it yet?" Flint asks.

"No way. She's probably called the school to make sure they keep my spot open, told everybody she'll have me there on day one even if she has to drag me."

Flint laughs at this. He knows I won't back down now. His eyes leave the road and flick over to my forehead as he is now often apt to do. "Your mom doesn't stand a chance against bear-survivor Dawn."

We talk more about my family and his. Our hopes for the school year. My worries about rooming with Gabby, and my guilt for abandoning Charlet so abruptly.

After a while our chatter peters out, and we mostly listen to music. We don't spot any wildlife, but the weather is clear and the mountains as dazzling as the day I first arrived.

I won't let him come inside the airport. He grumbles about wanting to park, but I insist on the curbside drop-off. I don't need to linger and fuss, especially now that we aren't waiting till our September concert date to see each other. We have another date planned for the day right after he returns in two weeks. And I have a lot of work to do between now and then to keep myself busy and my mind off missing him. He still gets out of the car to heave my suitcase from the trunk and places my Shelby bag on my arm. I'd sent the Dolly bag on knowing I'd want my Alaska friends' faces with me for this sad flight home.

He checks and re-checks the car to make sure I haven't forgotten anything.

"Oh come here and kiss me. If I forgot anything you can bring it with you," I say.

We kiss, slow and steady, until I release him to inhale, deeply committing to memory the mint of his aftershave and the piny scent caught in his sweater. His eyes are attentive, aflame in their mix of emotions.

"Two weeks," he says.

"Two weeks," I promise.

I grab the handle of my suitcase and roll toward the wide entrance. Flint calls behind me, "I only ever meant to split cab fair, save a little money."

I turn. "Sure you did."

He smiles, and I smile, and it takes everything in me to keep walking, leaving Flint and Alaska behind me.

CHAPTER THIRTY

I am up to the challenge of acquiring all seventy-five signatures of the guests at Dale and Jesslyn's wedding in their guest book. Check.

I'm also up to the challenge of babysitting Jessa and taking Mama and Daddy's money. More than they bargained for as I demand extra cash for activities—zoo, science center, children's museum. They are sparing no expense on their first step-grandbaby. Check.

I've registered for two classes at Houston Community College Central Campus, all I can afford till I get a new job. Check.

Rice University, where Dusty goes, is about two miles away, so he's found me an apartment in his same complex. Gabby's taken the online tour and has given it her okay. Big. Fat. Awesome. Check.

Once Flint gets back from Alaska, we have our first Texas date day at a state park picked for its halfway-ish location between Dallas and Longview. We rent a kayak, and it's the first time I've seen him in shorts, and, once we're underway, shirtless. There are advantages to being back in Texas.

Gabby and I pick the weekend just before my classes start to begin our apartment life together. I have so much to do in only a few weeks my head is spinning. Mama doesn't offer a dime of assistance. Not for gas when I use the twins' car to drive into the area to visit the apartment before signing a lease. Not when I ask Daddy if he'll rent a truck to get all my bedroom furniture out there. I'd do it myself, but I'm too young to rent a vehicle. Stupid laws.

When I announce my move-out date and ask about help with truck plans at dinner one night, it's Daddy who breaks.

"I am not sending my baby girl three hours away on her own," he tells Mama before turning to me. "I can borrow a cargo trailer, and I'll drive us out there, get you set up. And then," his gaze goes back to Mama, "we'll get you a car before I turn around and come back. No daughter of mine is going to be without wheels that far away from her family."

"That was never the deal," Mama says.

"Darlene dropping out of school and us paying her apartment for half a year till she got on her feet wasn't part of any deal I remember either, but that's what happened. And when Dale…"

"That's enough," Mama says.

"I like ETBU as much as you do since that's what brought you to the area. I like it because it's helped keep the twins close. Dale and Darlene stayed close even without it. Dustin left in spite of it. Maybe it's time to rethink our deals and accept that our kids

CHAPTER THIRTY

can pick what's best for them with or without our meddling."

Nothing on Mama's face indicates she agrees, but Daddy keeps on, "I'm mighty proud of Dawn for doing something none of her siblings did, heading off to Alaska like that. Proud too that she picked this new school, figured out her budget, and found a place to live. You don't have to offer any help, but I am. Dawn, we'll get you a good and safe car and any class you take that you get a *B* or an *A* in, I'll reimburse you for those credits."

"This semester?" I ask already thinking about the two classes I want to add if they're still open.

"Whole way through, where ever you end up. And there's not a principal of any school who should be against that kind of incentive," he says to Mama.

"You always did spoil the girls," she says, stabbing into her salad, but she doesn't argue his offer.

I jump from my spot at the table and wrap my arms around Daddy. He laughs. "I didn't get a hug for the dress and shoes we got you on your birthday, but a car offer gets the old man some love. Does this Flint guy know what a high-maintenance girl he's dealing with?"

Mama has her own helpful ways too. She makes Dale and Jesslyn take inventory of the household items they're upgrading with wedding presents and scores me their old toaster oven, pots and pans, and a set of dishes. She even comes away with a new waffle maker they got two of that Jesslyn didn't care about returning.

Of course Mama rides along to see my new apartment. I knew Mama would come through once she cooled. I just never can tell how long that will take.

The twins and Darlene make the trip with us too, so it's not Daddy's truck hauling my trailer, but Mama's Suburban. I'm grateful for their help and that the attention lacking on my birthday is now on me in full force. Especially since said attentions of all the Wilkes ladies at this moment will mean my piece-meal furniture gatherings adding up to something resembling a cute apartment.

I'm grateful that Mama's a reader, and my sisters are car-trip sleepers. As we start south on 59, I flip through my journal. The part of me that overpacked early summer is still with me as I head to college. The trailer is packed floor to ceiling, we still all have a box at our feet, and my bedding is stuffed in the back of the Suburban. Clearly some things won't change over one summer—not my terrible packing habits and not my family's support.

But some things do.

When I think about what changes still wait for me ahead on this road, I'm downright giddy. I've never been more ready for the unexpected.

Final Hike (no, you're crying)

<u>Where we went</u>: Polychrome
poly - Latin for many   chrome - color

<u>What we did</u>: climbed!
high as we could, higher still
climbed until we stood in
the clouds, wrapped them
around ourselves — shrouds for
summer's passing
melted a whisper of snowfall
on our faces

<u>What we saw</u>: wildflower fire
sweeping across the prairie
- wolf tracks in old snow
- discarded caribou antlers
  furry black
- rock faces split to tell
  sparkling geode secrets
- Mama dall sheep protective
  of two young
  and finally...
- Ourselves

stronger and better

and READY

THE END

DISCUSSION QUESTIONS

1. Dawn makes the very big decision to spend her summer in Alaska and acts on this idea quickly. Was she running away from her problems or seeking a necessary reprieve? Explain.

2. If Dawn had stayed in Texas for the summer, would she still be with Chris? How can new environments change our perspective?

3. Dawn struggles with her role as "the baby" in her large family. Sometimes the people who are supposed to know us the best, don't understand when we change. How can we support our loved ones or continue receiving their support even through big changes?

4. In Texas, Dawn's motto seems to be "it's easiest to agree." How does this serve her, and how does this limit her? When does this begin to change?

5. In many ways, Dawn is in over her head when she arrives in Alaska. Was it the boys or the wildlife that challenged her the most? Explain.

6. Dawn has three sisters back in Texas and three roommates in Alaska. How are these groups of women similar? Different? Who is your favorite? Why?

7. Dawn's mother is a demanding and overbearing force in her family. In what ways does she still show her love and support? How does Mama compare to Wanda? How did having Wanda as a maternal influence help Dawn through her summer?

8. Dawn and Gabby do not initially get along and this continues largely because Dawn doesn't move past her first impressions. Will they work as roommates, or was this decision too rushed? When have you misjudged someone? Is it important to move past a bad first impression?

9. Dawn struggles through the physical challenges of her first backcountry camping trip but feels she has to prove her right to be there and ability to keep up. Does she underestimate her friends in thinking this way? When she injures her knee, how does each member of the group react and why? Why is it important to have the right team in challenging situations?

10. When Dawn first sees Denali, the mountain, no longer cloud-cloaked, she thinks: "Everything in

DISCUSSION QUESTIONS

me knows this is the right place to be—held by vast, endless, empty spaces that are filled with freedom." Time spent in nature and beauty can be inspiring, but how can such moments sustain us when we return to the demands of everyday life?

11. Why isn't Dawn more assertive with Sugar? Why does she kiss him when she has a boyfriend *and* can't stop thinking about Flint? Mistakes are part of learning, but could she have avoided his one? How?

12. People often say, "Family first." What does this mean? At what times does Dawn put her family first? When does she put herself first? Do you agree with her decision to attend her brother's wedding? Why or why not?

13. A grand, romantic gesture is often celebrated in books and movies, but it does not work out at all for Chris. Why was Dawn so angry? Was Chris clueless, or did Dawn share some of the blame? Have you ever experienced or witnessed a romantic gesture that failed?

14. If the summer staff were to give out superlatives, the Most Likely to Downplay a Bear Attack definitely goes to Dawn. Are her reactions only due to shock? Why doesn't she want more attention or just take a minute to let herself be hugged and cry? How has she changed from when she first hurt her knee to this injury near the end?

DENALI SUMMER

15. In what ways has her Denali summer helped prepare Dawn for the next stage of her life? If you could spend an entire summer in a place different from where you live, where would you go?

ACKNOWLEDGEMENTS

From inspiration to publication, books can take a very, very long time. Here are the highlights of how this book came to be, and who helped make that happen:

I worked at the Denali Park Hotel (which is no longer there, so Denali Summer is set at a fictional resort) in the summer of 1999. While this book takes place twenty years later, some of the experiences (white water rafting, volunteering with the huskies, camping party for summer solstice, and more) were part of my summer, and I do not doubt they have been part of the experiences for seasonal employees both real and imagined for the decades since. This is a work of fiction, and the characters are indeed fictional characters, not based on anyone from real life, but I still have to acknowledge the incredible people I met that summer. They put up with my had-never-camped-once, didn't-own-any-gear, why-not-start-with-Denali, ridiculous self and showed me one of the best times of my life. That summer empowered me and continued my love of the outdoors to this day. Thank you.

DENALI SUMMER

In 2016, I needed a book project to attend a retreat, so I pulled up a short story from my MFA thesis collection titled "Me and the Boys in Alaska" and reimagined it as a full-length young adult novel. I think I wrote the fifty pages I needed to submit to the retreat leaders in order to gain acceptance over two nights. I didn't necessarily have plans to finish the book—I just wanted to meet Jennifer Mathieu and Julie Murphy and talk writing with them. Some of their ideas are still in the final draft, but it was the enthusiasm of fellow attendees (Amy! Tia! Cassie! Shelli! Kim! Ashley! Charlotte-Ashley! Domino!) who convinced me to finish the book. Thank you.

Thanks also goes to Serena Schreiber, Amber Garr, and Amanda Sandifer, authors I met through the Florida Writers Association who were my critique partners through the first draft. After this, Rebecca Petruck came through with an extremely helpful plot critique edit letter. With all these cheerleaders and minds (there are a few online connections I know I've missed) on one story, *Denali Summer* still did not find a home until Arielle Haughee believed in it and took it on for publication with Orange Blossom Publishing. For this, I am grateful.

Kendra Gurkin Dew was one of the nicest people I knew. We lost her while I was first drafting this book, so I named one of the nicest people in the book after her. F*@k cancer, but thank you, Kendra for your beautiful life.

ACKNOWLEDGEMENTS

Finally, thank you to my family for their love and support, especially Kevin, who has made this life the best adventure I could have hoped for.

ABOUT THE AUTHOR

Faydra Stratton has also written the young adult novel *Devil Springs*. She resides in Florida with her family. Her day job involves trying to teach teenagers how to correctly use an apostrophe. Find her online at <u>faydrastratton.com</u>.

Other Books from Orange Blossom Publishing

After getting dragged out of her school's winter formal, seventeen-year-old Percy Bloom needs to escape her controlling mother. Fleeing into the cold night, she's lost, alone, and freezing.

Ditched by his date and attacked by bullies, Hayden Addams wants nothing more than to be done with high school forever. He finds Percy shivering in the woods and brings her back to the first place he can think of--his family's funeral parlor.

Percy is charmed by Hayden and his unusual family. Eager to help her get away from her problems and forget his own, Hayden offers Percy everything she needs: a truck, a destination, and the prettiest blue eyes she's ever seen.

Together, the two hit the road, letting their hopes, dreams, and sparks fly along the way. But can the two arrive at a future without confronting their pasts?

Helene Denny worries about everything, even the prospect of leaving home to attend college. It doesn't help that she's fascinated with serial killers.

In her final semester of high school there's a string of missing girls. Helene immediately thinks a serial killer is loose. When Fred Thompkins arrives in town to become mayor he becomes her primary suspect.

No one takes her seriously. Unfortunately, her sister disappears. Is Fred guilty? How could Helene cope with the loss of her only sibling?

Printed in the USA
CPSIA information can be obtained
at www.ICGtesting.com
LVHW050319111123
763646LV00036B/181